IMAGES
of America

OROVILLE
CALIFORNIA

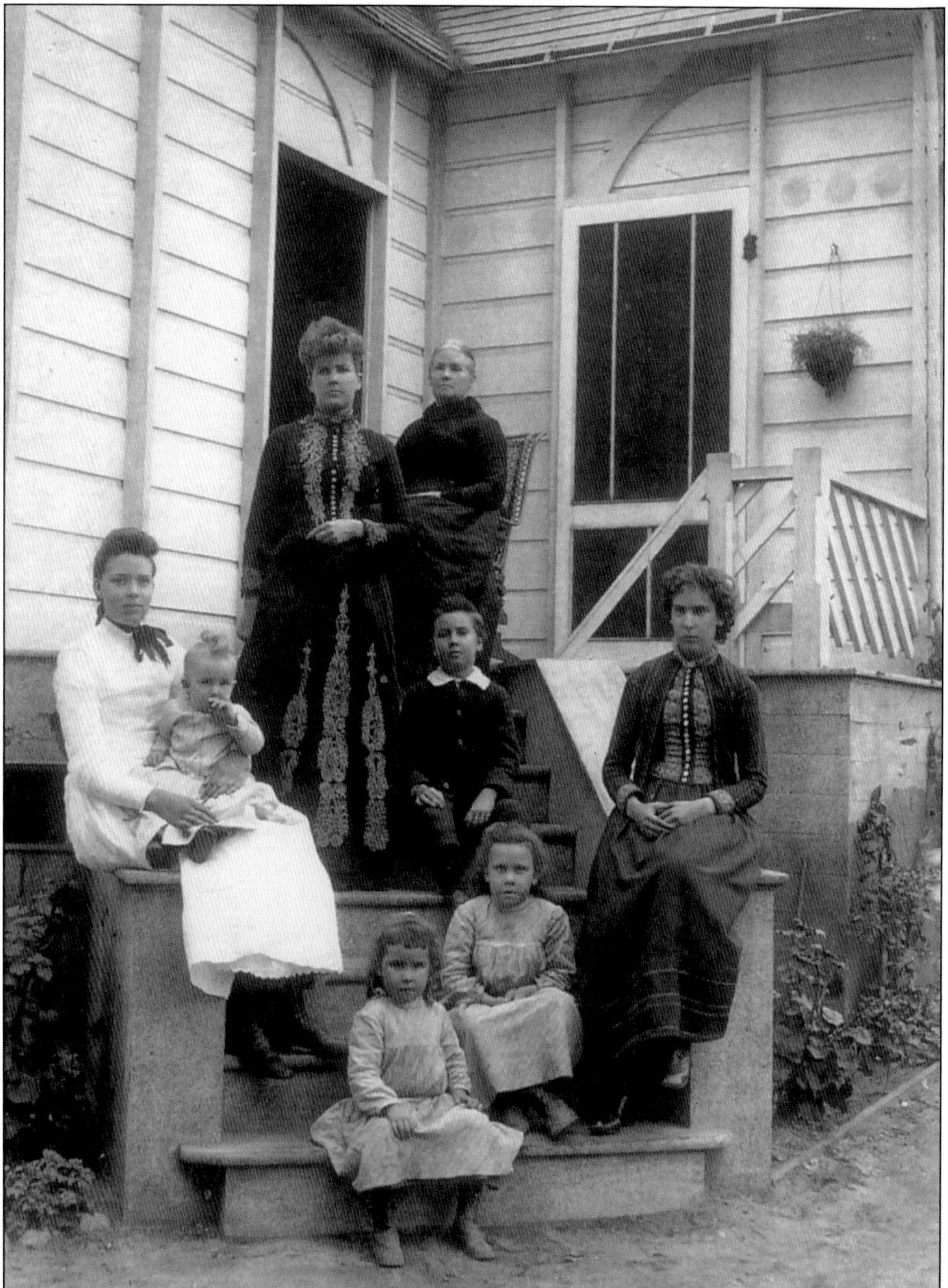

Two pioneer Oroville families were joined when the daughter of Mary and Ebenezer Sparks married David Perkins, brother of Governor George Perkins. This family portrait shows Mary Perkins standing in front of her mother Mary Sparks. Six of her children are shown in foreground. Mary Sparks' marriage certificate was the first recorded in Butte County, while daughter Mary is credited with being one of the first white children born in the county. Thomas Lovelock is credited with being the first white child born in Oroville.

IMAGES
of America

OROVILLE
CALIFORNIA

James Lenhoff

ARCADIA
PUBLISHING

ISBN 978-0-7385-1854-1

Published by Arcadia Publishing
Charleston, South Carolina

Printed in the United States of America

Library of Congress Catalog Card Number: 2001090253

For all general information contact Arcadia Publishing at:
Telephone 843-853-2070
Fax 843-853-0044
E-Mail sales@arcadiapublishing.com
For customer service and orders:
Toll-Free 1-888-313-2665

Visit us on the Internet at www.arcadiapublishing.com

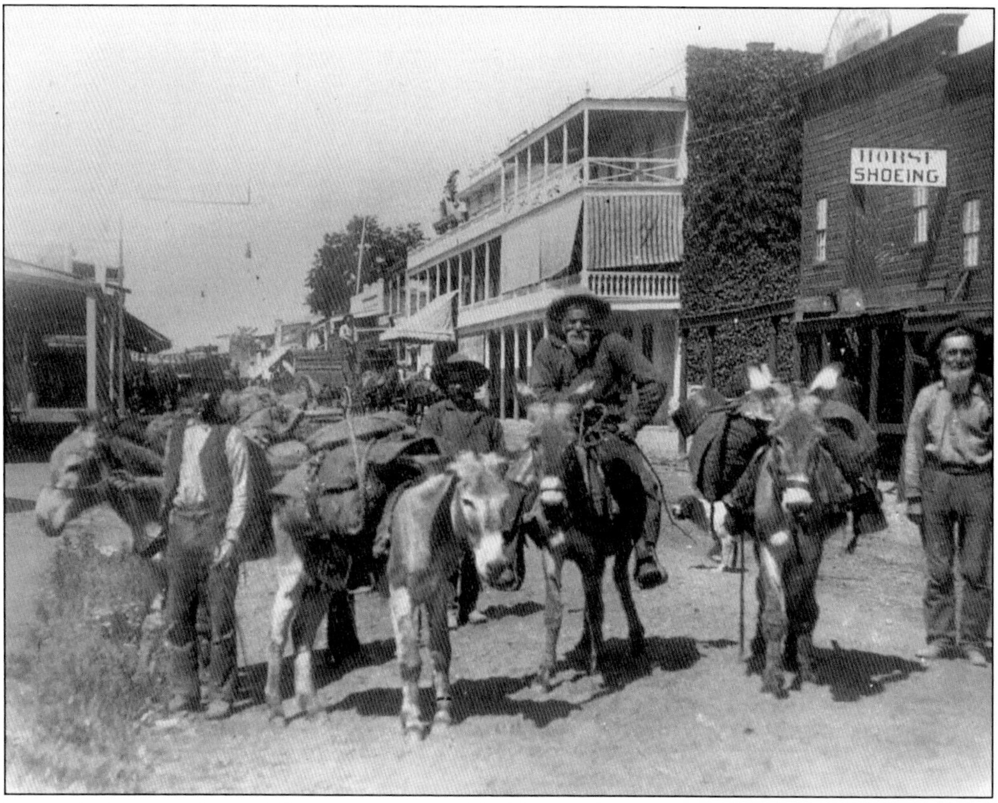

This c. 1890 photo by prolific photographer J.H. Hogan shows miners heading up Montgomery Street returning to their gold claims in the foothills.

Contents

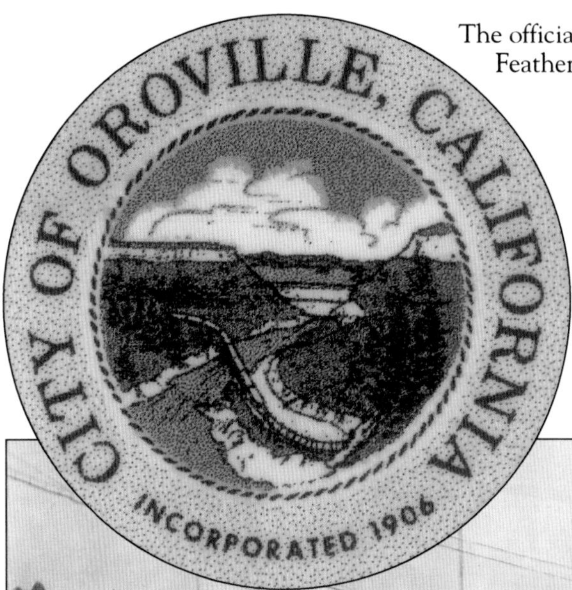

The official seal of Oroville depicts the railroad, Feather River, and Table Mountain.

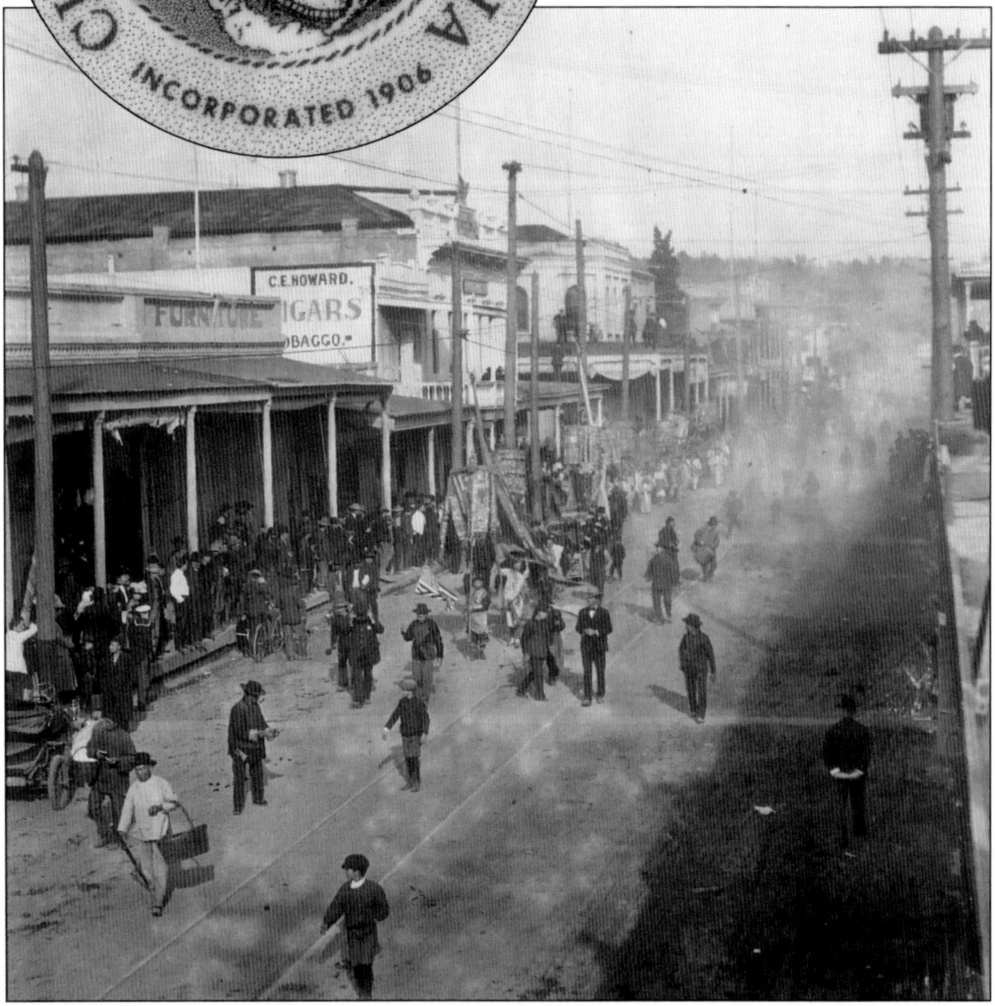

Hundreds of Chinese once occupied Oroville, building their own residential and commercial area along the Feather River. Their parades attracted many viewers such as this one down Montgomery Street around 1900. (Oroville was fortunate to have several professional photographers who recorded much of the town's history, which otherwise might have been forgotten.)

INTRODUCTION

Every town has its own unique history, and Oroville is no exception. Because of its place in time and varied natural resources, Oroville is blessed with an ever-growing heritage that is second to none. After John Bidwell discovered gold in the Feather River in 1848, thousands of young adventurers combed the hills and gullies, hoping to lay claim to their rightful share of the precious but often elusive metal. Tent towns sprang up everywhere, and for a time, Bidwell Bar held sway as the official seat of Butte County, one of California's original 27 counties. Following the completion of the ambitious South Fork Ditch, which brought water to sluice the rich, dry diggins around Ophir in 1855, this struggling little village on the banks of the Feather River would suddenly mushroom into the most populated mining town in California and become its fourth city in importance. In 1853, John Tatham, Ralph Bird, Benjamin Myers, Dewitt Downer, and others held title to most of the future town site in the form of placer mining claims. In 1854, Captain Bird and Jacob Morris secured title to most of these claims and laid out the town in 1855, promptly selling lots to enthusiastic buyers. Ophir was re-christened Oroville and became the county seat following a spirited election in 1856.

The following year would prove even more auspicious for Oroville. It was briefly incorporated as a city, boasted two theaters, three banks, a music hall, a race track, and numerous hotels, the most fashionable being the United States, St. Nicholas, and Orleans. Scores of saloons lined the streets. One of the most famous of those was the Bank Exchange, operated by debonair Harry Hunt, who was instrumental in founding the first newspaper in Panama on his way to California. Stages came and went hourly, and two newspapers kept the literate informed about the latest local events and "the States." There was a talented dramatic association, plus a popular debate club, and one permanent church, founded by Rev. Bela N. Seymour from Massachusetts. This was a boisterous society—young, vital, and full of energy—with attributes that would remain a part of the town's social fabric down to modern times.

Although gold would remain the cornerstone of the local economy for several years to come, farming and logging soon asserted themselves as prosperous adjuncts. At the turn of the century, when giant gold dredgers crawled over the outskirts of Oroville, extracting more millions in gold, local citizens became increasingly aware that the region was blessed with a remarkable thermal belt that made planting of orange and olive trees practical. Thousands of acres were gradually developed and harvests shipped to various parts of the country. Later, rock tailings not leveled for expansion of the city were used to manufacture gravel and build the nation's largest dam. Years ahead of its time, in 1906, one of America's first electric railways would connect Oroville with other cities in the valley. Completion of the Western Pacific Railroad in 1909 boosted the local economy measurably, augmented still further when the scenic Feather River Highway to Reno was opened in 1937.

The mighty Feather River had supplied generous fortunes in gold, plus a year-round travel route over the Sierra Nevada, and now it would be harnessed by power companies to generate electricity for the region's growing number of industries and homes. This period of history would culminate in 1968 with completion of the Oroville Dam, highest and widest in the nation. This grand engineering feat provided water not only for thirsty cities and farms throughout the length and breadth of California, but also resulted in one of the state's important new recreational areas, featuring a spectacular lake with 167 miles of shoreline.

Down through the decades, Oroville's entrepreneurial ventures (often on a scale that excited national attention) have lured numerous luminaries to walk the streets of the city. Herbert Hoover, Ronald Reagan, Gertrude Atherton, Richard Burton, Erle Stanley Gardner, Phoebe Hearst, Black Bart, Sabu, and Ishi are only a few who made their imprint on the town's diverse and robust life. The mining exploits of men like Frank McLaughlin still rank among the world's most impressive. Freda Ehmann, Wendell Hammon, and George C. Perkins were three long-term residents who went on to statewide and national fame. Their memories are kept alive locally by streets or buildings named in their honor.

Today, Oroville is a progressive community that attracts new investments and families on a regular basis. While modern structures are erected continuously, scores of historic buildings and homes are proudly maintained by their occupants. Despite its constant expansion, Oroville has managed to retain its congenial small-town ambiance. The rustic majesty of Table Mountain, combined with other spectacular landmarks such as Feather Falls, the foothills, and the Feather River Canyon, insure that Oroville will continue to recognize its pleasing contrast between past and present, its delicate balance between human enterprise and natural wonders.

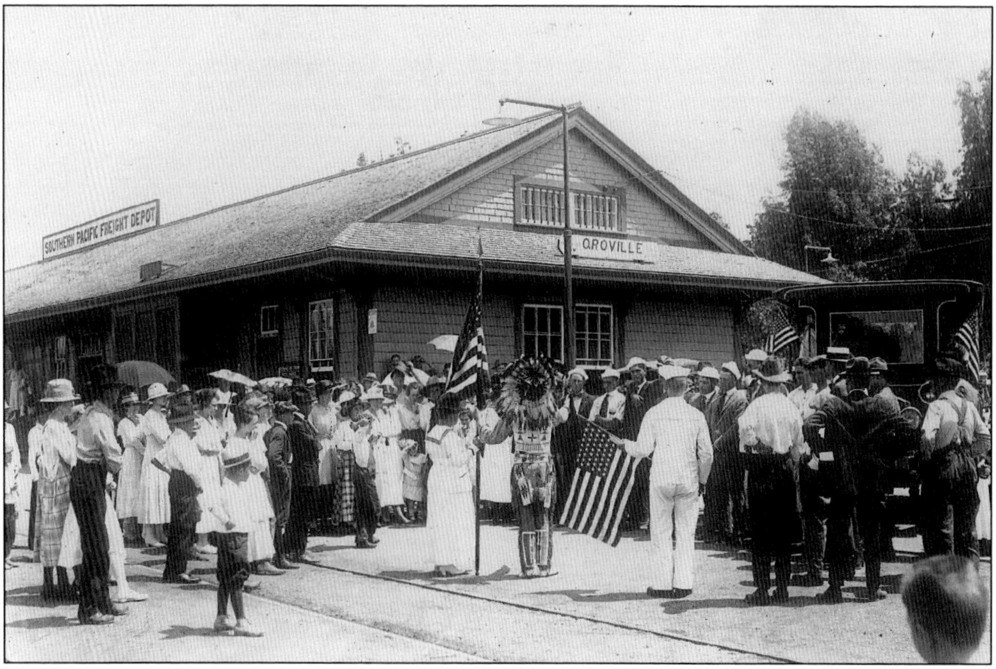

In 1864, the California Northern completed the first railroad to Oroville, later absorbed by the Southern Pacific system. In 1950, citizens gathered at the depot site to dedicate a monument commemorating the fourth railroad built in California.

One

In the Beginning

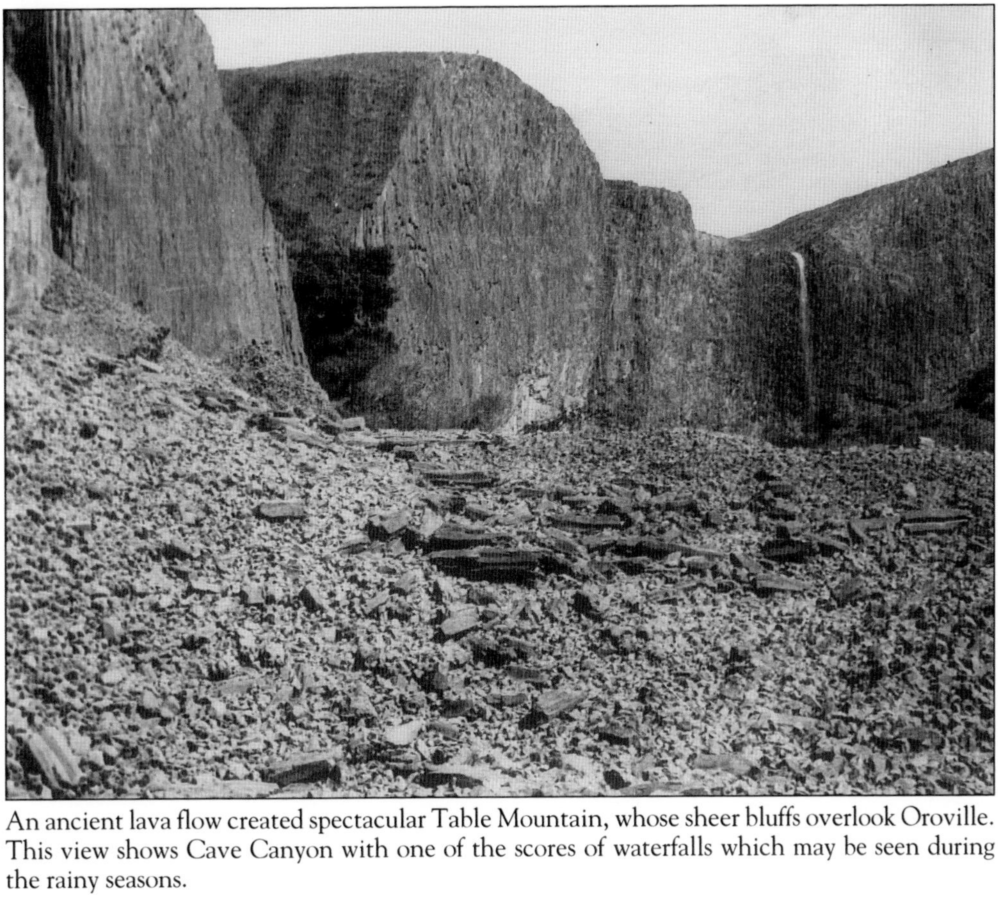

An ancient lava flow created spectacular Table Mountain, whose sheer bluffs overlook Oroville. This view shows Cave Canyon with one of the scores of waterfalls which may be seen during the rainy seasons.

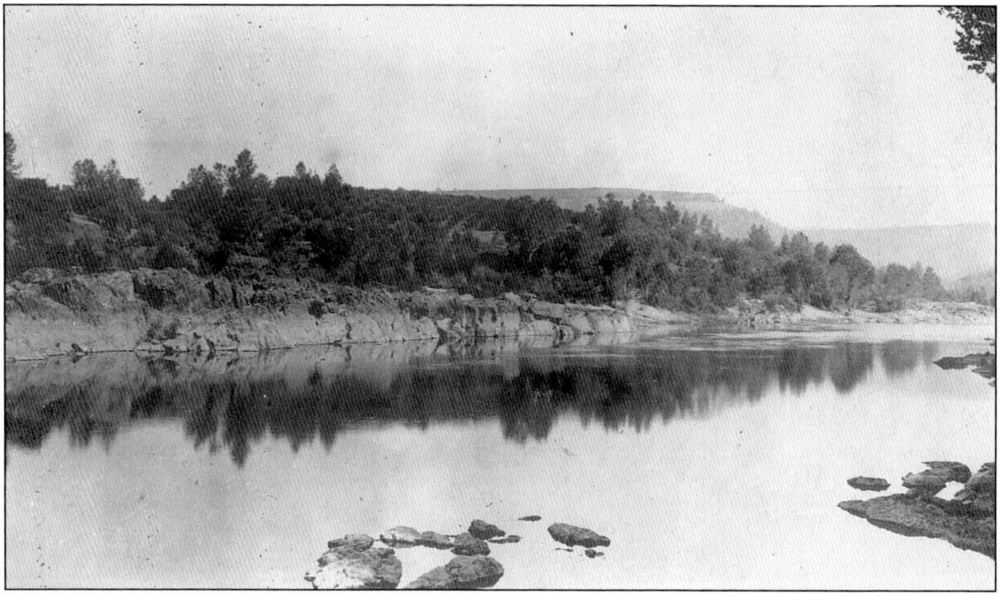

The Feather River as it appeared to early explorers in the area. Table Mountain is shown in the background.

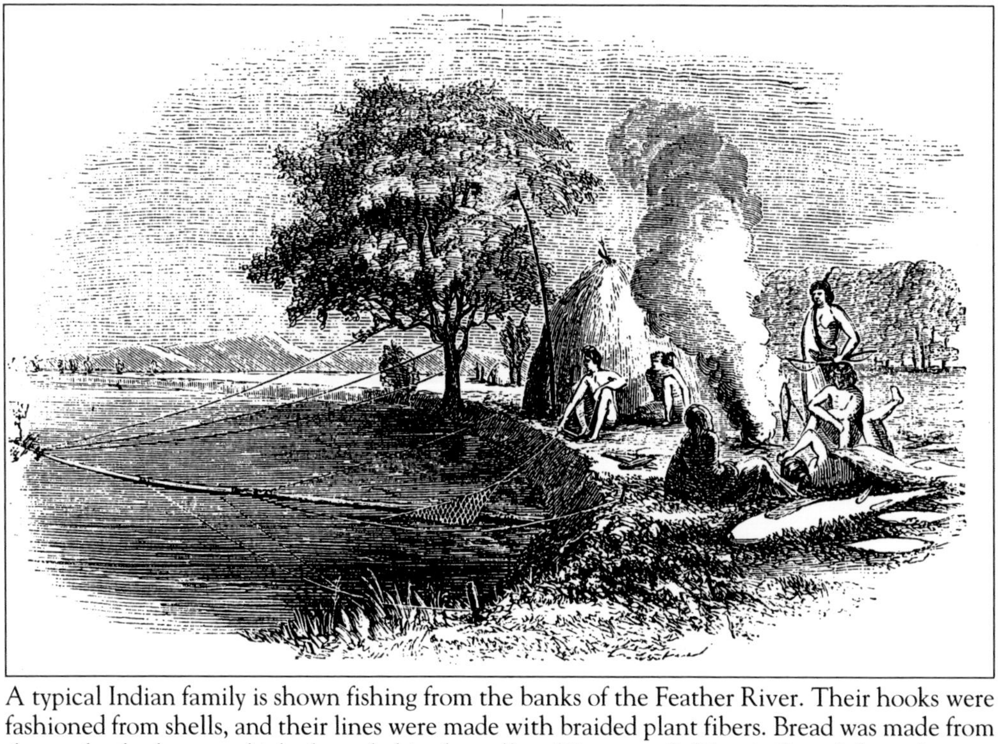

A typical Indian family is shown fishing from the banks of the Feather River. Their hooks were fashioned from shells, and their lines were made with braided plant fibers. Bread was made from the seeds of oak trees which abounded in the valley. (Courtesy California State Library.)

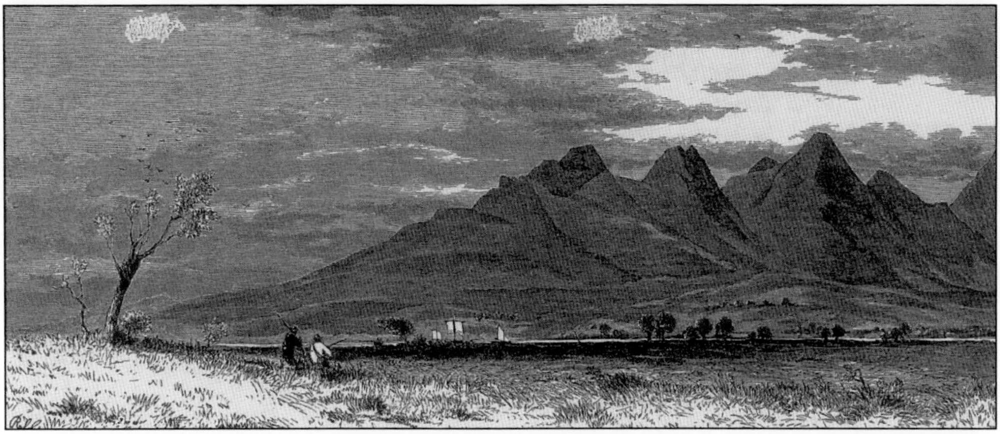

The Sutter Buttes south of Oroville, in whose honor Butte County was named, is the smallest complete mountain range in the world. They are the remnants of an ancient volcano that blew out of the heart of the Sacramento Valley eons before the advent of man. (*Pictorial History of Northern California*, 1893.)

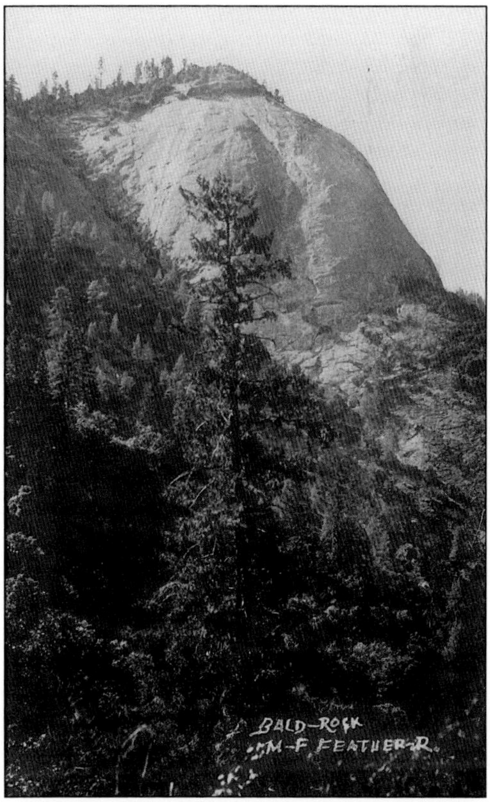

Mammoth Bald Rock east of Oroville overlooks the Middle Fork of the Feather River. It is one of numerous granite formations which rise in the Feather River Canyon east of town.

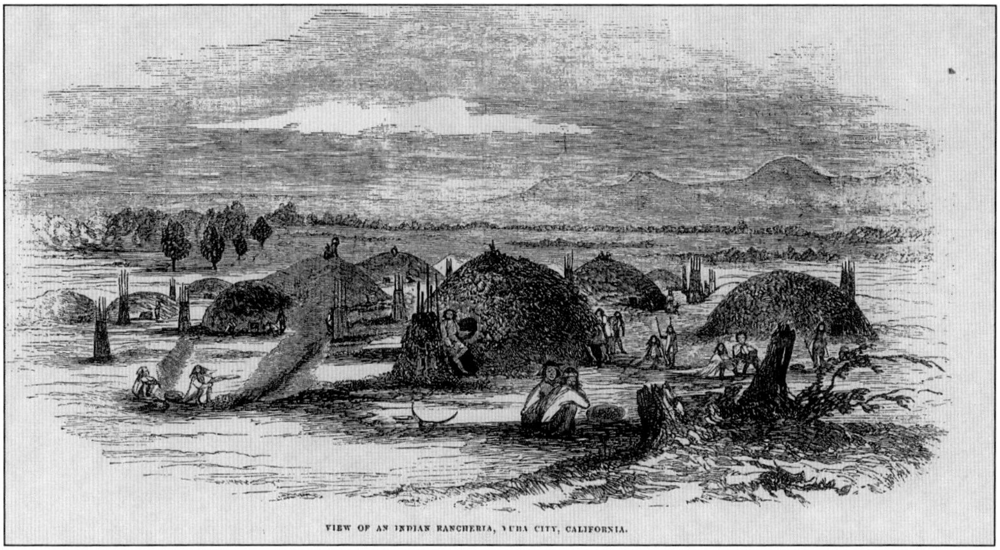

This is what a typical American Indian village looked like in the Sacramento Valley between Oroville and the Sutter Buttes, shown in the background. (*Gleason's Pictorial*, 1851.)

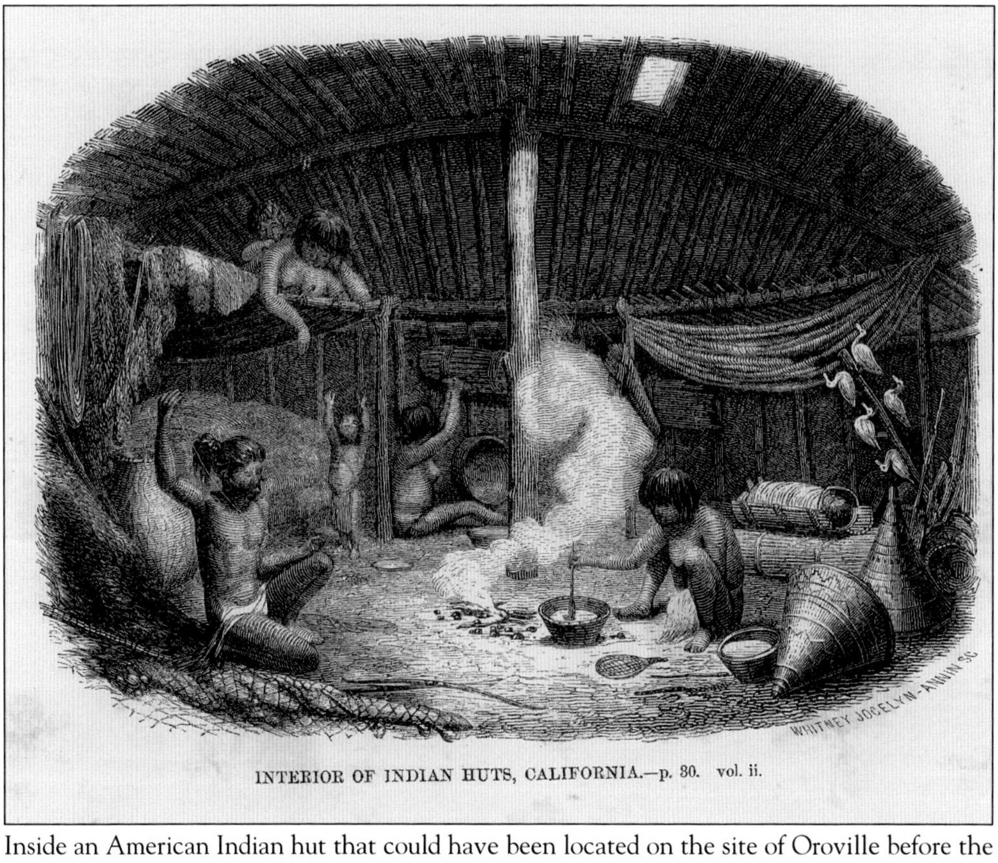

Inside an American Indian hut that could have been located on the site of Oroville before the Gold Rush. Huts were made from tree limbs, bark, and mud. Those who lived around Oroville were known as Tancows, part of the Maidu nation.

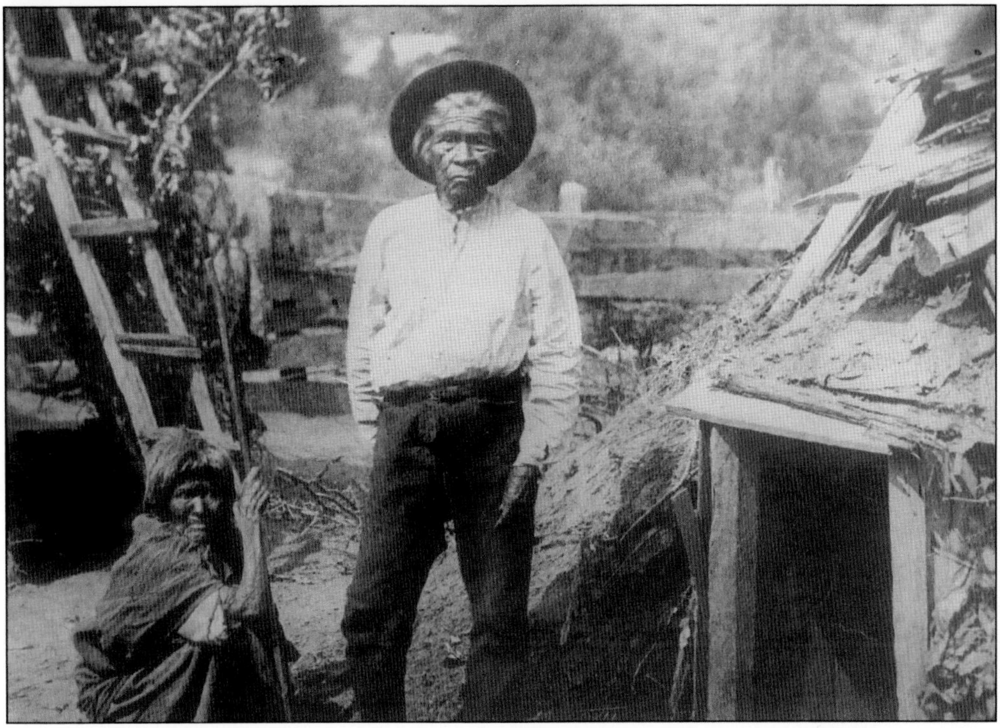

This photograph of a Table Mountain Indian and his mate was taken in the 1880s by local photographer J.H. Hogan.

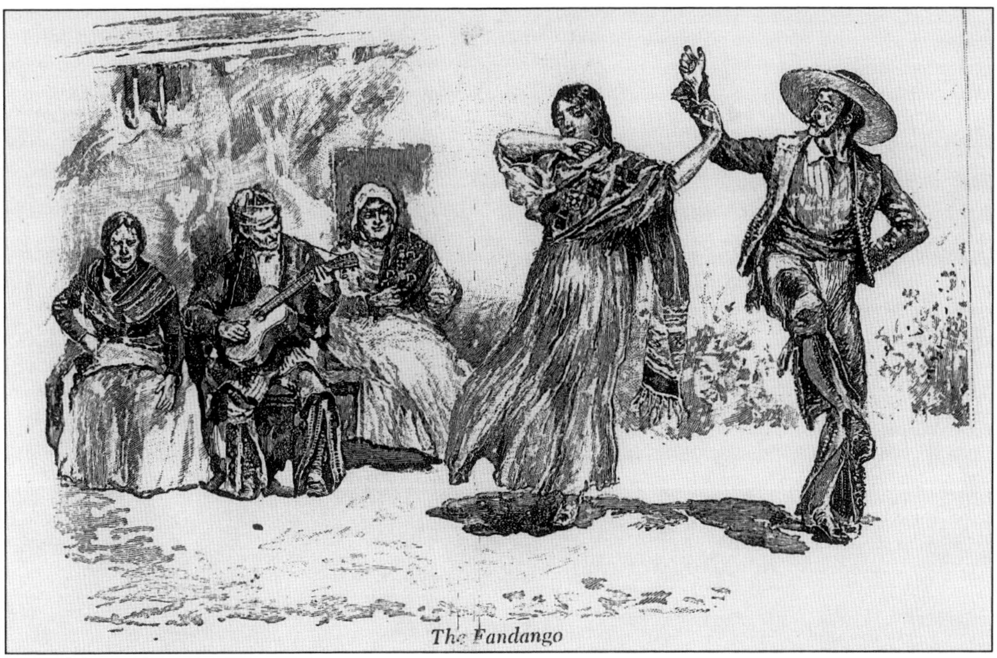

Early Spanish and Mexican explorers would occasionally travel through northern California but never made any permanent settlements. Historian H.H. Bancroft noted, however, that they may have discovered gold under Table Mountain as early as 1818.

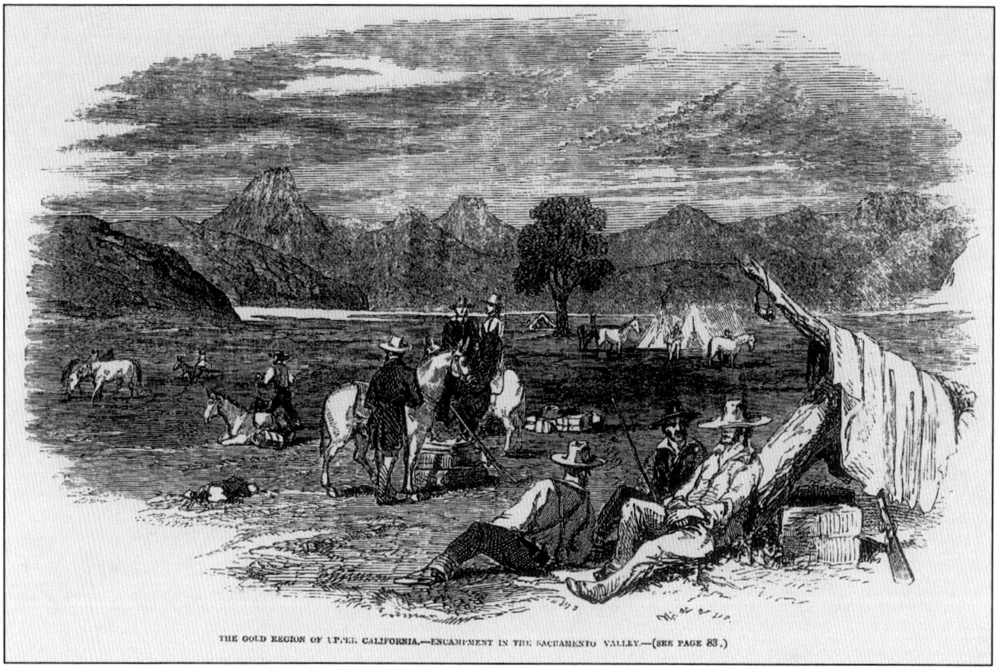

The world got its first view of California's gold region through engravings such as this one, which shows an encampment in the Sacramento Valley in 1849. (*Illustrated London News*, 1849.)

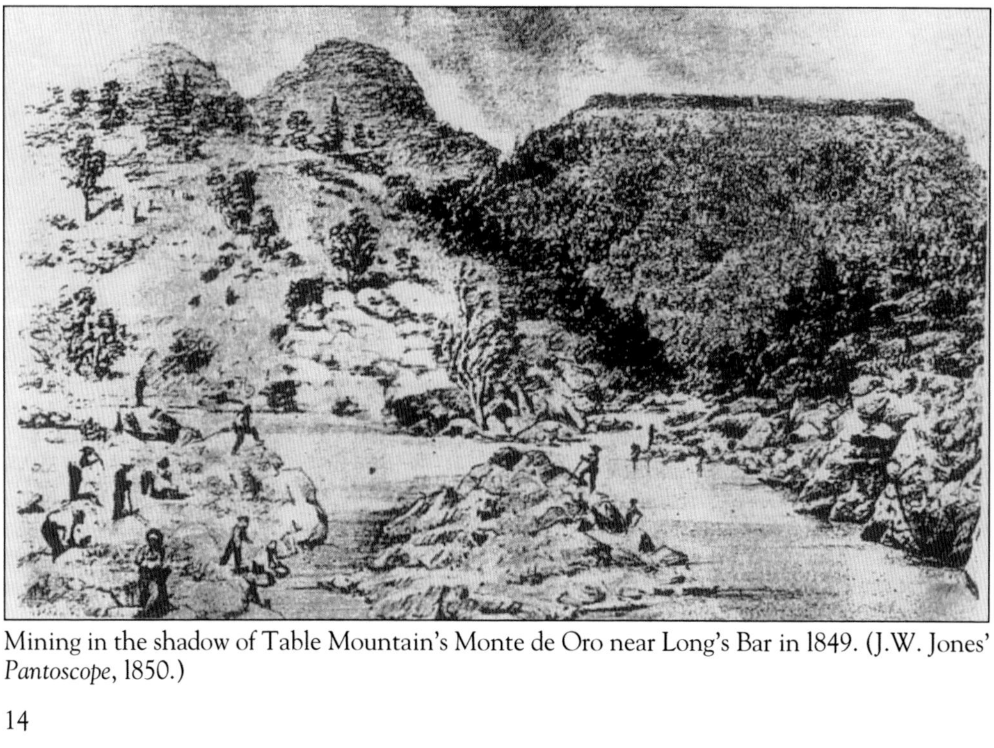

Mining in the shadow of Table Mountain's Monte de Oro near Long's Bar in 1849. (J.W. Jones' *Pantoscope*, 1850.)

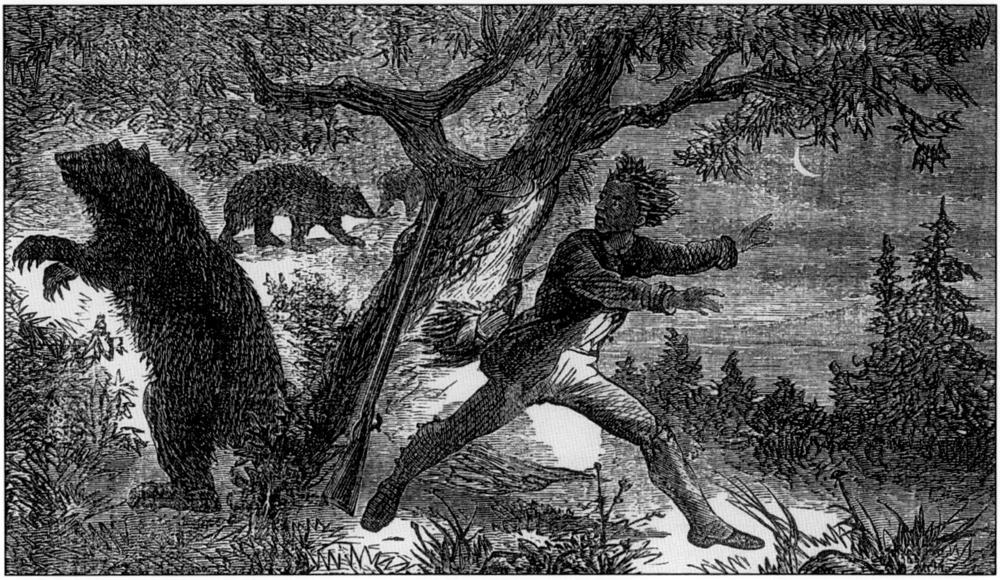

The area around Oroville originally abounded with such wildlife as grizzly bears, deer, antelope, and elk. The grizzlies were known to be particularly aggressive. (*A La California*, 1874.)

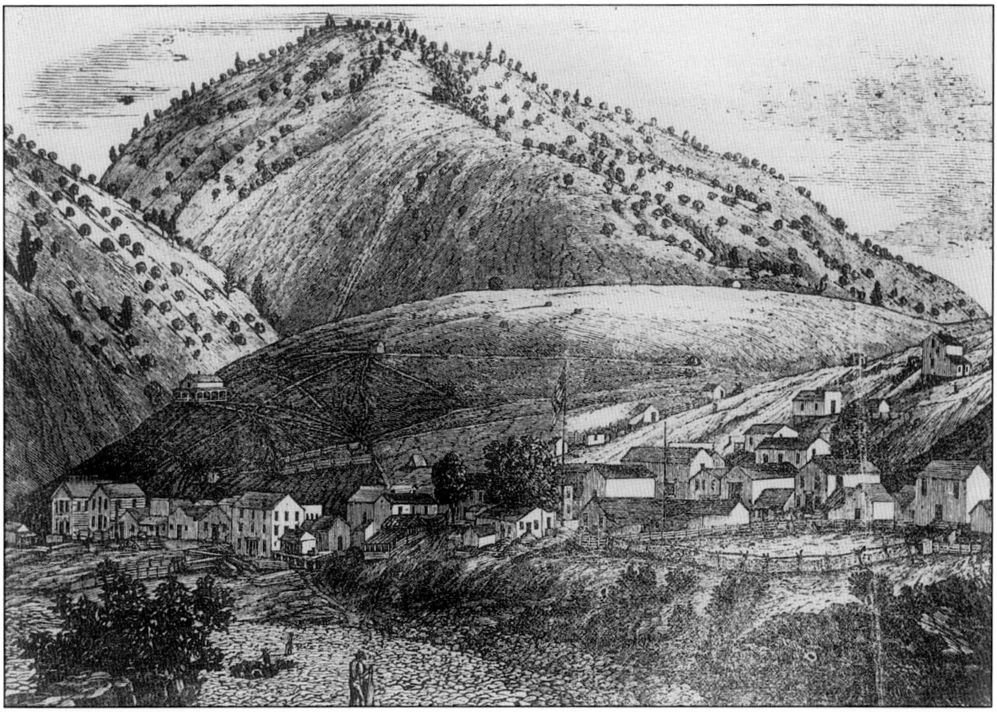

The first major mining settlement in the Oroville area was Bidwell Bar, which became the county seat in 1853. Townspeople built the first suspension bridge in the West in 1855, but a year later, Oroville became the mining center of Butte County, and Bidwell Bar was hauled lock, stock, and barrel to Oroville. (*Sacramento Pictorial Union*, 1854.)

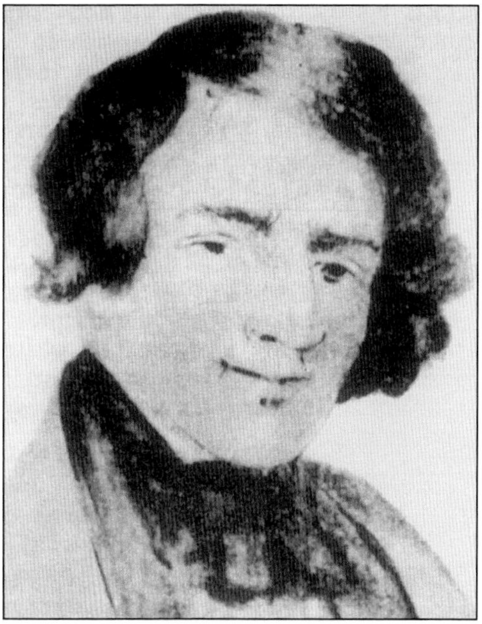

Jebediah Smith was the first American to explore the Sacramento Valley, arriving in 1827. A fur trapper by trade, he was looking for beaver habitats.

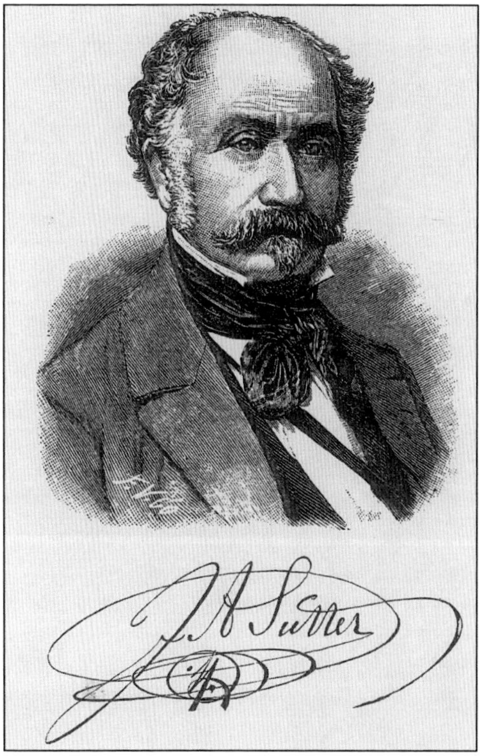

John Sutter was instrumental in securing Mexican land grants for associates in the Oroville area. He hired John Bidwell to search the region for a possible location for his sawmill, later built at Coloma.

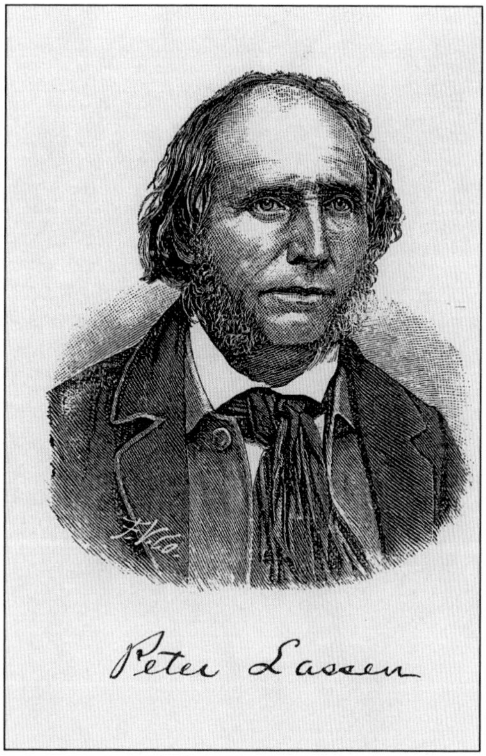

Peter Lassen led a party from Missouri to settle his holdings north of Oroville in 1848, but members of the party were quickly lured away to such gold camps as Long's Bar on the Feather River.

John C. Fremont explored the Sacramento Valley near Oroville and camped at the foot of the Sutter Buttes in 1845. (Courtesy California State Library.)

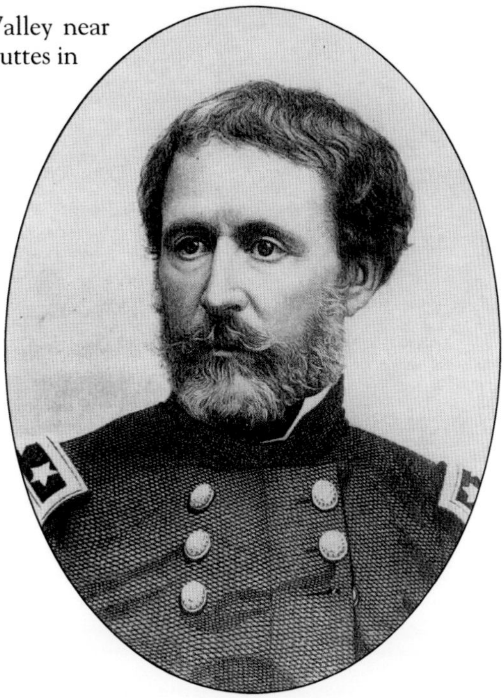

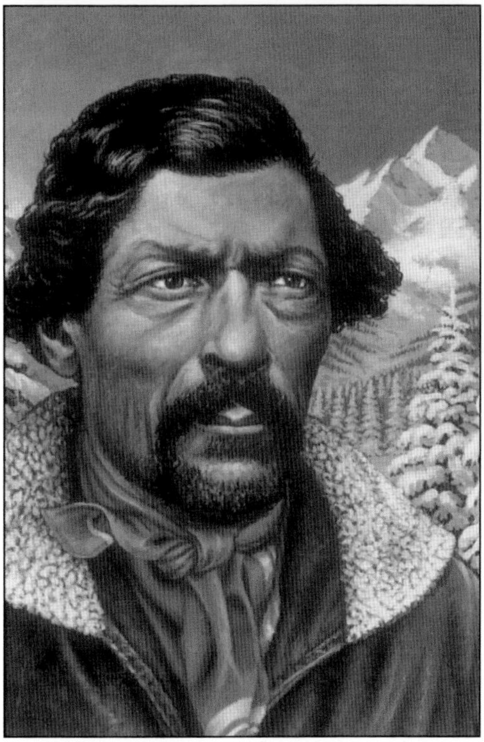

Jim Beckwourth was an early mountain man who discovered the mountain pass later named for him. He pioneered the first wagon road over the Sierra Nevada to Bidwell Bar, Oroville, and Marysville. Dame Shirley described meeting him in her famous letters.

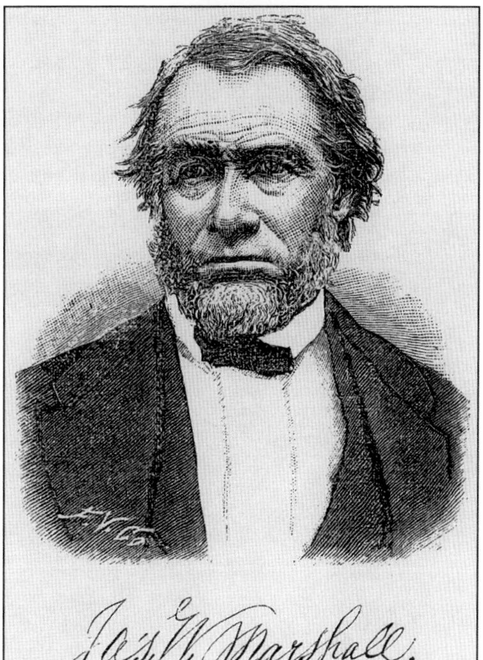

James Marshall, who discovered gold on the American River, also acquired a Mexican land grant in the valley north of Oroville, thanks to his employer, John Sutter.

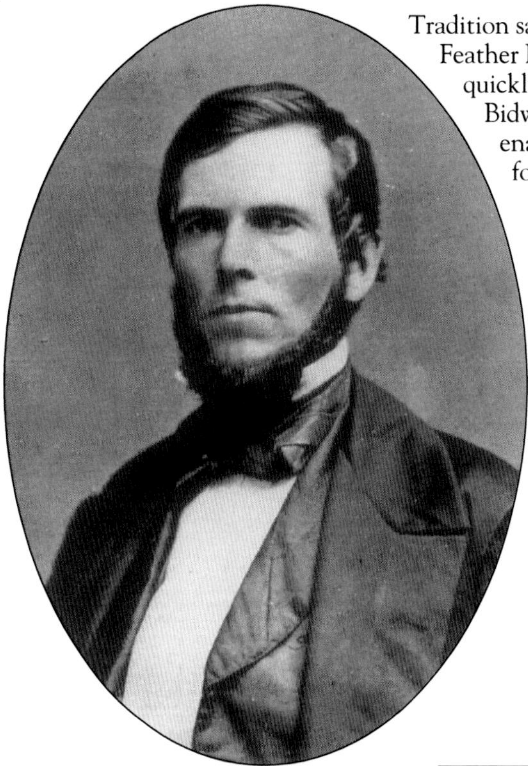

Tradition says John Bidwell discovered gold on the Feather River below Oroville on July 4, 1848. He quickly formed a mining expedition and settled at Bidwell's Bar, where he made the fortune that enabled him to purchase a vast land grant and found the city of Chico.

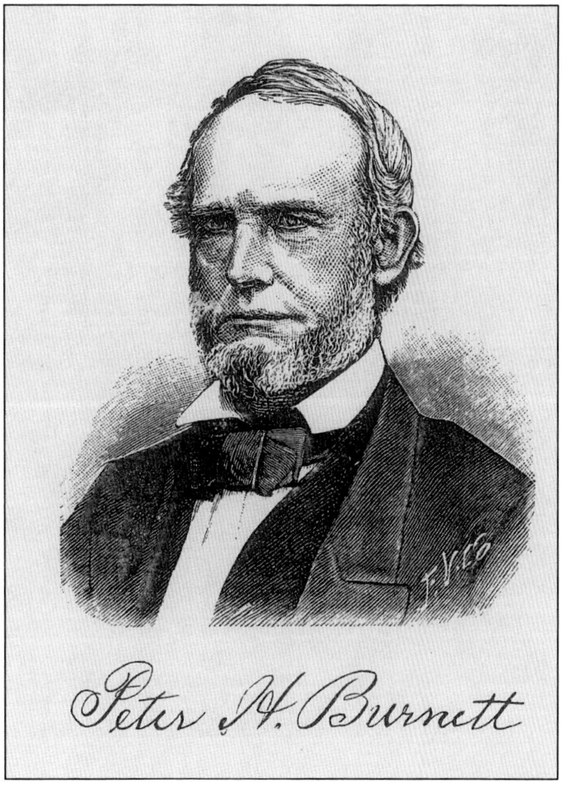

In 1848, Peter Burnett led the first wagon train from Oregon Territory in search of gold. Members of his party founded Oregon City on Table Mountain. While Burnett became the first civil governor of California, others returned to Oregon and struck the first gold coins in the West.

Two

THE AGE OF GOLD

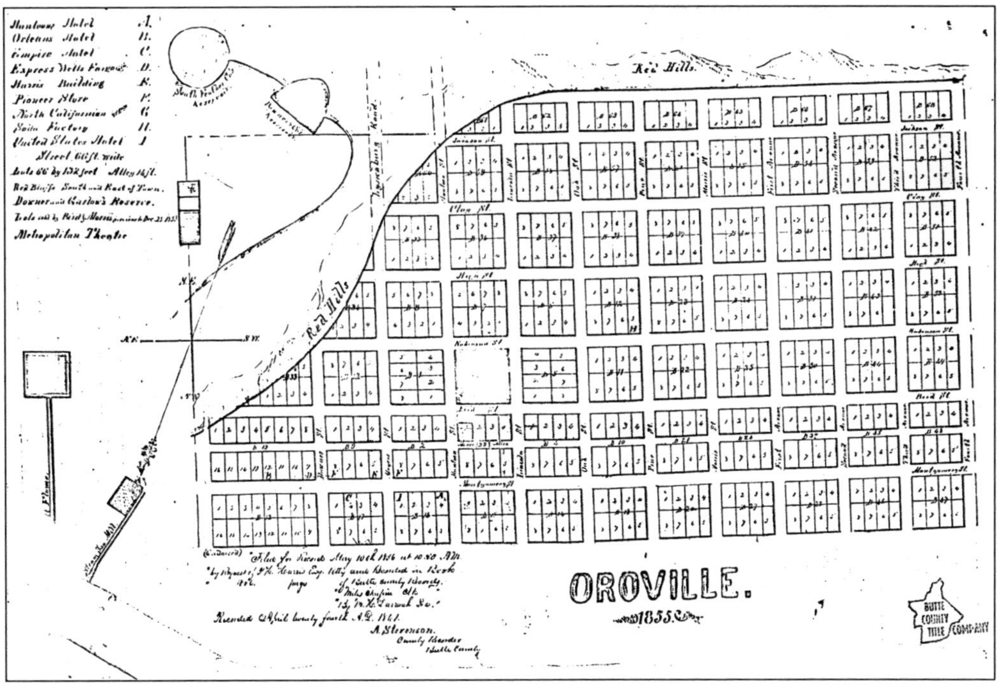

Shown above is the official map laying out the city of Oroville in 1855. The following year it would be declared the county seat and the most populated mining camp in California.

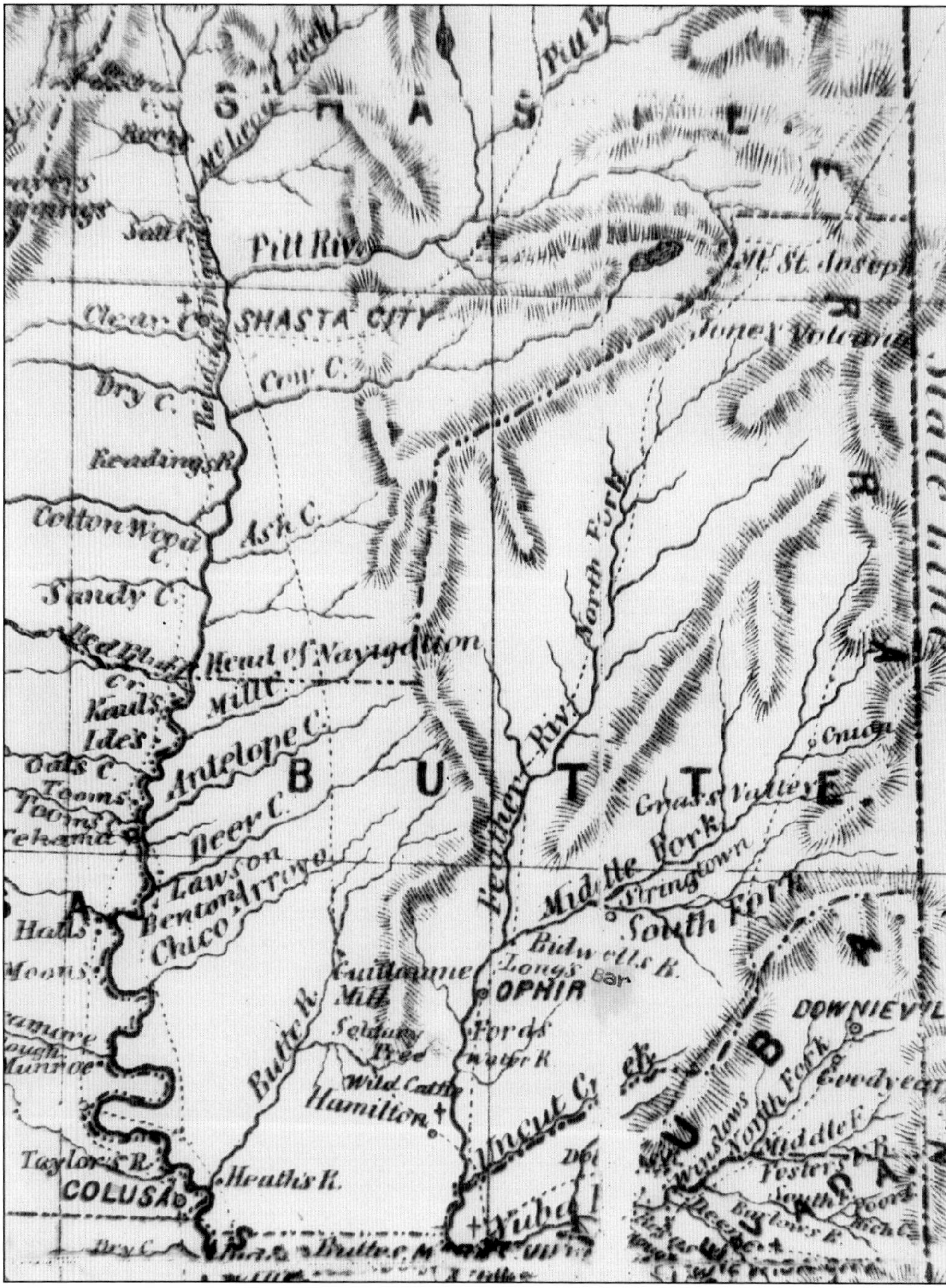

A map made during the Gold Rush shows Oroville when it was originally called Ophir. When it secured a post office in 1855, the new name was suggested by 49ers J.M. Burt and C.F. Lott.

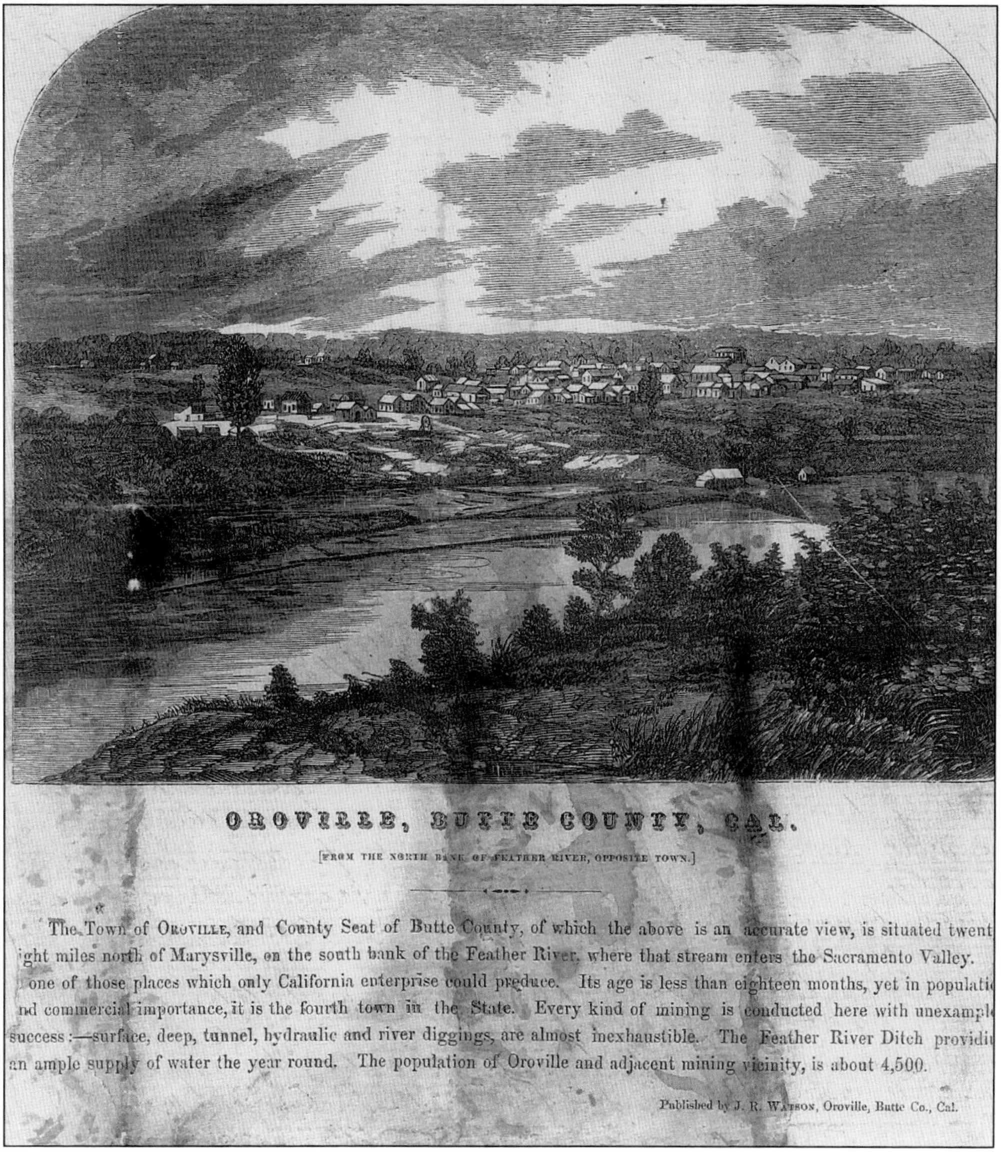

OROVILLE, BUTTE COUNTY, CAL.

[FROM THE NORTH BANK OF FEATHER RIVER, OPPOSITE TOWN.]

The Town of OROVILLE, and County Seat of Butte County, of which the above is an accurate view, is situated twent ight miles north of Marysville, on the south bank of the Feather River, where that stream enters the Sacramento Valley. one of those places which only California enterprise could produce. Its age is less than eighteen months, yet in populati nd commercial importance, it is the fourth town in the State. Every kind of mining is conducted here with unexampl success:—surface, deep, tunnel, hydraulic and river diggings, are almost inexhaustible. The Feather River Ditch providi an ample supply of water the year round. The population of Oroville and adjacent mining vicinity, is about 4,500.

Published by J. R. WATSON, Oroville, Butte Co., Cal.

A pictorial lettersheet shows Oroville on the banks of the Feather River in 1856. The caption states that although less than 18 months old, its commercial growth and population of 4,500 made it the fourth most important city in the state. (Published by merchant J. R. Watson.)

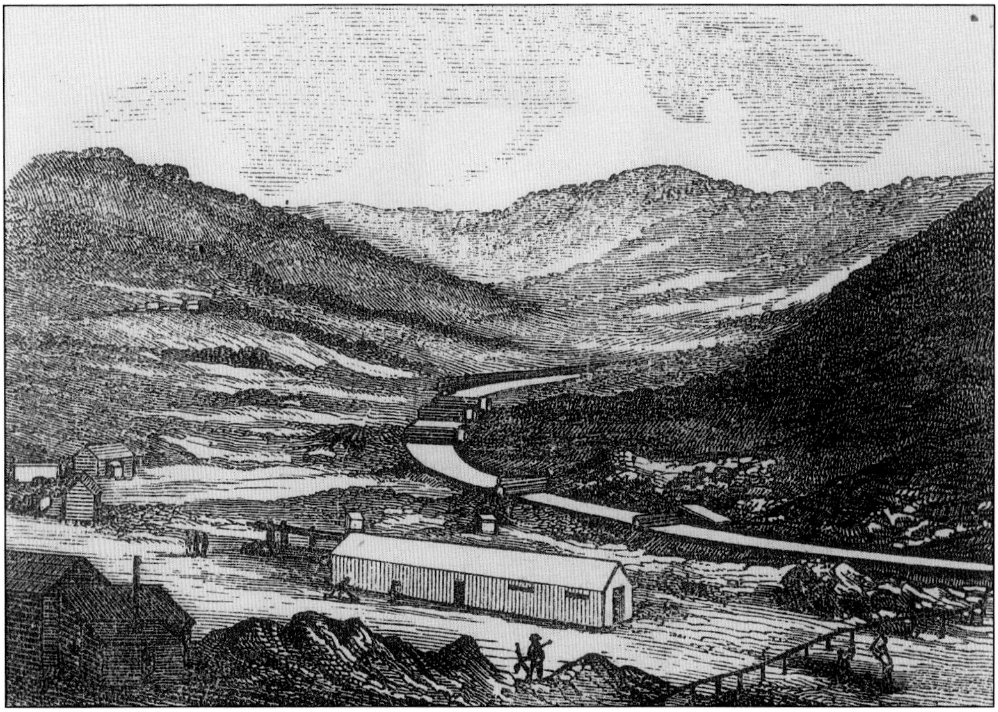

As early as 1856, miners diverted the Feather River just east of Oroville for the gold that lay beneath. This view of the Cape Claim was published by the *Sacramento Pictorial Union* in 1855.

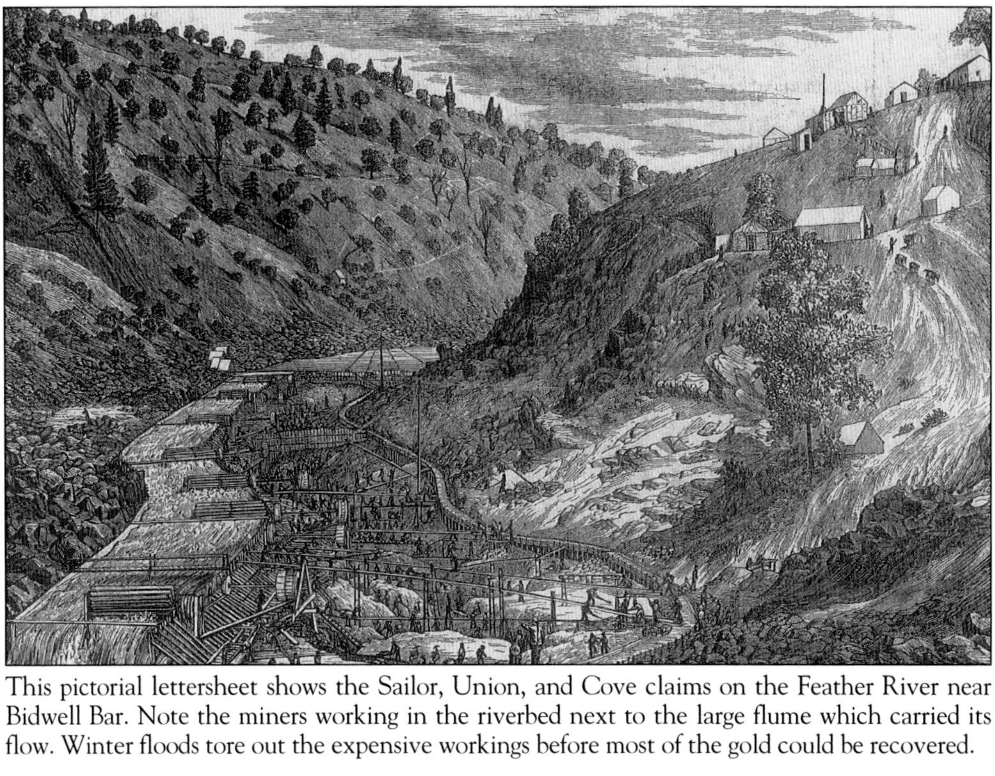

This pictorial lettersheet shows the Sailor, Union, and Cove claims on the Feather River near Bidwell Bar. Note the miners working in the riverbed next to the large flume which carried its flow. Winter floods tore out the expensive workings before most of the gold could be recovered.

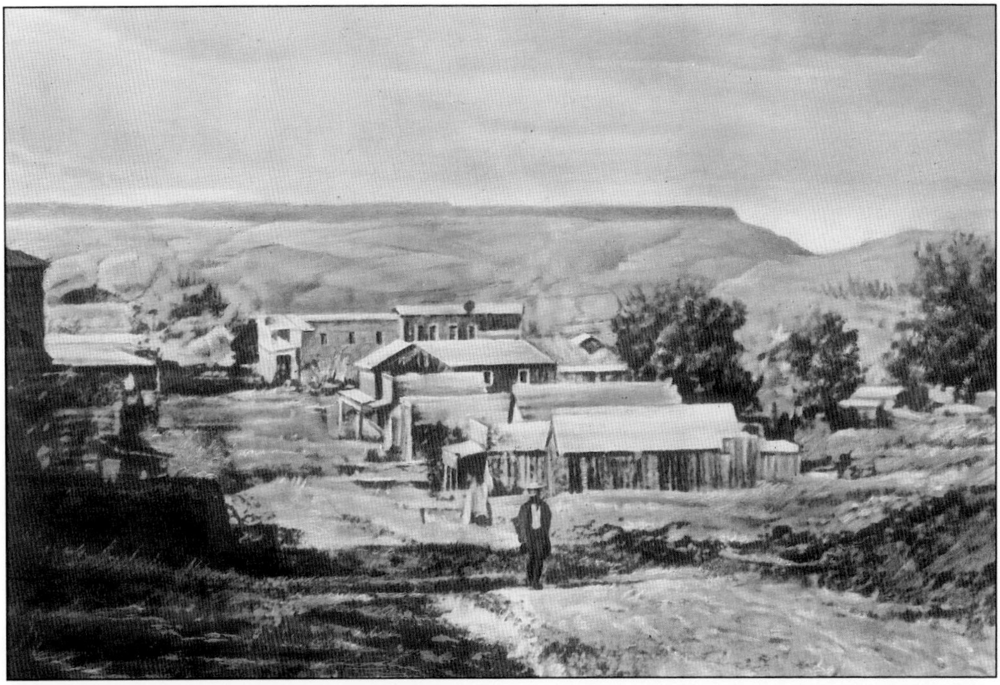

One of the earliest photographs taken of Oroville in 1854 shows Myers Street before construction of a water flume and canal which brought new life to the partially abandoned mining camp.

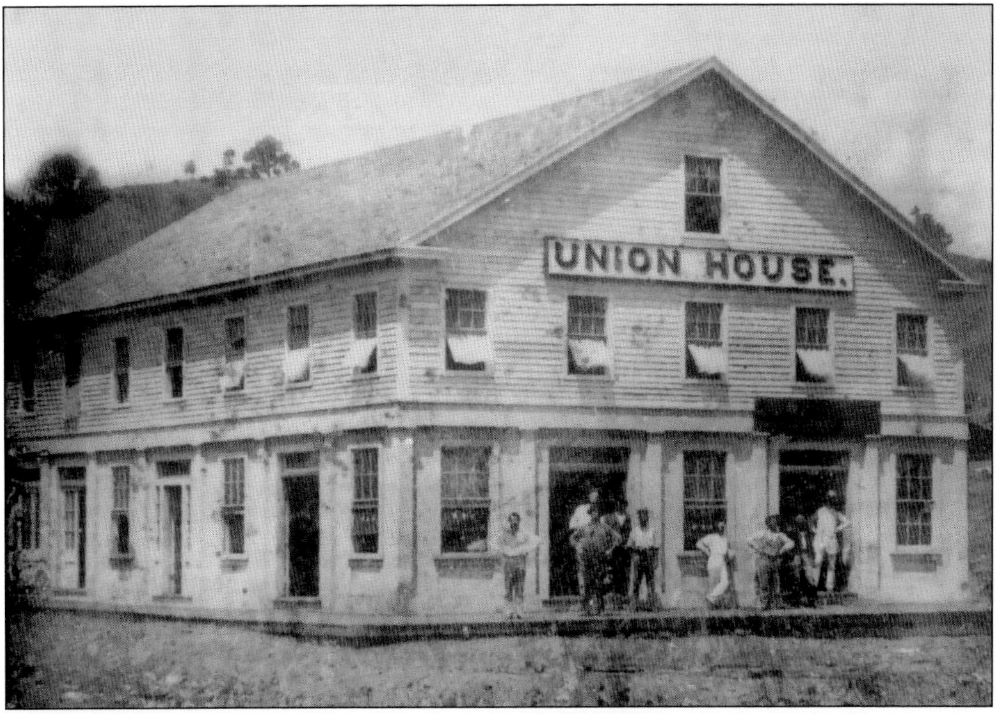

Inscribed Union House, Oroville, 1853, there was also another establishment by the same name at Bidwell Bar that burned in 1854. During their heydays, Oroville and Bidwell Bar boasted numerous hostelries, with stages arriving and leaving by the hour.

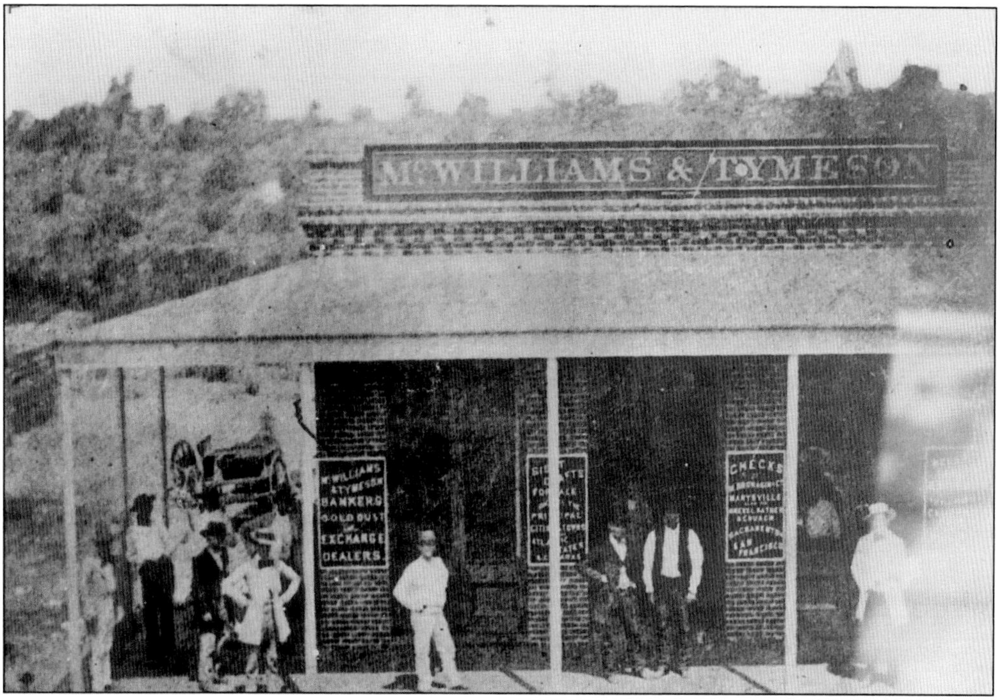

The first bank in Oroville was erected in 1855 on the northeast corner of Myers and Montgomery Streets by bankers McWilliams and Tymeson. It also served as agent for Wells Fargo & Company Express. The bank survives today as a branch of Bank of America.

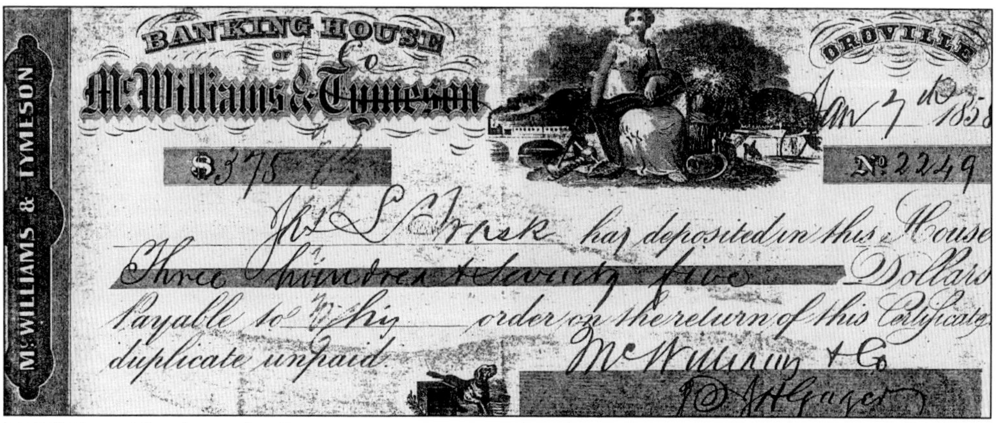

McWilliams' banking checks were impressive works of art.

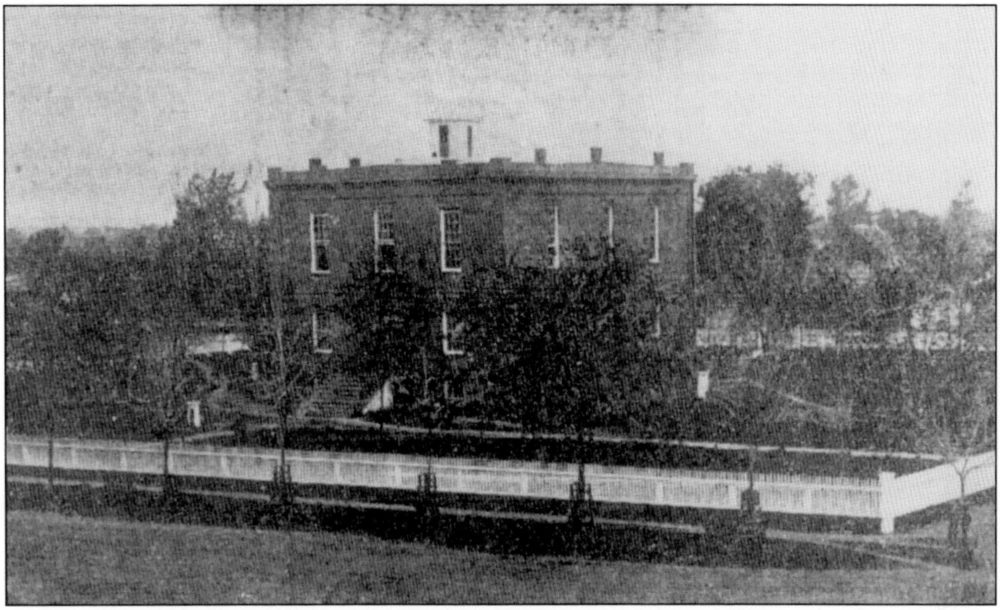

Taken in 1856, this photo shows the newly completed courthouse erected on the plaza in downtown Oroville. Expanded over the years, it would remain in use until the earthquake of 1975 inspired politicos to build a new one across the river. (Photo by pioneer photographer E. Kusel.)

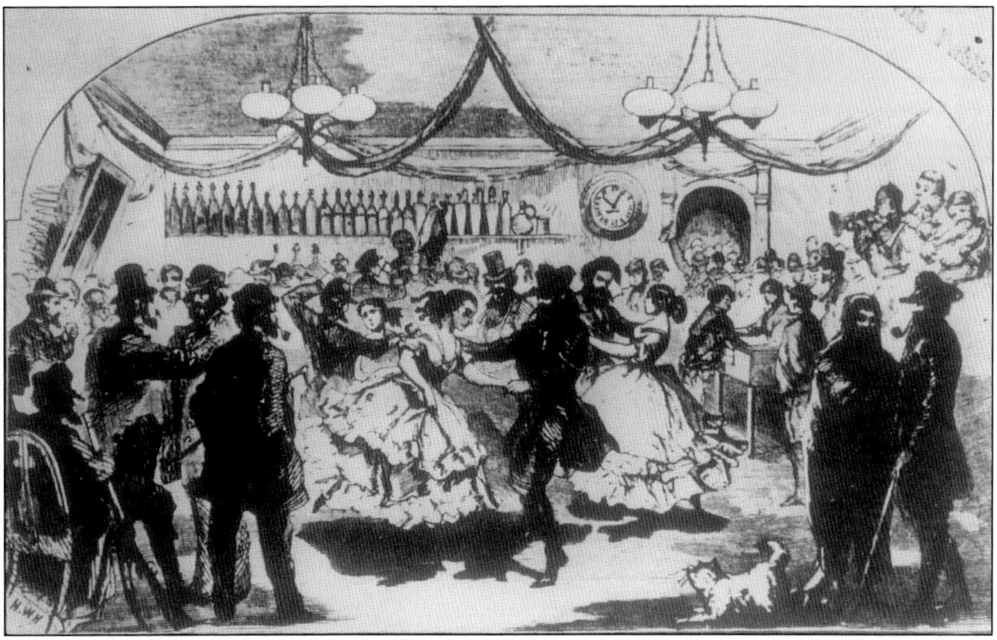

Some accounts say Oroville had as many as 100 saloons during the Gold Rush era. The most famous was Harry Hunt's Bank Exchange in the basement of the Washington Block on the corner of Myers and Montgomery Streets. It operated for over 50 years, and the ghostly rooms survive to this day.

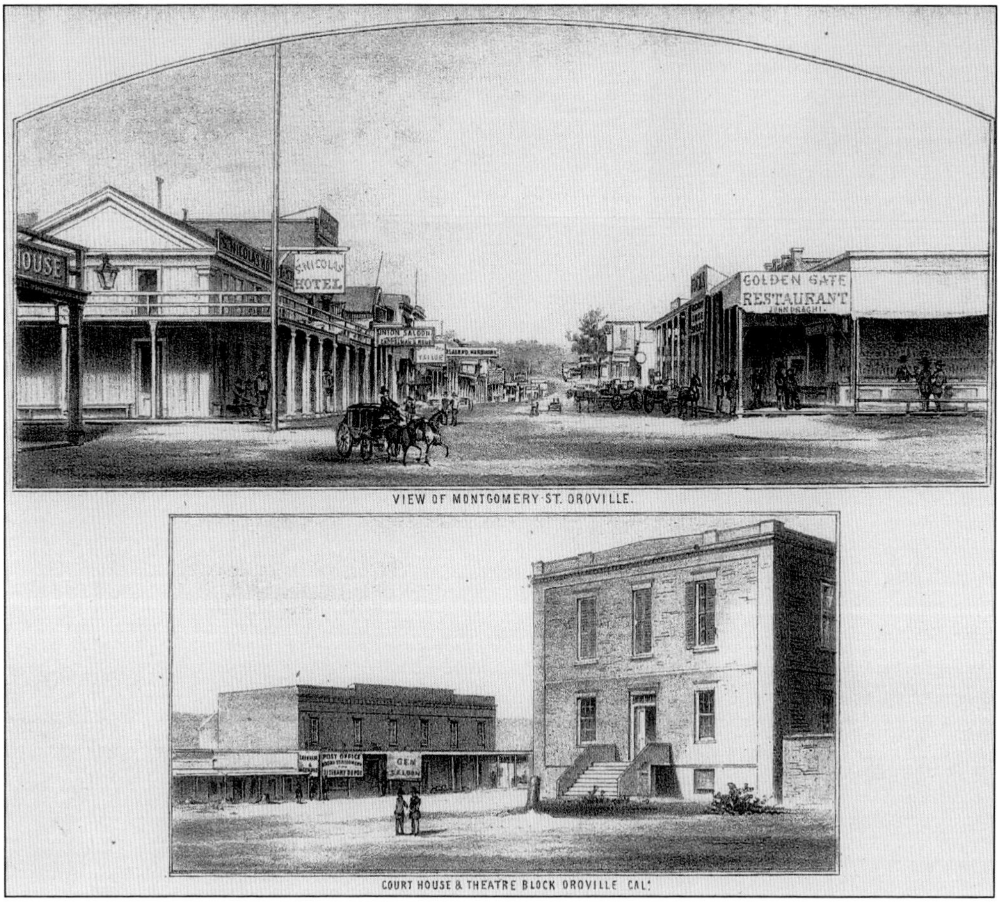

This pictorial lettersheet published by Lockwood's Literary Depot in 1858 shows Montgomery Street looking east from Huntoon Street, plus the courthouse and Metropolitan Theatre on Bird Street. The American Theatre was the first in Oroville, located on Montgomery Street.

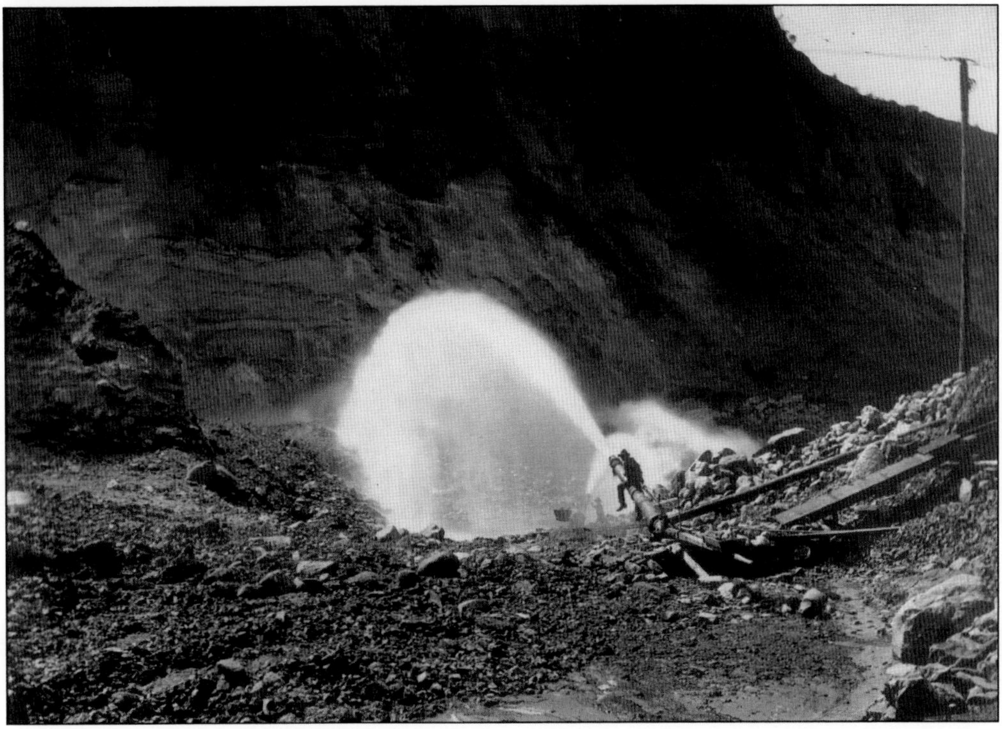

Oroville was the commercial hub for such surrounding towns as Cherokee, Oregon City, Forbestown, Bangor, Bidwell Bar, and Honcut. Shown above is a hydraulic monitor working the bluffs of Cherokee, site of the most complete hydraulic mine in the world during the 1870s and 1880s.

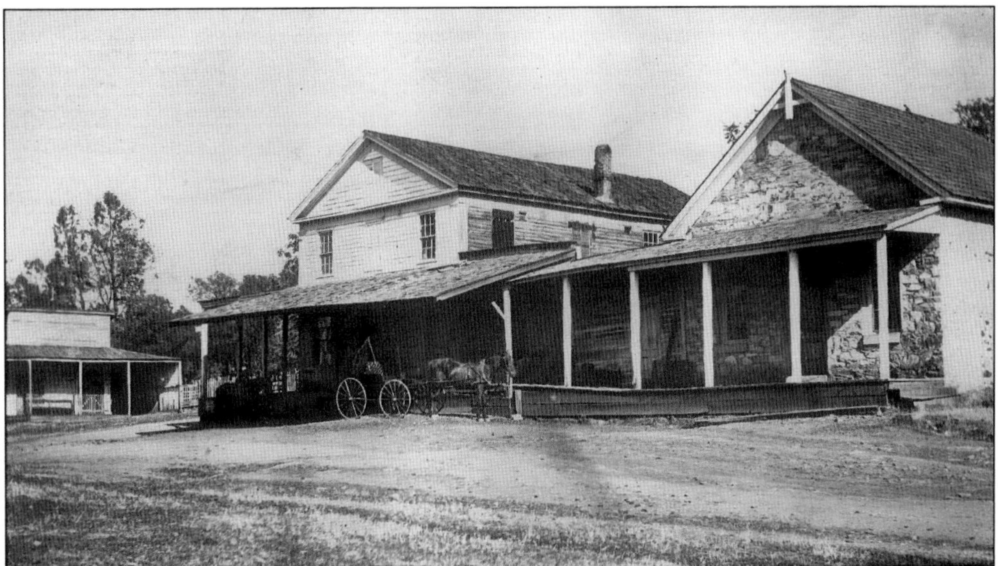

Shown above are the remnants of downtown Cherokee in 1900. A vault in the stone mine office at right once held gold and the first diamonds discovered in the U.S. Across the street today is the Cherokee Museum.

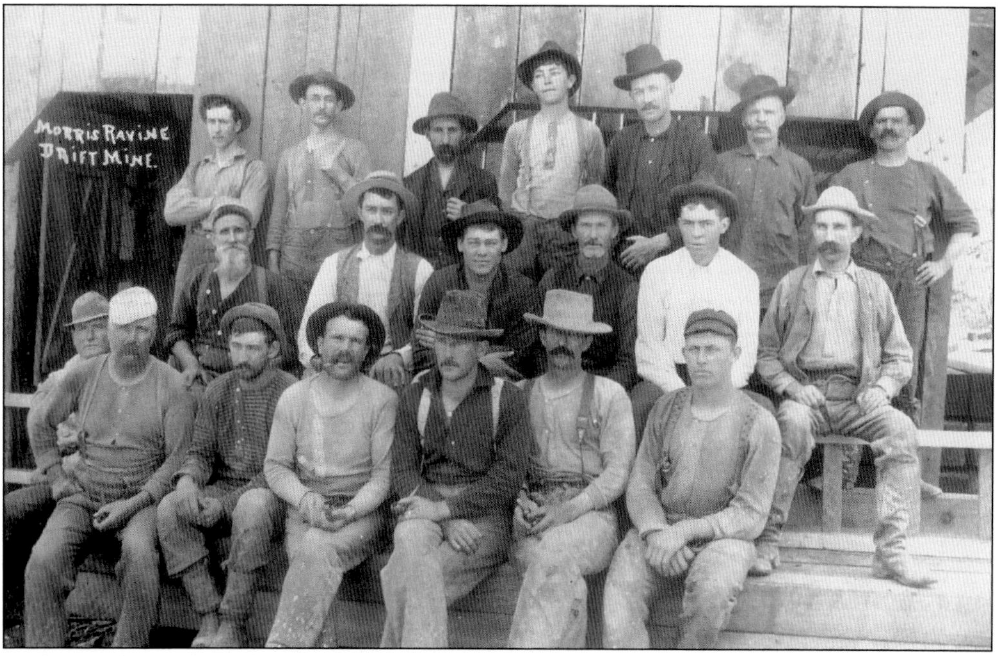

A photo taken in 1885 shows men who worked in the Morris Ravine Drift Mine between Oroville and Oregon City. Tunneling under Table Mountain, miners were able to tap the rich placer deposits beneath, producing gold that was the purest found anywhere in California.

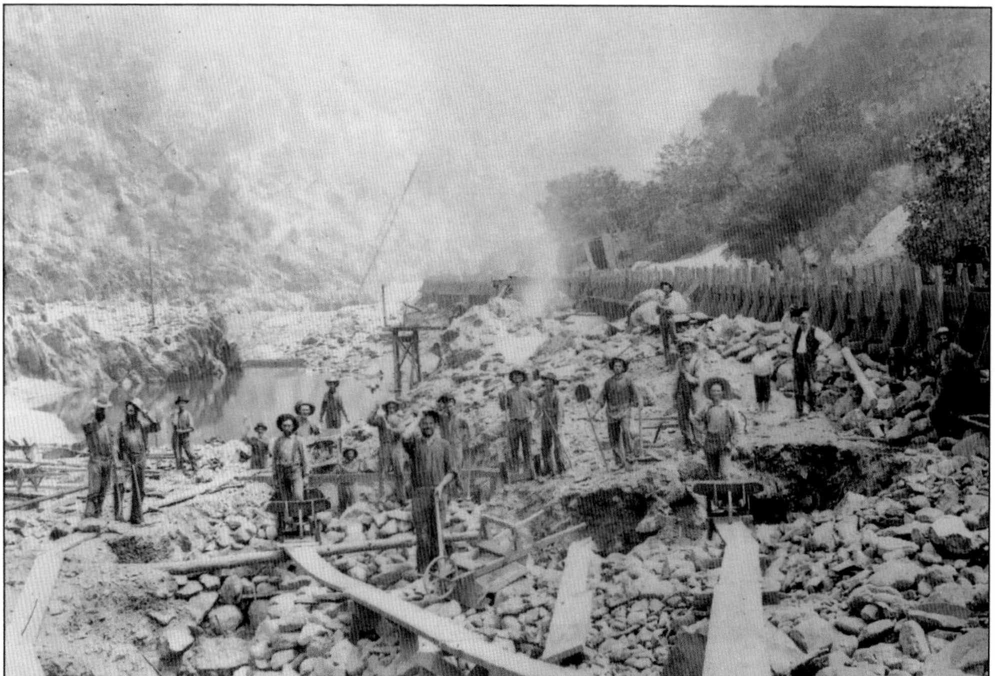

After diverting gold rich streams, miners would dig down through many feet of stone rubble to reach the heaviest gold deposits. It was back-breaking labor, requiring derricks to move the heaviest boulders.

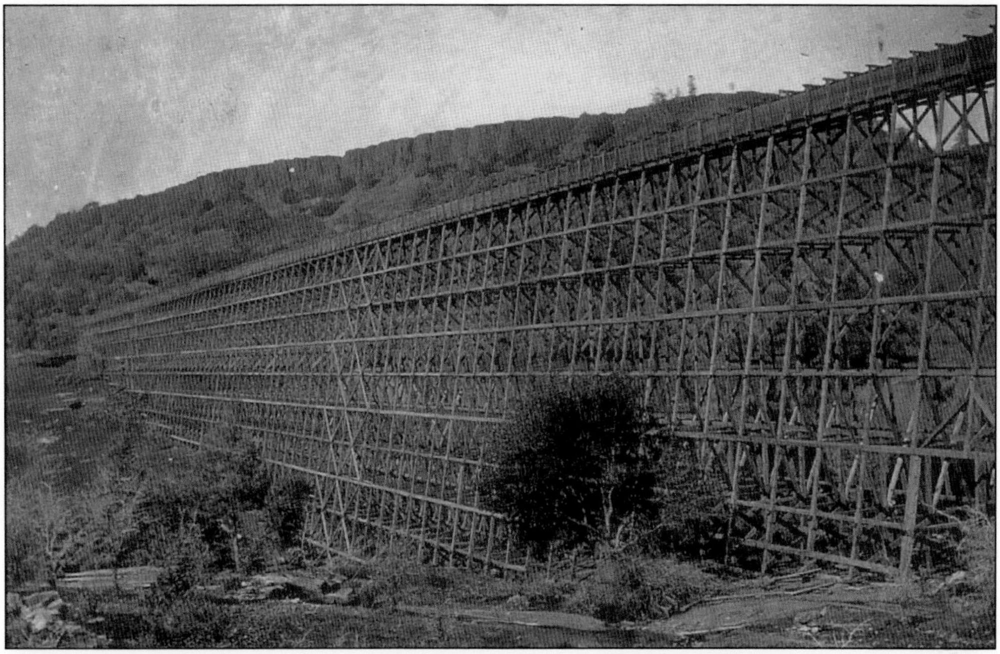

Massive flumes like this one below Table Mountain were built to supply water for "dry diggin's." Below this flume in Schirmer Ravine was located the Hurry Back Saloon.

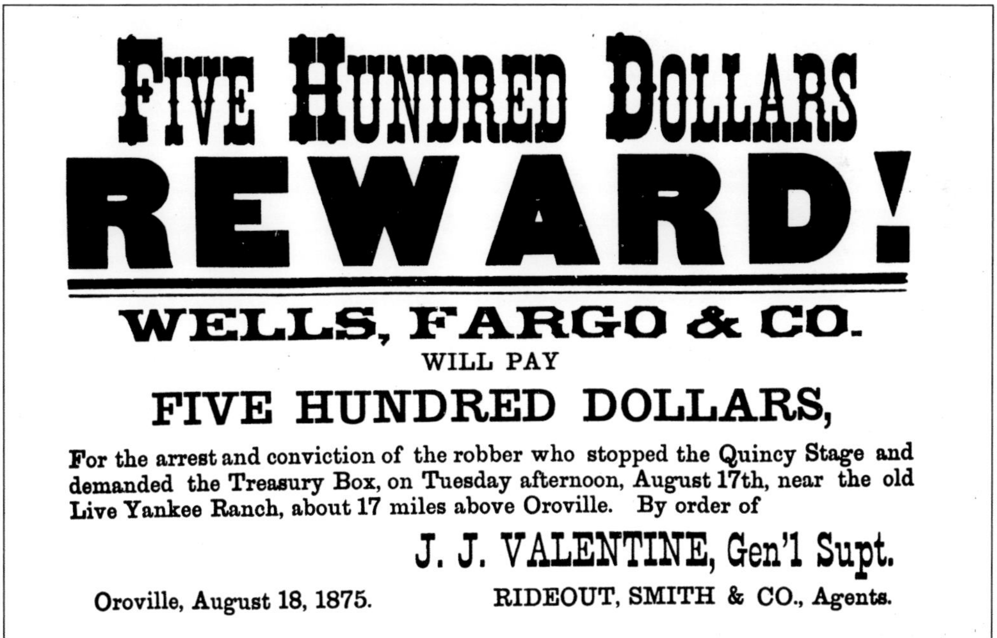

Although there were not many stage robberies around Oroville, it was Black Bart who robbed at least three, posing as a gentleman gambler at local saloons. He was even invited to serve on the book selection committee of the Ladies Library Association. A subsequent wanted poster printed one of the poems he left after robbing another local stage.

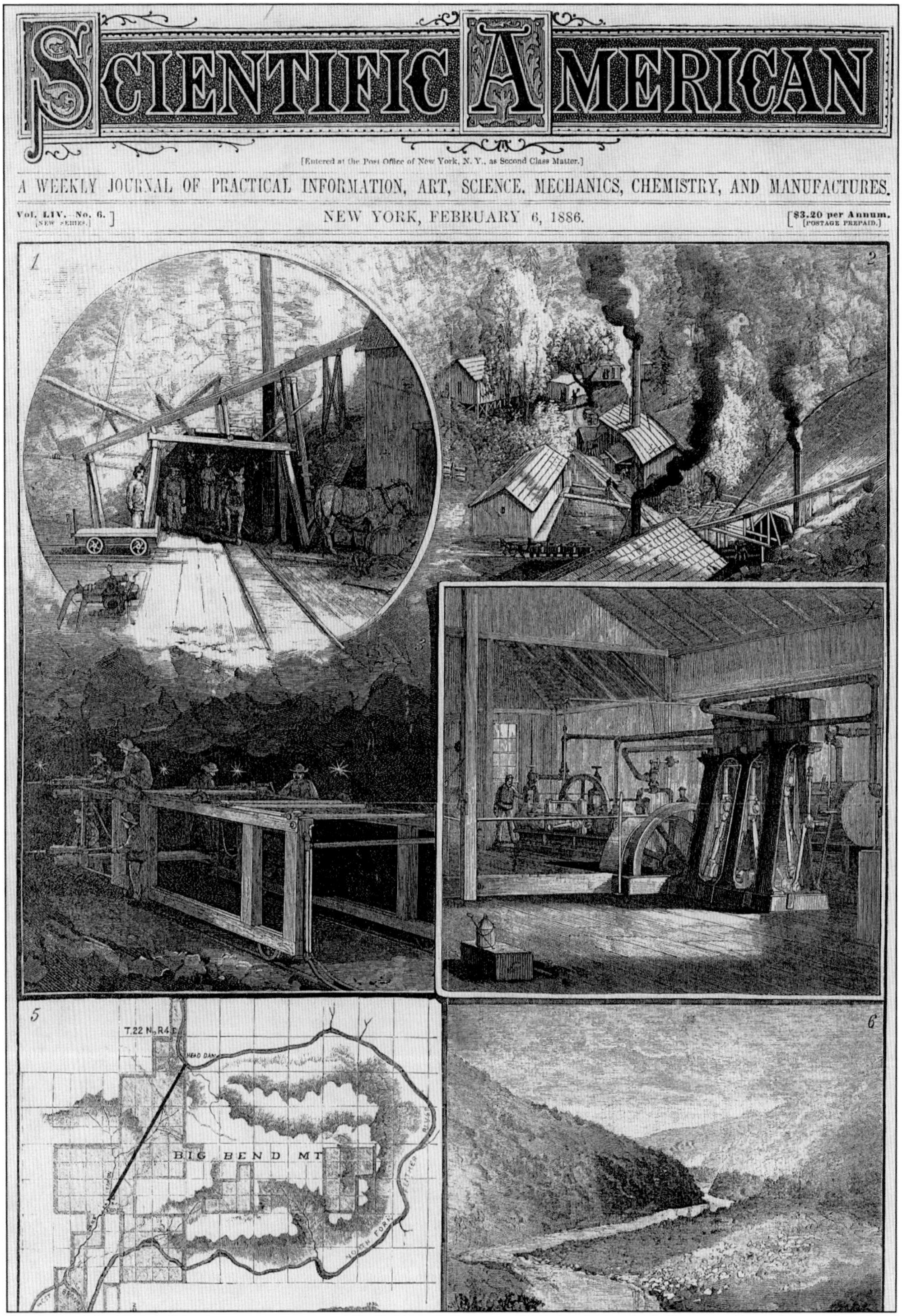

SCIENTIFIC AMERICAN

[Entered at the Post Office of New York, N. Y., as Second Class Matter.]

A WEEKLY JOURNAL OF PRACTICAL INFORMATION, ART, SCIENCE, MECHANICS, CHEMISTRY, AND MANUFACTURES.

Vol. LIV.—No. 6. [NEW SERIES.] NEW YORK, FEBRUARY 6, 1886. [$3.20 per Annum. [POSTAGE PREPAID.]

One of the grandest mining operations in history was diversion of the Feather River through a tunnel at Big Bend north of Oroville in the 1880s. It would be masterminded by Major Frank McLaughlin and financed in part by Dr. Pierce of patent medicine fame.

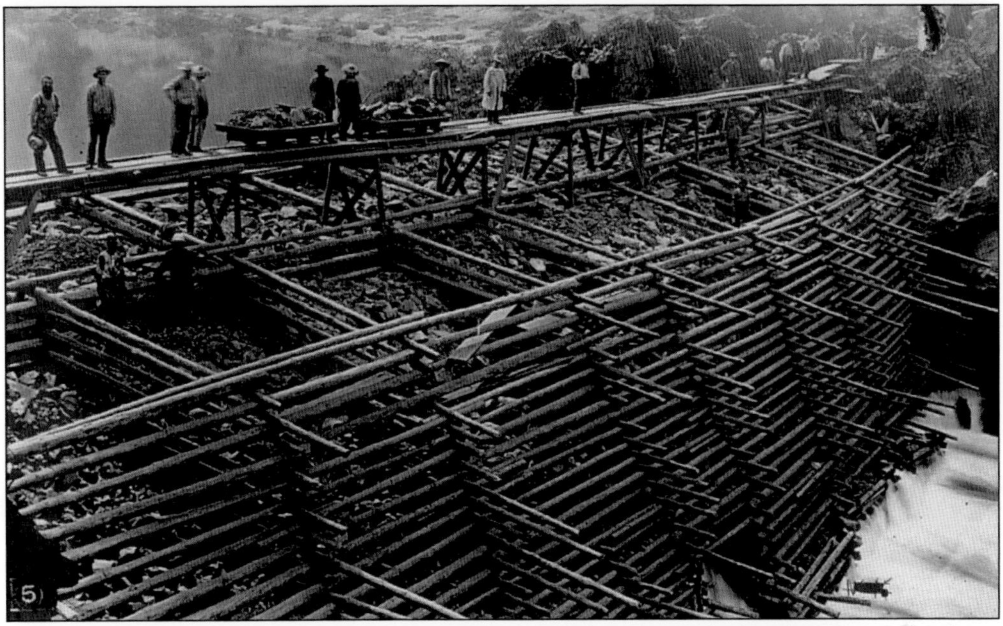

After the Big Bend project, Major McLaughlin decided to divert the Feather River just above Oroville for the gold which earlier miners hopefully left behind. Shown above is the dam he constructed with the help of Chinese laborers. He named the operation the "Golden Gate." (Photos by Hogan.)

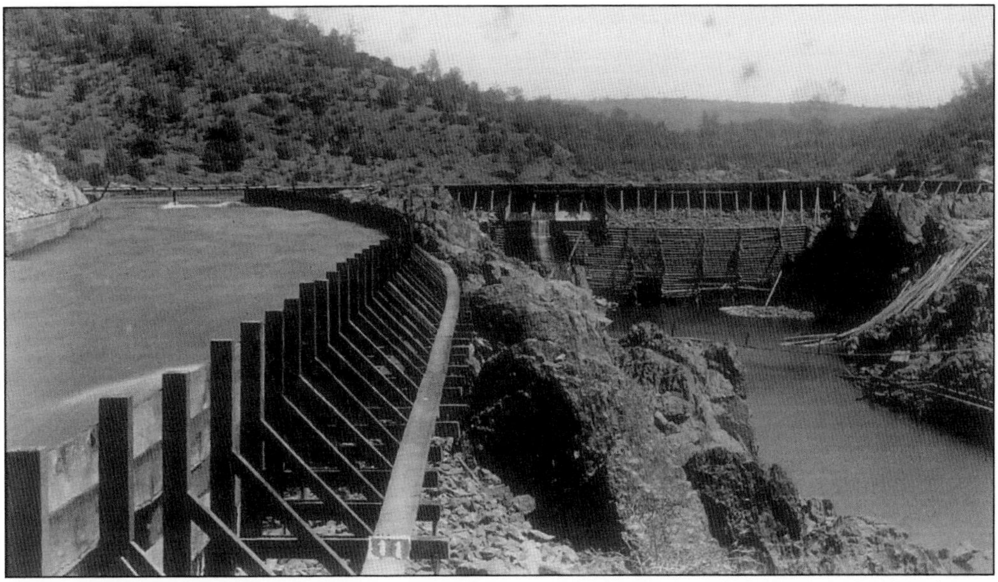

The Feather River was diverted into the large flume at left, continuing its course further downstream behind a massive stone wall, which was a favorite walking site until submerged in the 1960s by the Oroville Dam Diversion Pool.

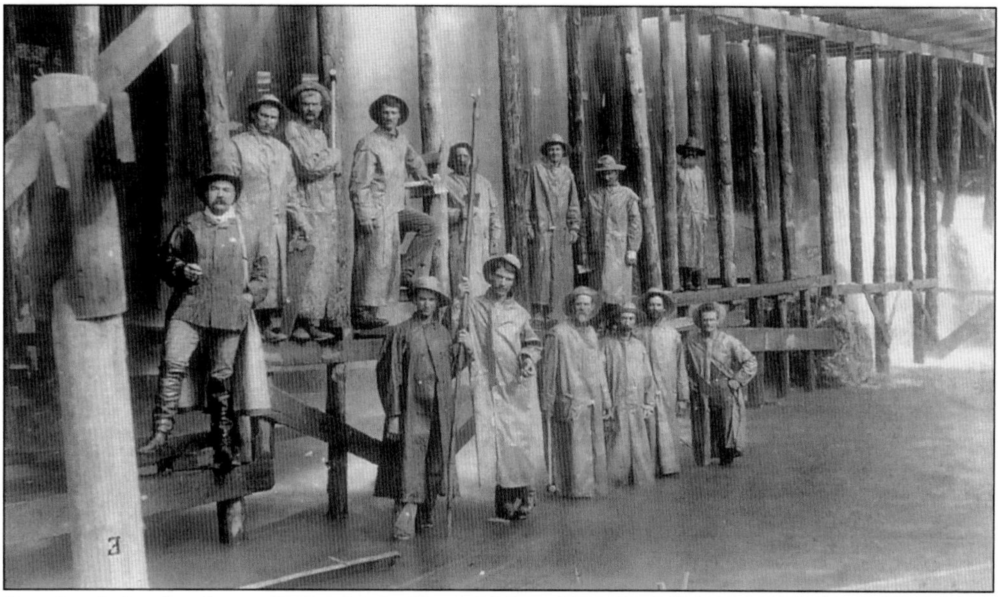

Standing below his dam in 1888 is Major Frank McLaughlin (far left) and some of his workers. English investors were disappointed with profits, and the project was ultimately abandoned. Nevertheless, McLaughlin gleaned enough to build a stately mansion on Beach Hill at Santa Cruz.

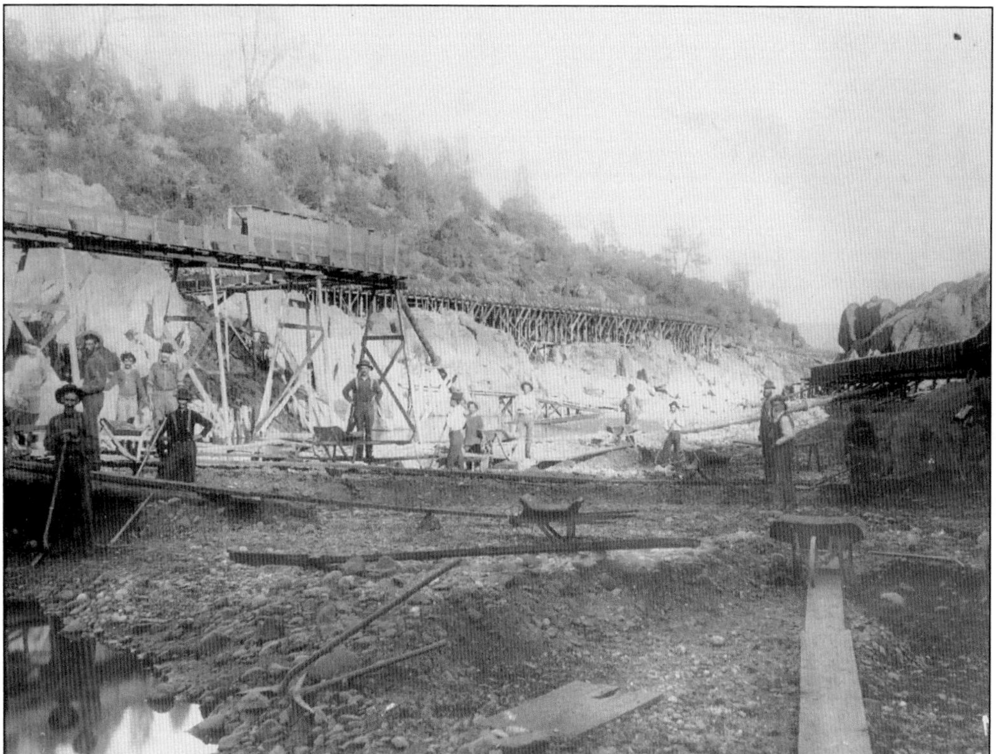

Although mining operations were often on a grand scale, workers still had to use picks, shovels, and wheelbarrows to get at the elusive grains of gold and tucked-away nuggets.

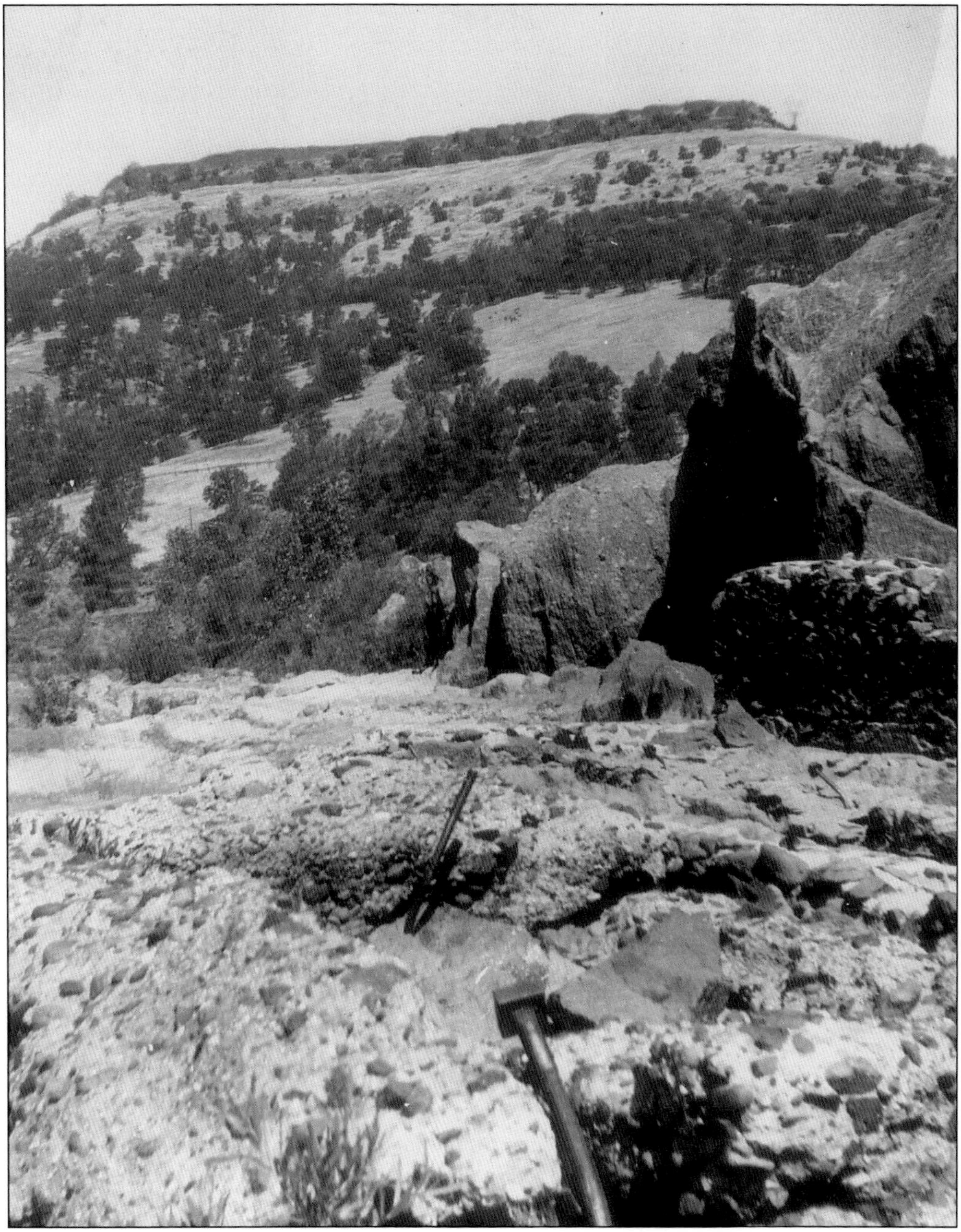

In this photo taken by the author in 1954, all that remained of McLaughlin's river diversion dam were a few bolts imbedded in concrete. Majestic Table Mountain towers in the background, most of its fabulous riches still hidden beneath.

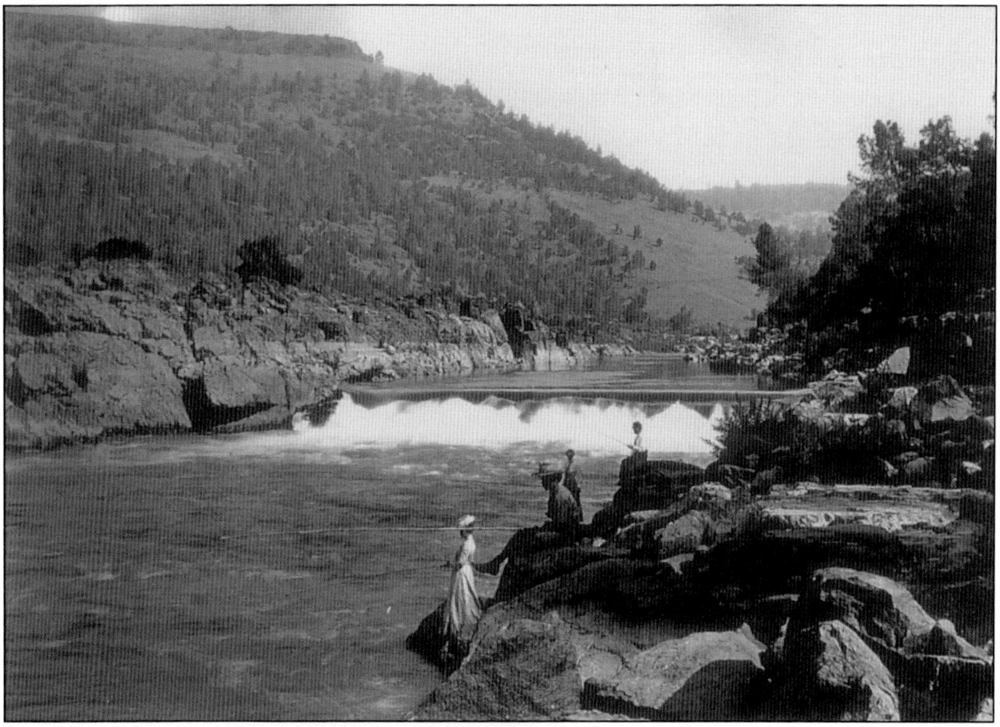

The Feather River at Oroville quickly reclaimed itself by 1900 when these ladies were shown fishing from its banks. Tall rocks and deep pools made popular swimming and diving sites.

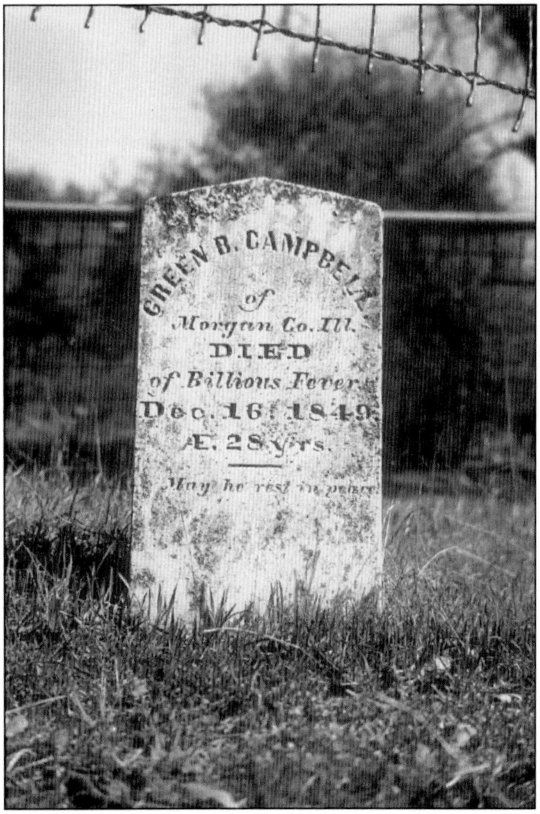

Not all those who sought fortunes from the gold fields of California found success. Often the adventure was reward enough, while for others it was the end of the trail. The oldest dated tombstone is at Long's Bar near Oroville.

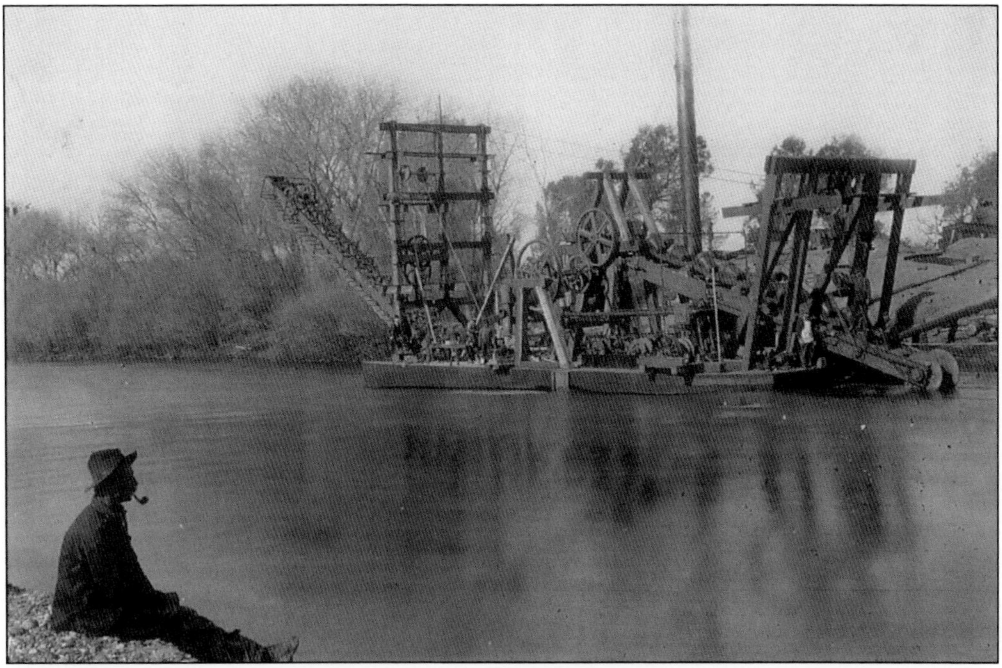

The next big era of mining at Oroville was the advent of what was called the gold dredger. Wendell Hammon and Col. Thomas Couch constructed the first continuous bucket elevator dredger at Oroville in 1898. It would soon be covered to protect the intricate machinery aboard.

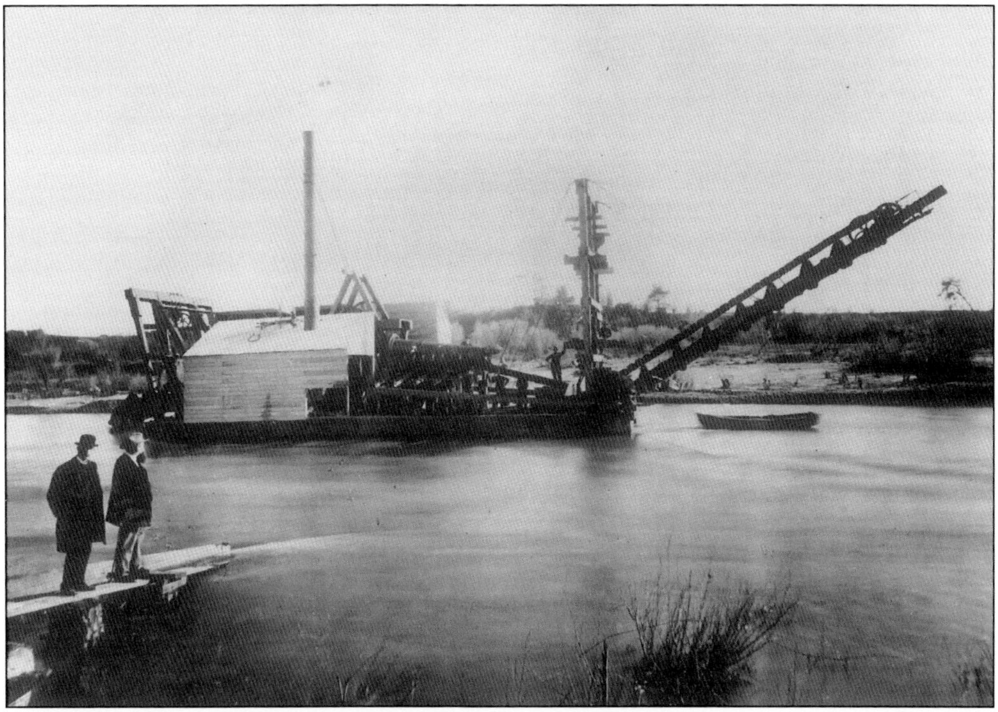

Wendell Hammon and Col. Couch view their completed Feather River No. 1 gold dredger as it fires up to roam the gold-rich placer deposits below Oroville.

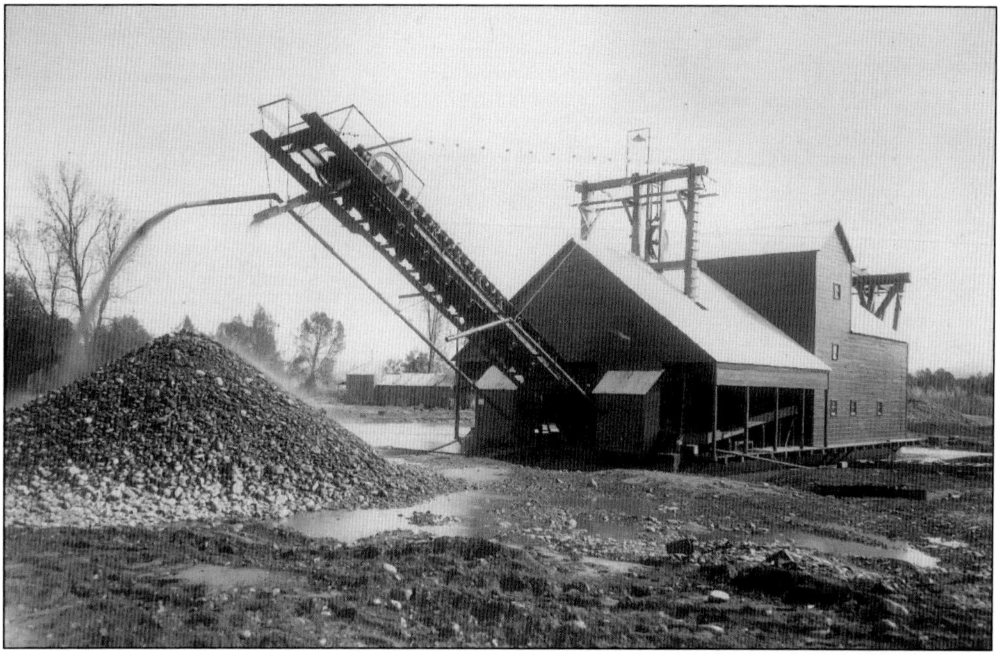

It was not long before the first gold dredger was dwarfed by giants such as this one, shown spewing out rock debris. This debris would later be used to build the great Oroville Dam, highest and widest dam in the U.S.

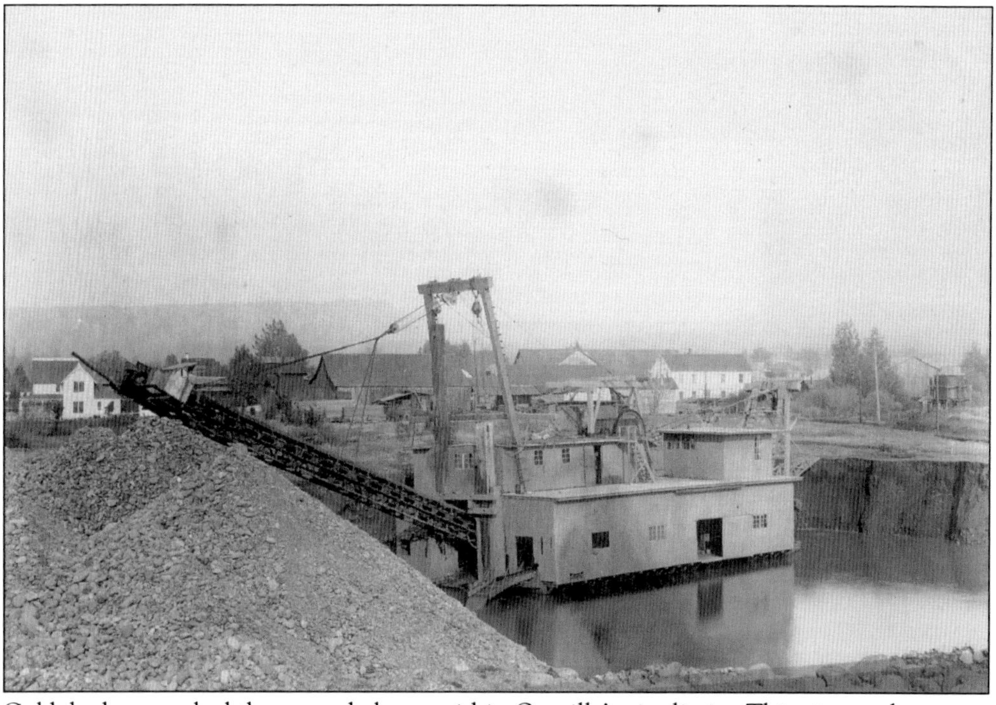

Gold dredgers worked the ground almost within Oroville's city limits. This picture shows one working in the Gray Addition. At their peak, 35 dredgers worked at the same time in the 6,000-acre gold fields south of town.

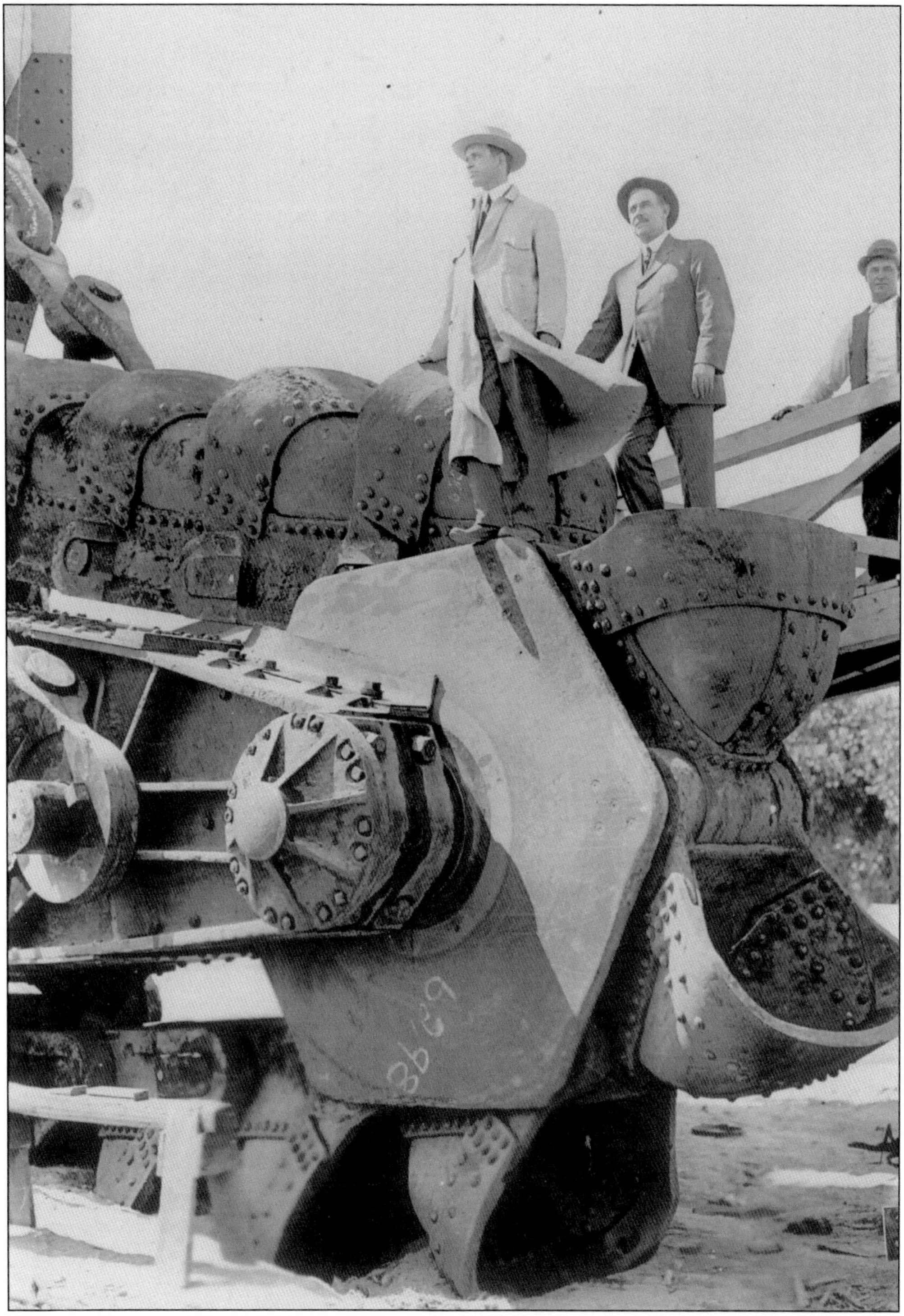

Future millionaire Wendell Hammon (center) poses with associate Will Cleveland on one of the giant buckets of their dredgers. The buckets were able to scoop 75 feet below the surface where the heaviest deposits of gold lay hidden.

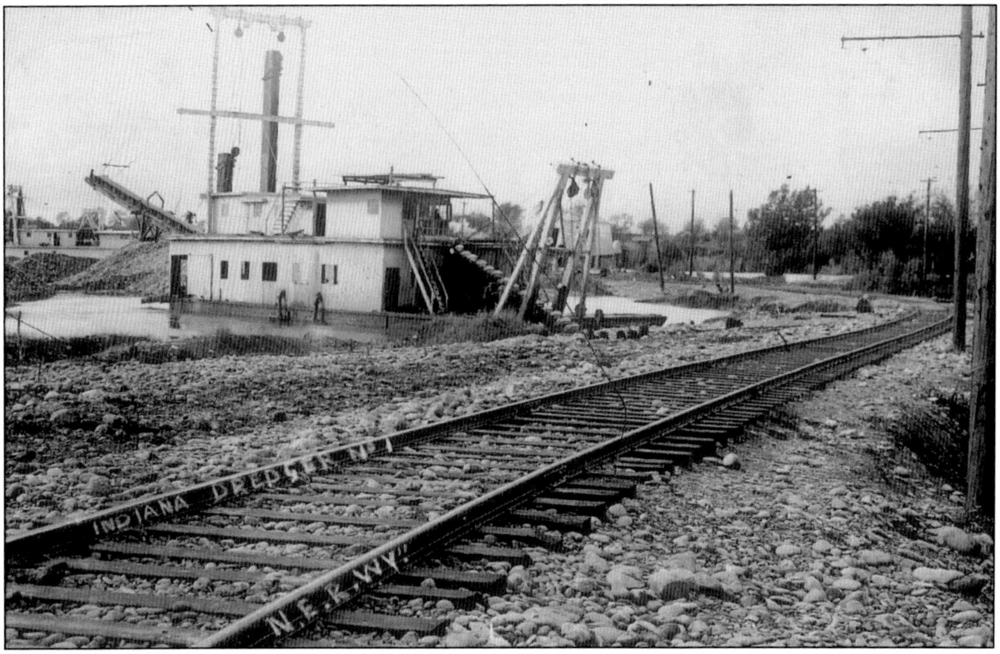

Indiana Dredger No. 1 is shown chewing its way through the gold fields up to the very tracks of the Northern Electric Railway which connected Oroville to Sacramento and Oakland.

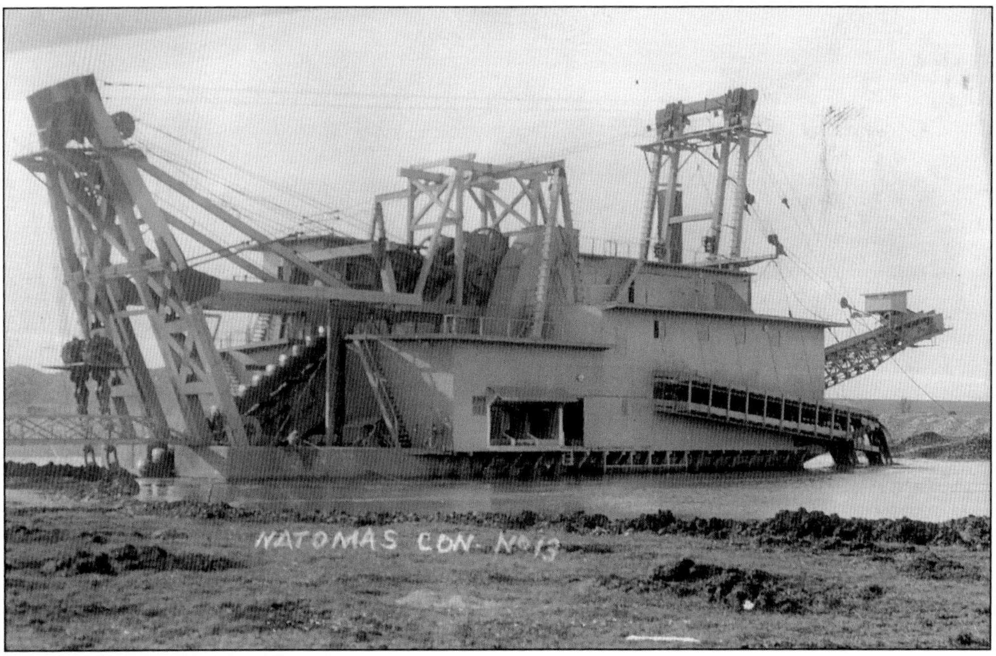

The giant Natomas Consolidated No. 13 was one of the largest gold dredgers in the world. Some were later moved to Columbia and Alaska.

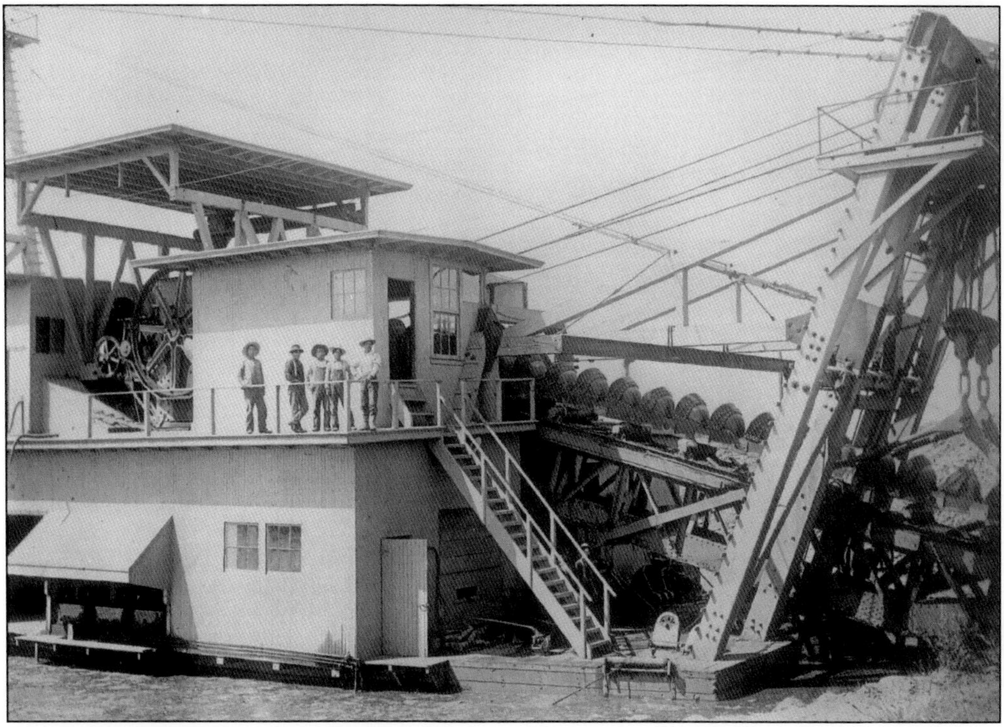

During the dredging era, many Japanese came to the area and worked on the gold dredgers as well as starting their own farms and businesses. Six of them are shown standing by the control room of this dredger.

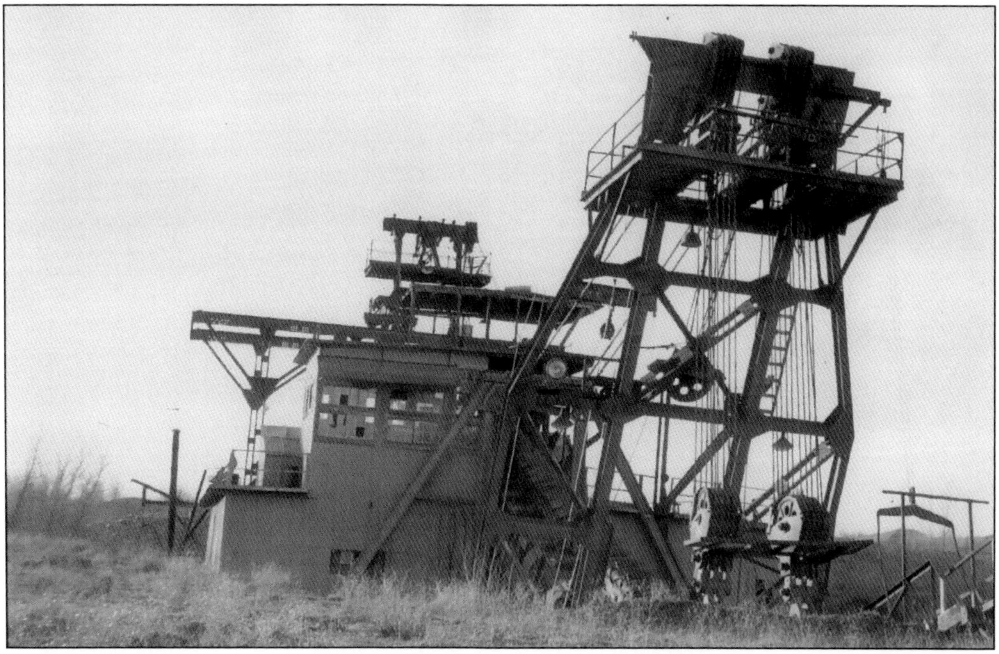

Gold dredging operations ceased altogether a few years after World War II. This photo of the last dredger was taken by the author in 1957.

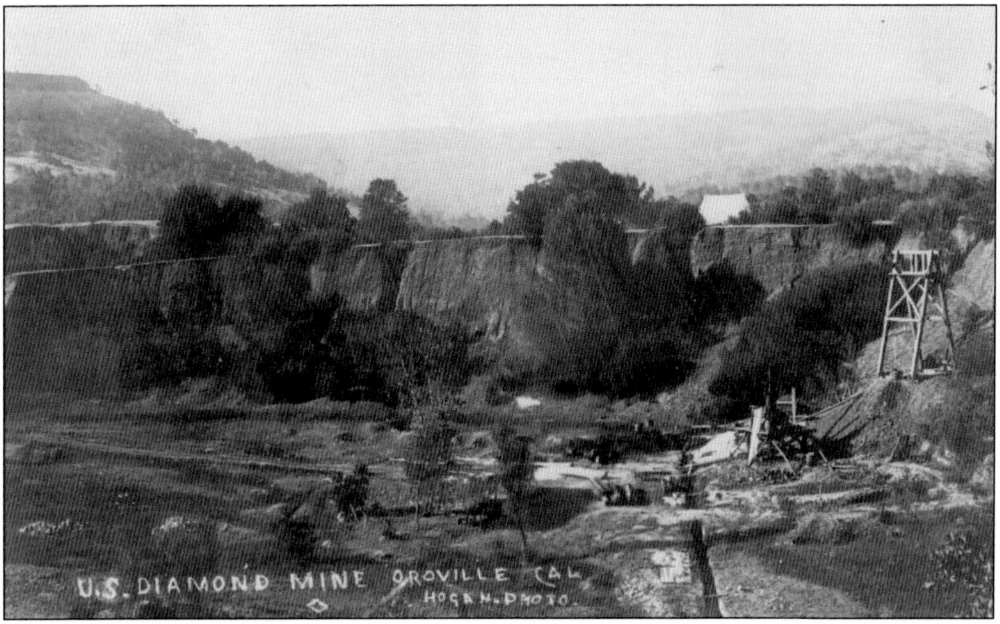

Gold wasn't the only mineral sought at Oroville. Shown here is the U.S. Diamond Mine across the river from town. In 1907, Michael J. Cooney drilled shafts at Cherokee and Oroville in search of the kimberlite pipe that produced diamonds found earlier in the area.

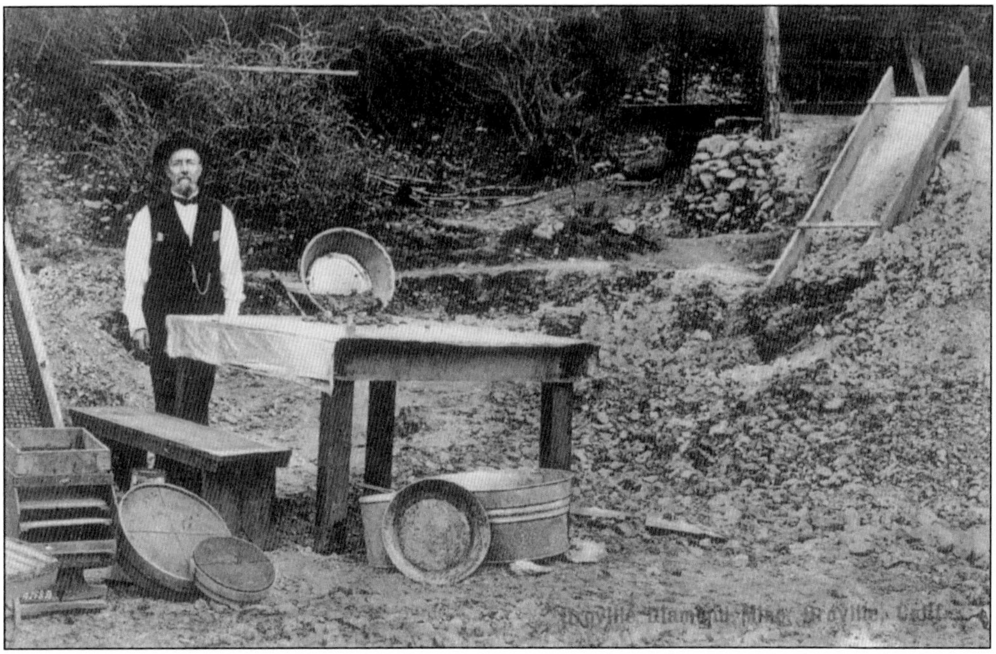

M.J. Cooney stands beside the table he used to pan tailings for possible diamonds. A controversy still exists whether he found the precious stones or not. His remains rest in the Old Oroville Cemetery.

Three

COMMERCE AND ENTERPRISE

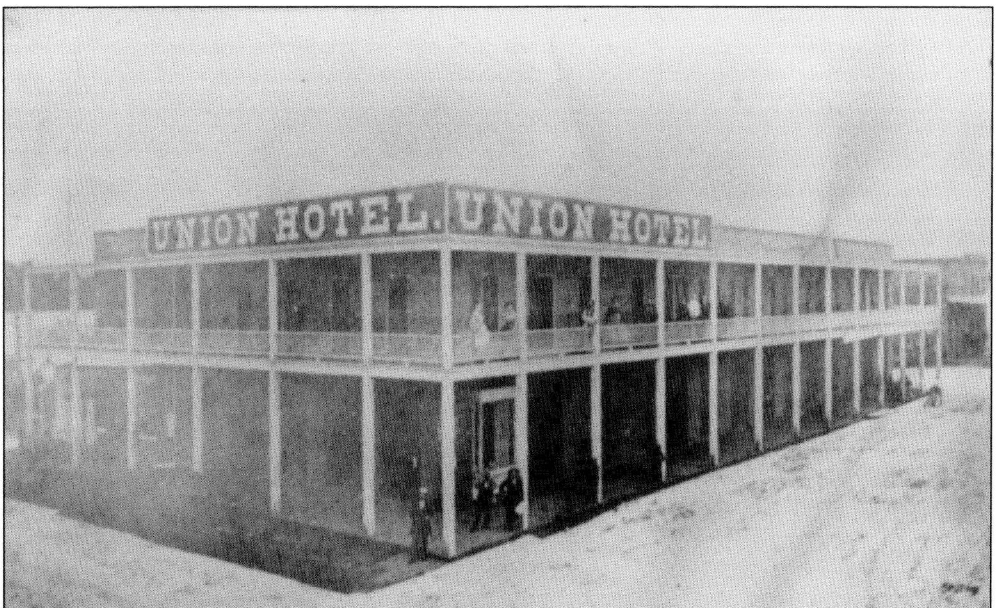

The historic Union Hotel on the corner of Myers and Montgomery Streets was started in 1864 by several prominent local pioneers, including George Perkins, D.N. Friesleben, and J.M. Brock. Over the years it would expand, and it survived until 1944 when destroyed by fire.

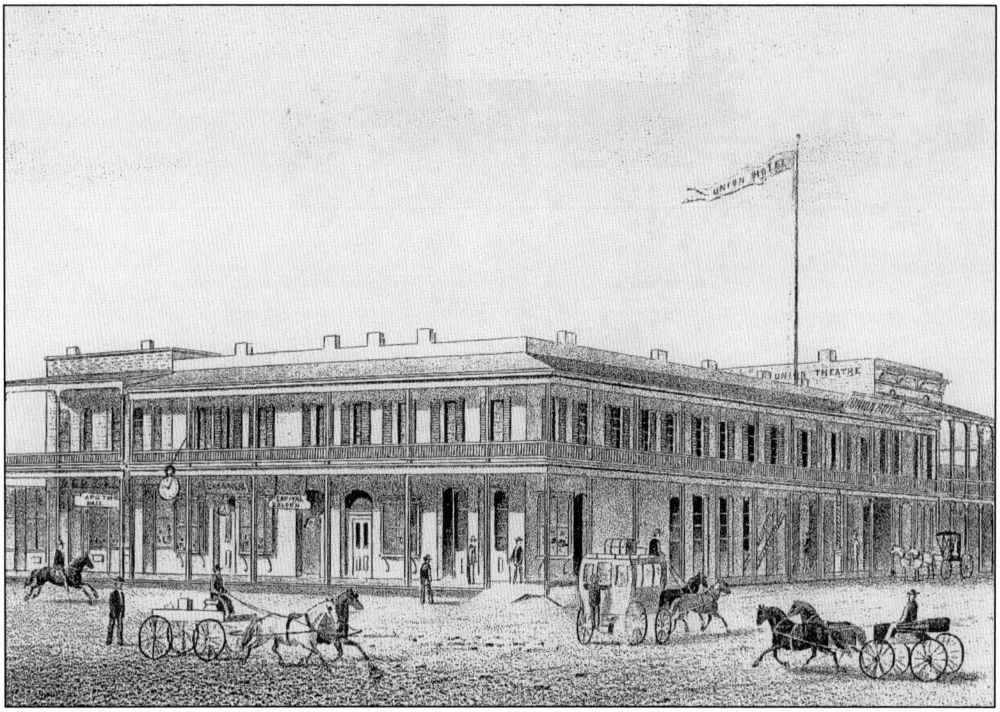

By 1882, the Union Hotel incorporated a splendid theater in addition to several businesses on the ground floor. (Wells & Chambers, *History of Butte County*, 1882.)

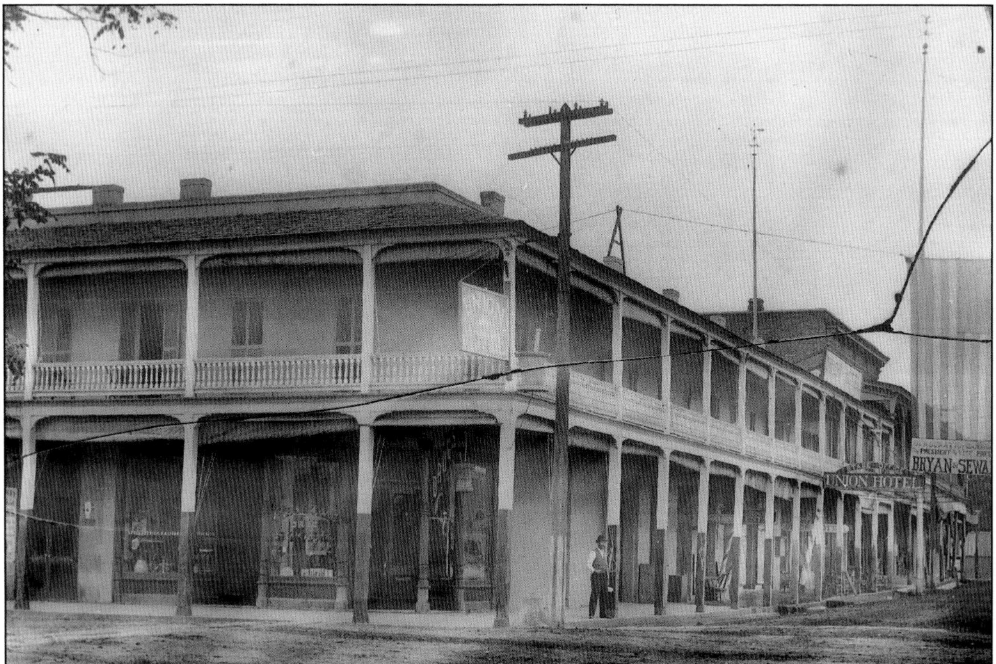

Union Hotel as it appeared in 1896. Parker Drugs was at the corner location. A flag and banner over the street promoted William Jennings Bryan for president.

A formal portrait of the employees of Perkins & Co. store around 1888 was taken by J.H. Hogan. Seated are Milton Green, David Perkins, William Perkins (brothers of Gov. George Perkins), and Ed Hollins. Standing are Dan Carter, George Sparks, Jeff Brown and Ed Ward. Perkins' store served mining camps as far away as Magalia and Rackerby.

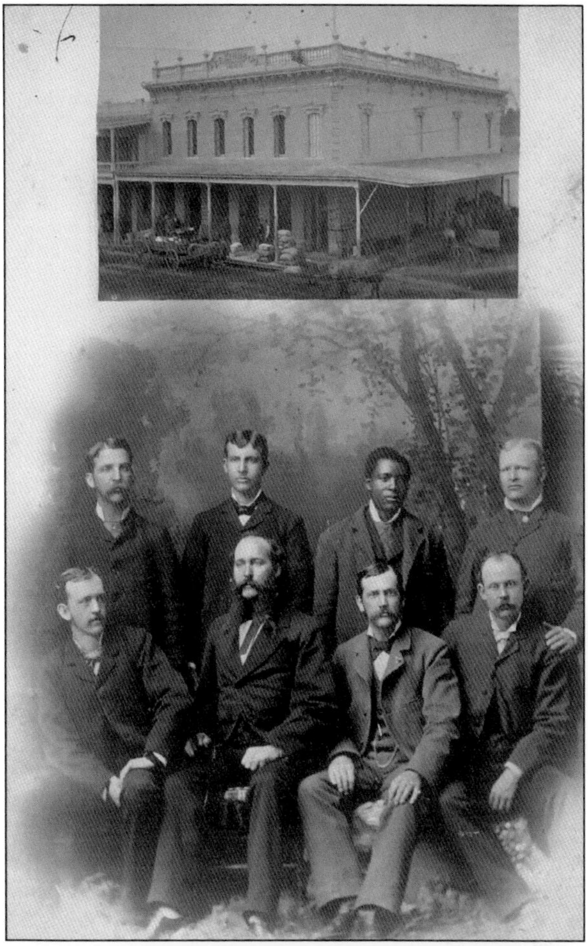

When originally built in the 1850s, Perkins' store at the corner of Myers and Montgomery Streets was one story. Like many homes and stores in town, second floors were added later. (Photo by E. A. Kusel.)

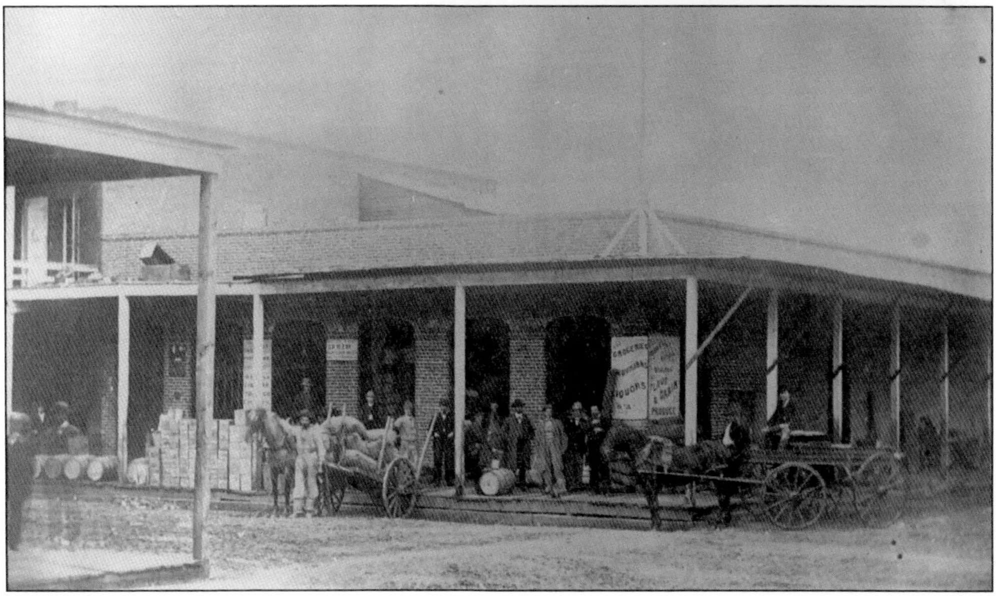

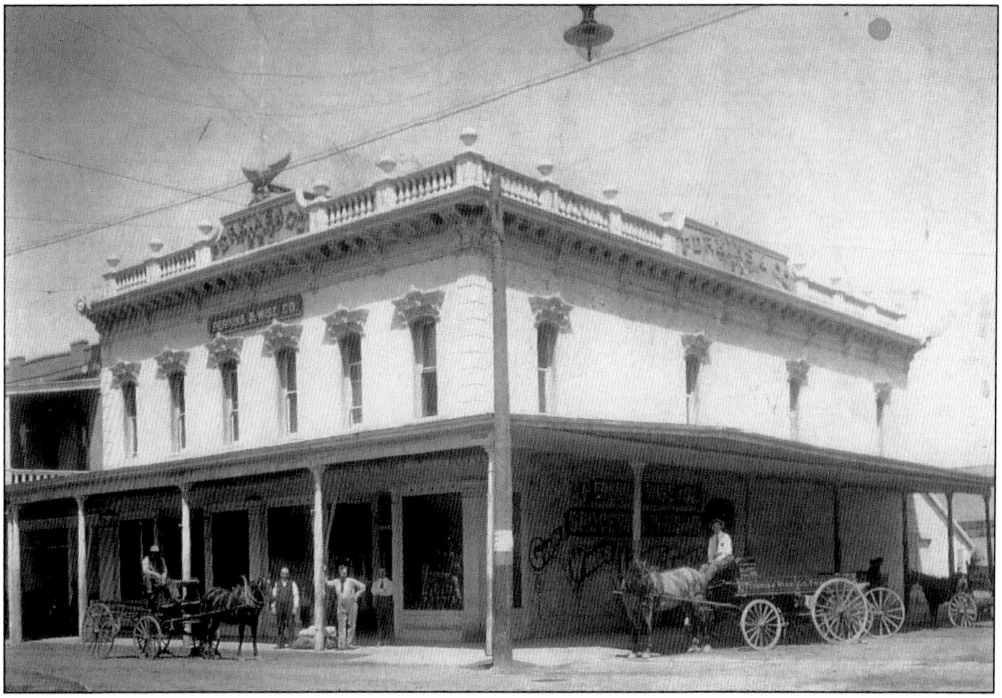

In 1860, George Perkins purchased the store of Hedley & Knight and added the fancy second floor with eagle on top. He opened a second location at Cherokee during the peak of its hydraulic operations. Subsequently he sold out to his brother, moving to Oakland where he operated the Pacific Coast Steamship Lines and became governor and U.S. senator for nearly two decades. The store operated into the 20th century.

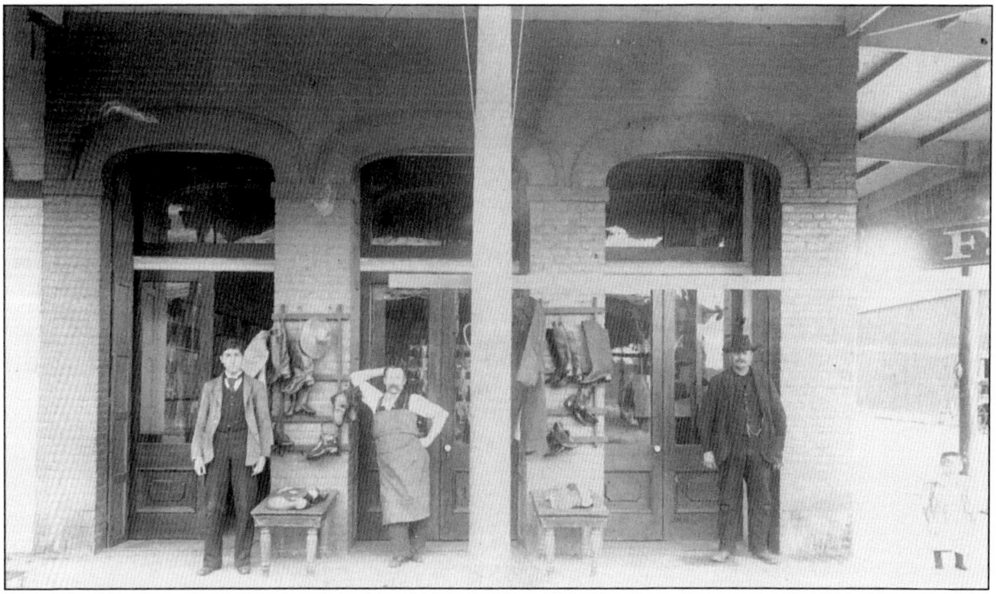

Hecker Shoe Store, on the corner of Huntoon and Montgomery Streets, continued in business for over a century. Shown here are Sam Marks, Pat Jolly, an unidentified customer, and child. Unusual brick arches were replaced with a cast iron facade. A second level was added around 1900.

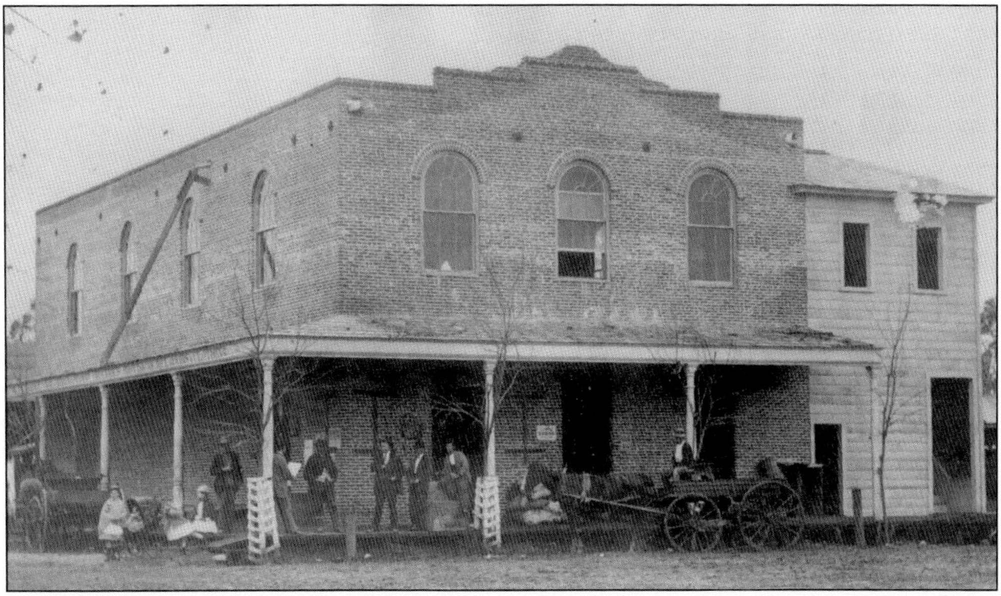

St. Sure Building was located on the southwest corner of Lincoln and Montgomery Streets. The store sold bag grain, flour, groceries, dry goods, and clothing. In later years, it housed Meyer's Furniture Store.

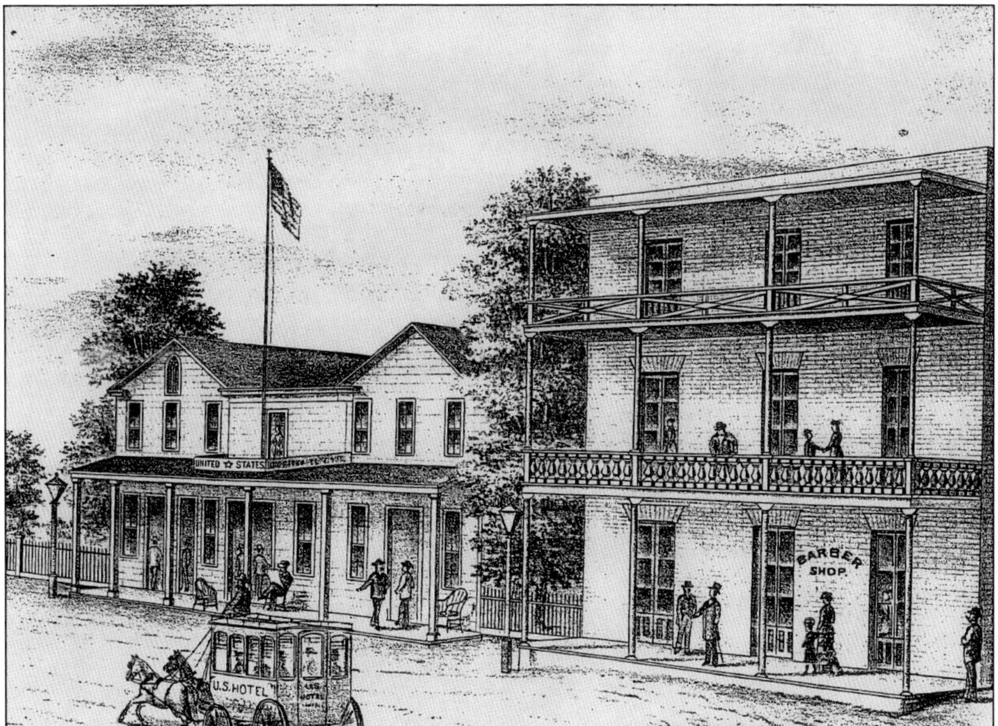

The original United States Hotel on Montgomery Street dated from the 1850s. It burned in the Fire of 1858 but was quickly rebuilt and gradually expanded by Louis W. Hoops. This engraving appeared in Smith & Elliott's *History of Butte County*, 1877.

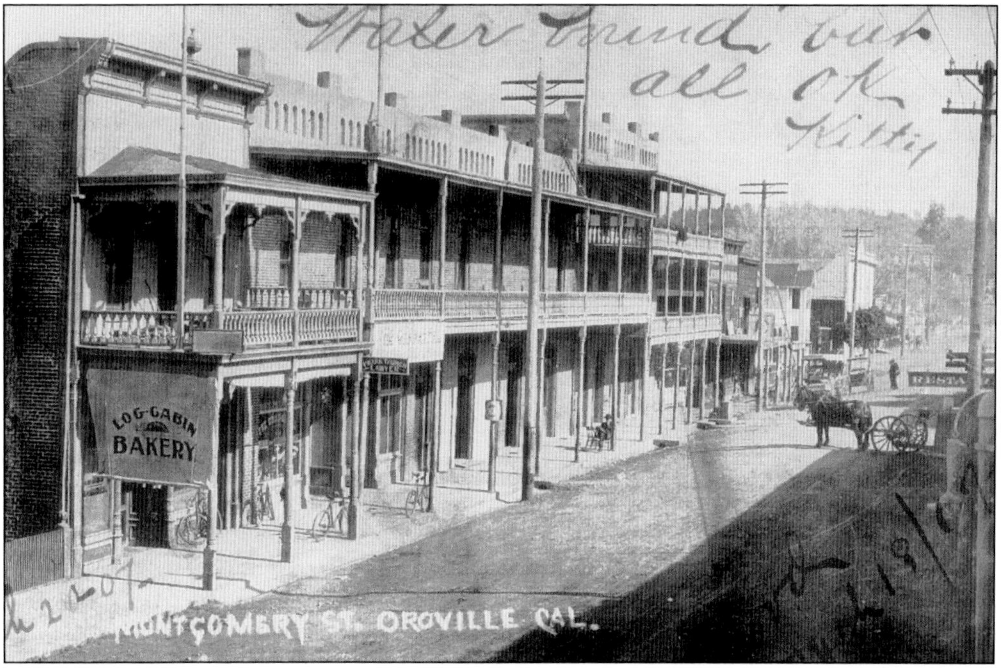

This photo of the U.S. Hotel on Montgomery Street was taken in 1907, showing the brick structure that replaced an earlier wooden section and the historic Log Cabin Bakery, which operated well into the 20th century.

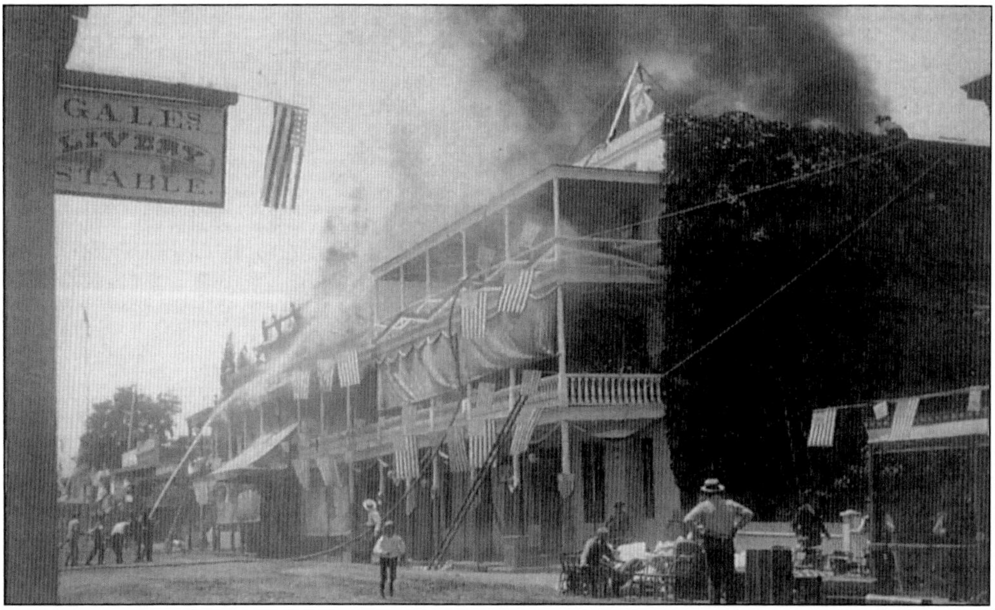

On July 4, 1893, a portion of the U.S. Hotel caught fire, creating much excitement in town. Fortunately, most of the hotel was saved, becoming an annex of the Union Hotel in later years.

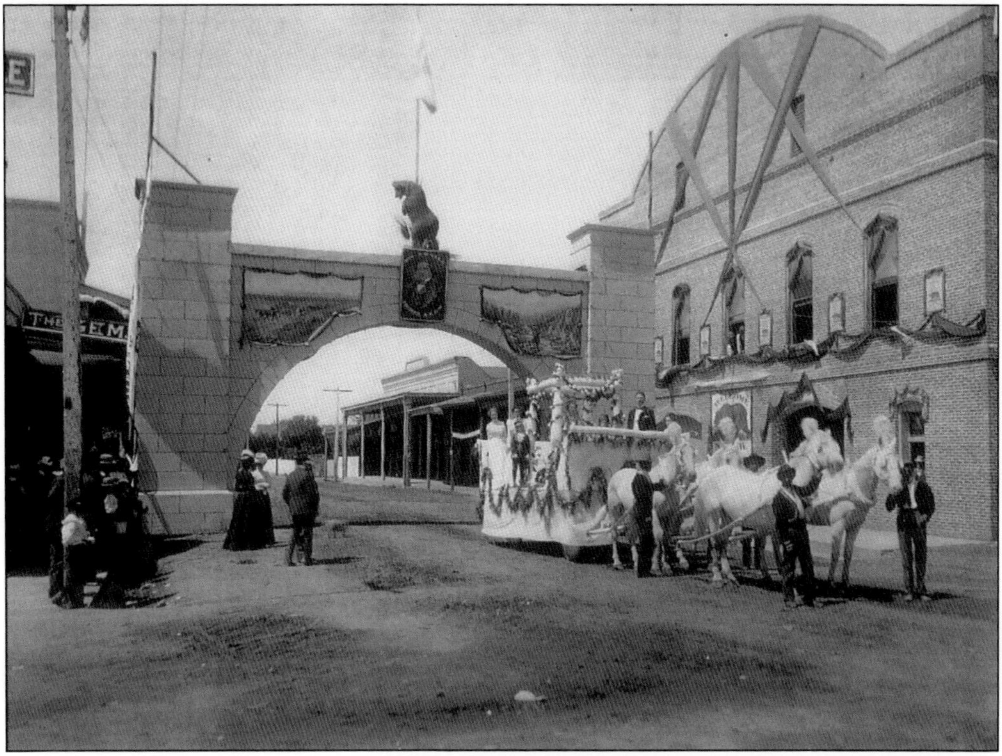

In 1900, the Native Sons of California staged a major celebration in Oroville. At right is the Atkins Theatre & Stables, on the corner of Montgomery and Huntoon Streets.

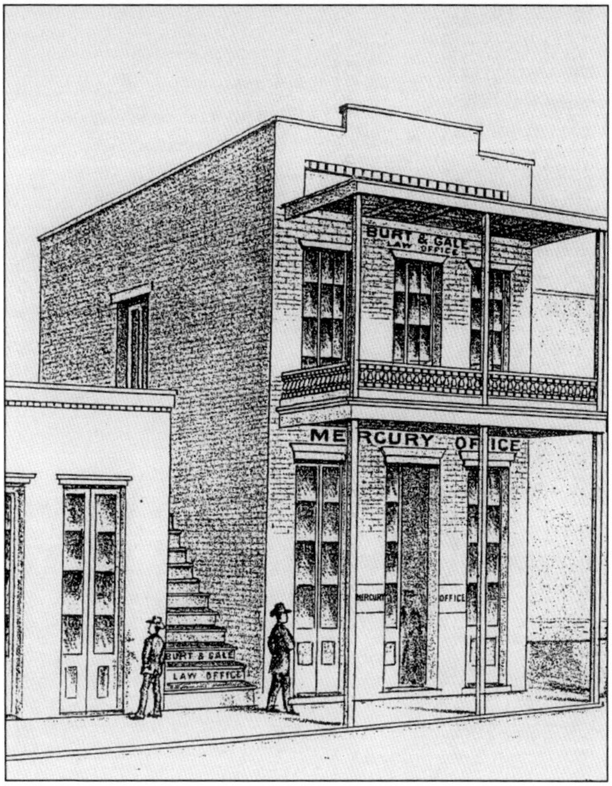

The *Oroville Mercury*, founded in 1873, is shown in the Burt Building on Bird Street. Built by 49er J.M. Burt in 1856, the building still stands. He and Alexander Simpson opened the first stores in Oroville. The *Register* was started in 1879 and merged with the *Mercury* in 1927 when Dan Beebe became long-time editor and publisher.

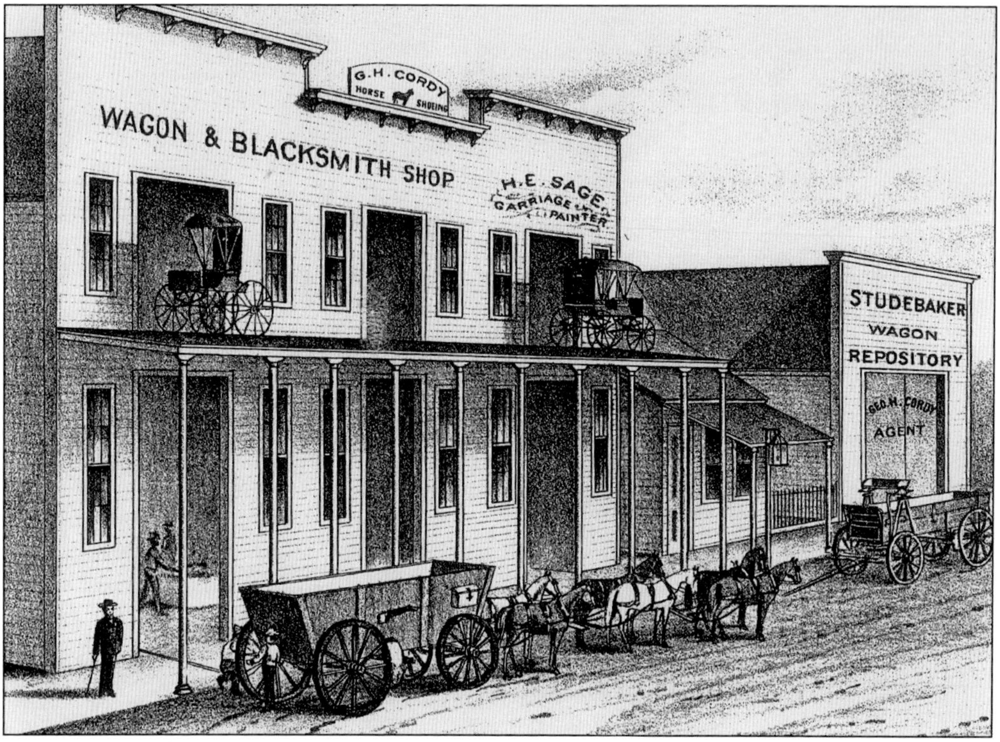

George H. Cordy's wagon and carriage manufactory on Montgomery Street was a busy place in town. He was also an agent for Studebaker wagons. (Smith & Elliott's *History of Butte County*, 1877.)

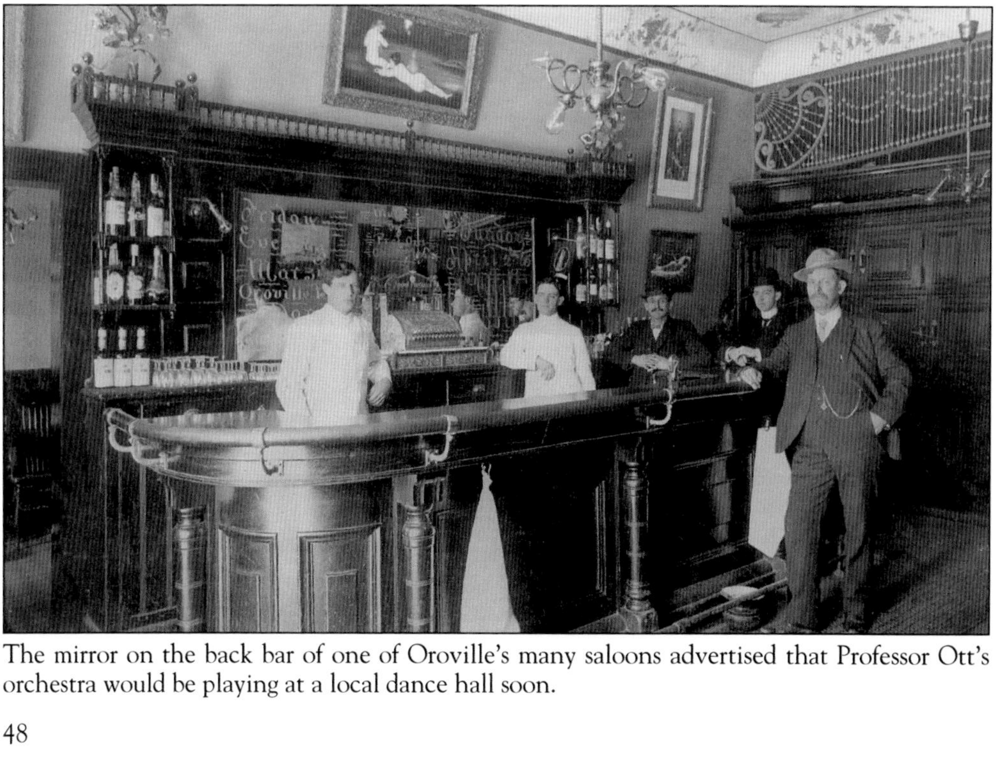

The mirror on the back bar of one of Oroville's many saloons advertised that Professor Ott's orchestra would be playing at a local dance hall soon.

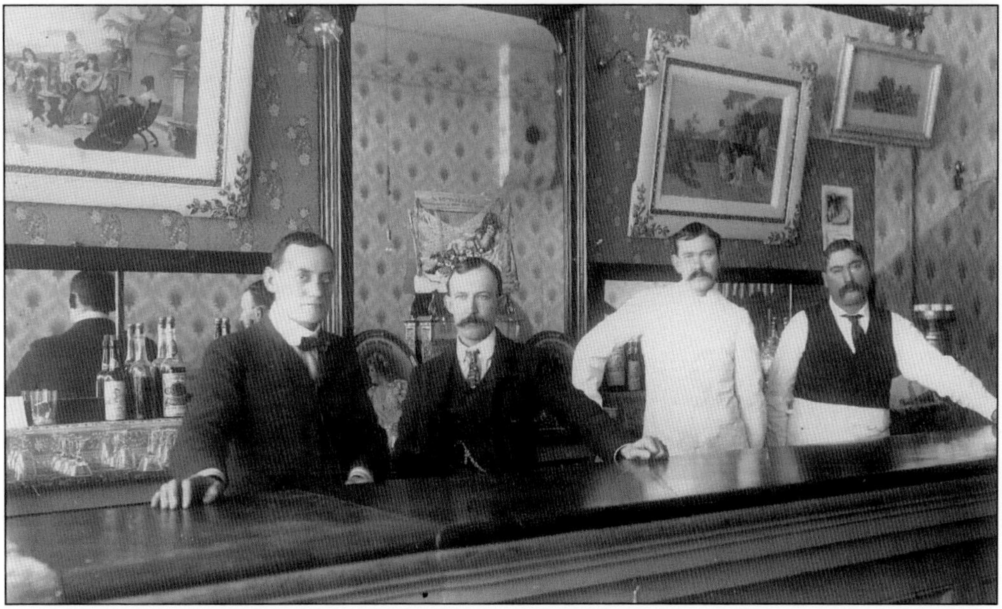

Oroville's Grand Saloon had a fancy interior in 1902. Shown, left to right, are owners Bill Fitch and John Finlayson. Next to them are bartenders Tom Tuhey and a Mr. Hollohan.

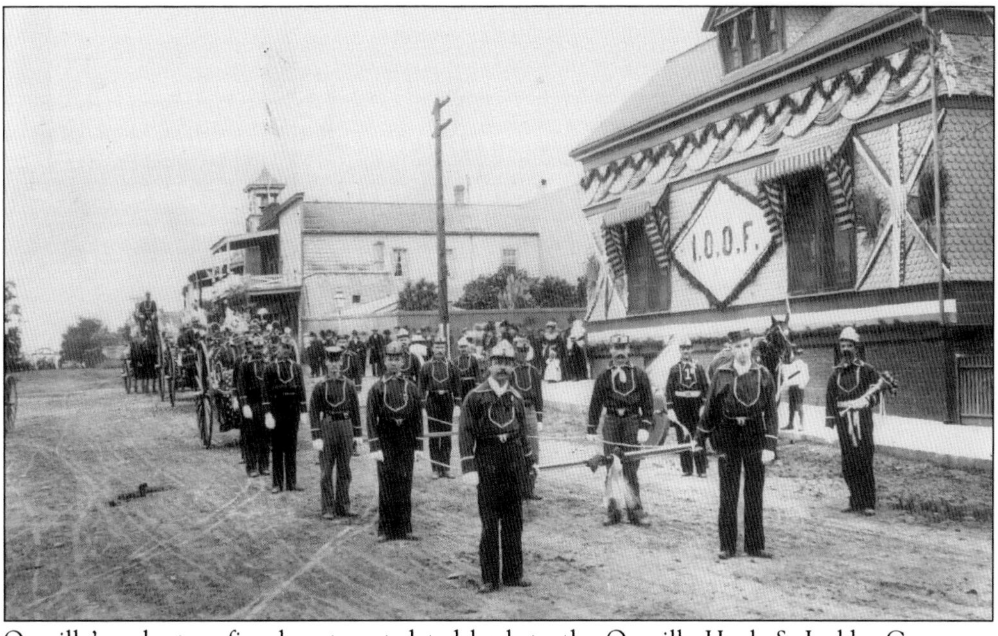

Oroville's volunteer fire department dated back to the Oroville Hook & Ladder Company, founded in 1873. It occupied a two-story brick building on Bird Street with bell tower on top. This photo was taken in 1887 as firemen prepared for a parade. Shown at right is the office of the Edison Ore Milling Company, where Frank McLaughlin started his amazing Oroville adventures, representing America's most famous inventor in 1879.

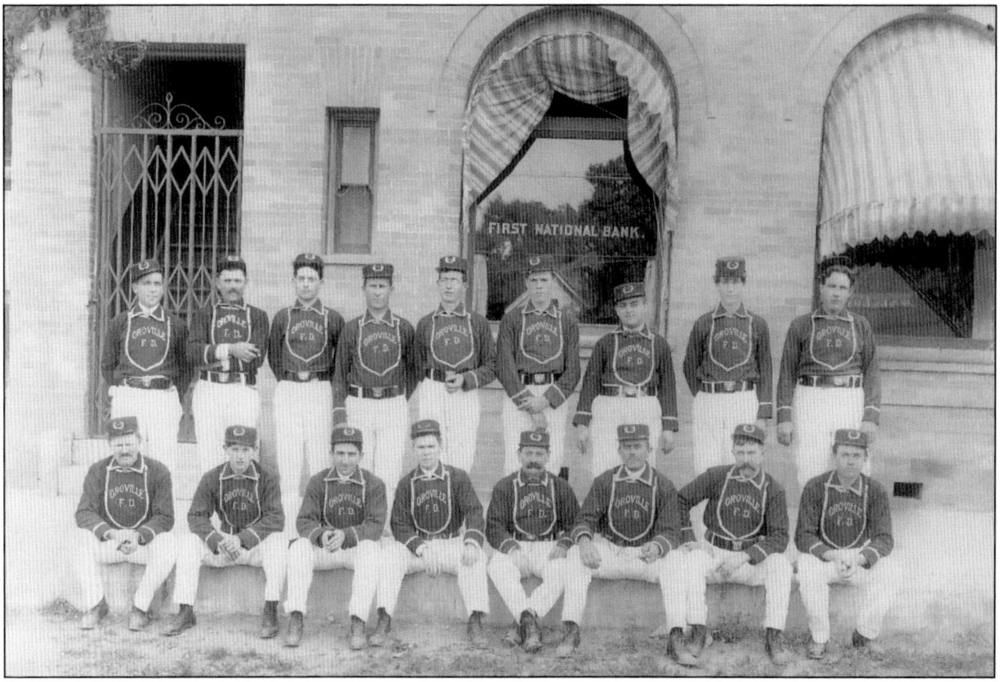

A later portrait of Oroville's firemen was taken in front of the new First National Bank Building on the corner of Myers and Bird Streets. Among those pictured (not in any order) are Jack Williams, Ben Boydson, Fred Hall, Harry Jacobs, Harry Sadowski, Chris Mathews, Albert Boynton, Joe Marks, and August Johnson.

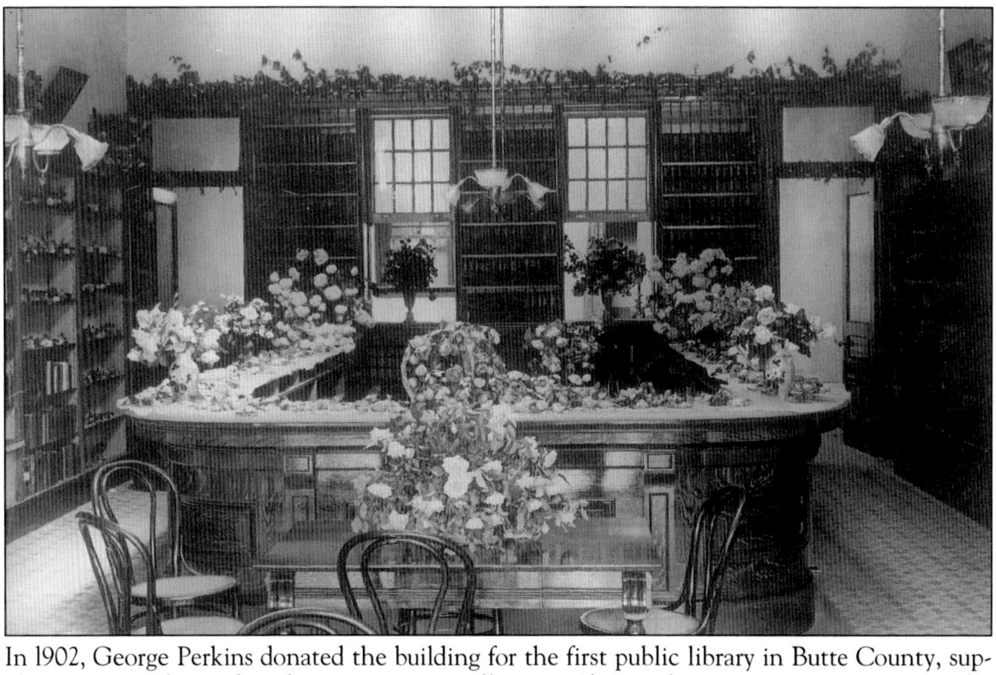

In 1902, George Perkins donated the building for the first public library in Butte County, supplying many volumes from his own private collection. Shown above is an interior view on the day of its dedication.

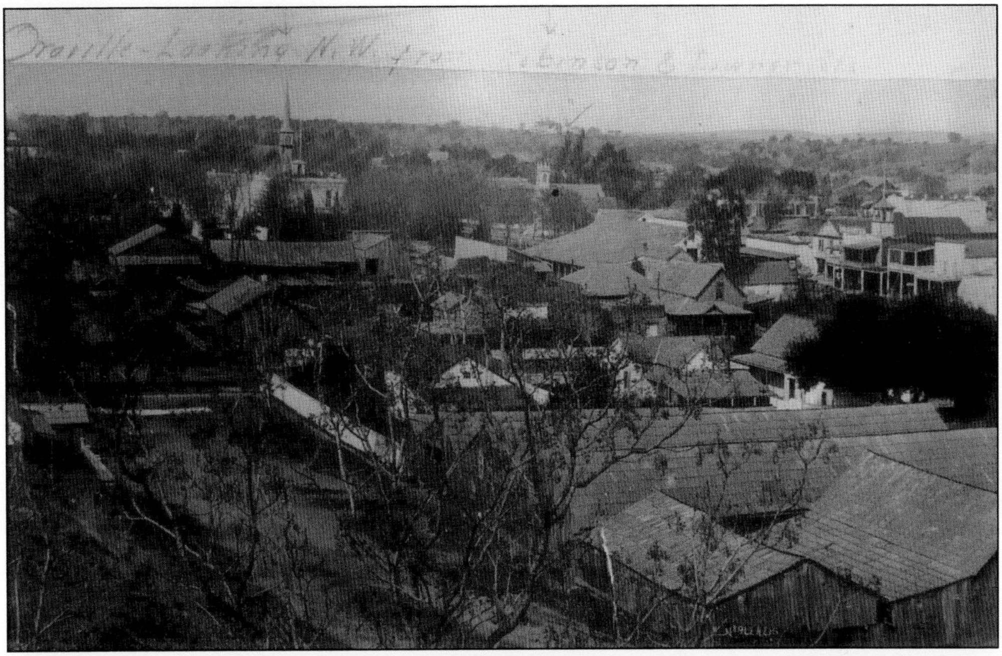

Bird's-eye view of Oroville taken from the bluff behind the town around 1890. Looking west one can see the courthouse, towers of the Congregational and Methodist churches, and business houses along Bird Street.

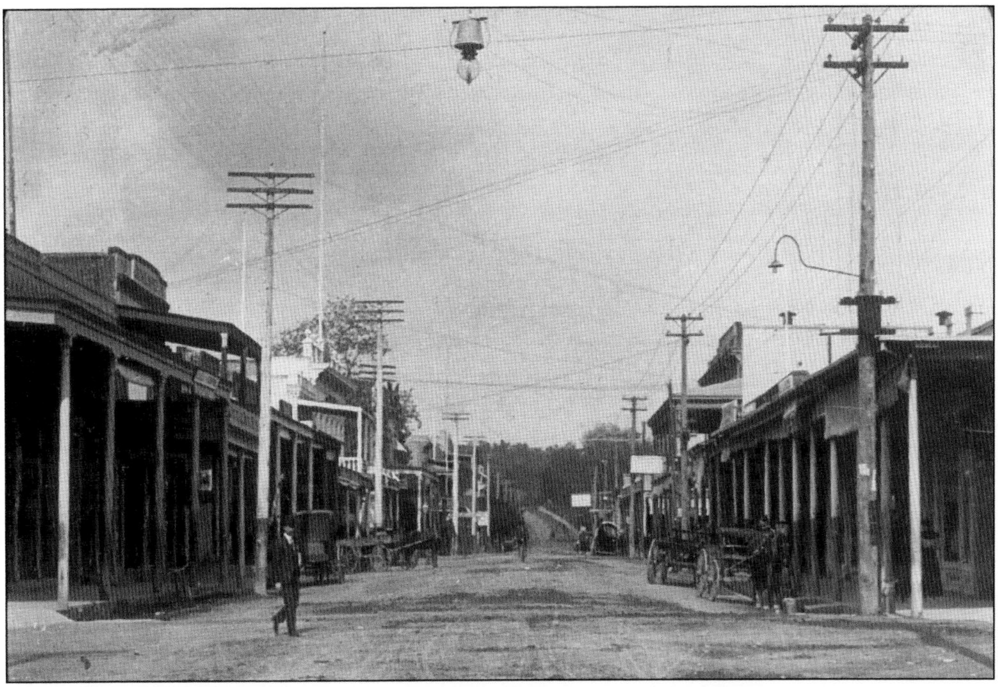

Photo around 1895 is looking east from corner of Montgomery and Huntoon Streets. Note arc lights hanging over center of the street, a major innovation in those days.

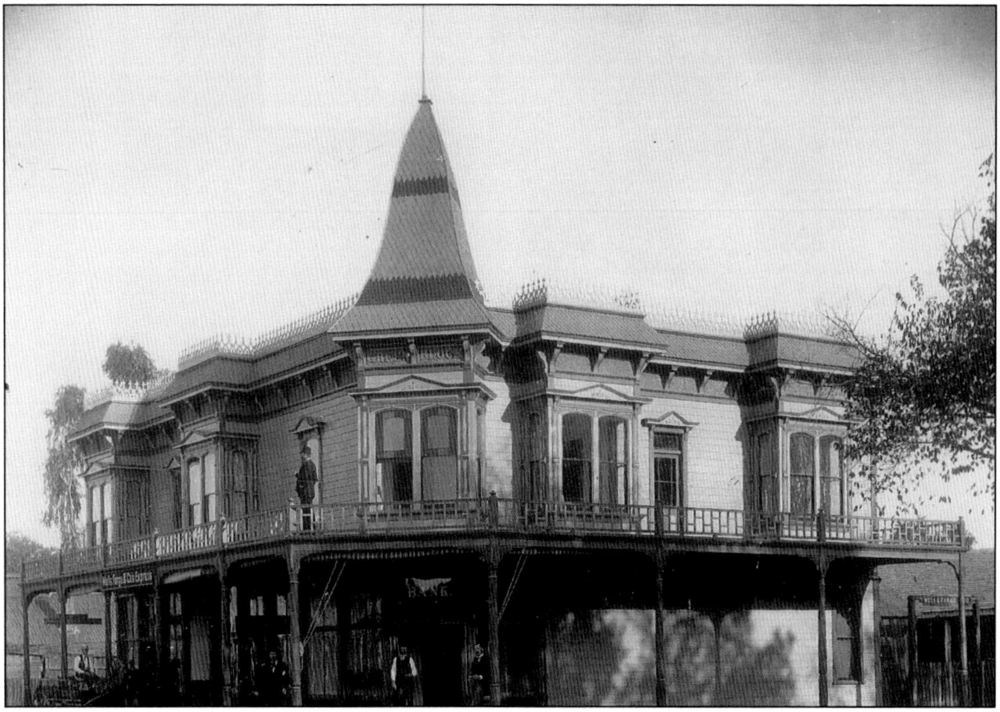

The ornate Green Block was erected on the corner of Huntoon and Bird Streets during the 1890s. It housed the drug firm of Robert M. Green, the short-lived *New Era* newspaper, the Bank of Oroville, and the Butte County Title Company.

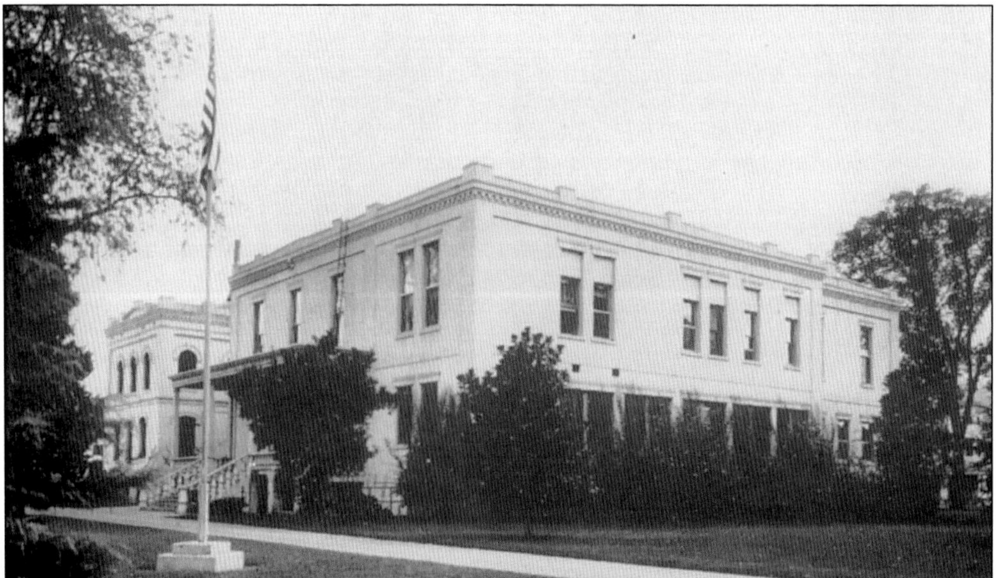

Down through the years, the courthouse in Oroville was gradually expanded around the original structure. The jail was later removed from the basement and lodged in the annex shown at left.

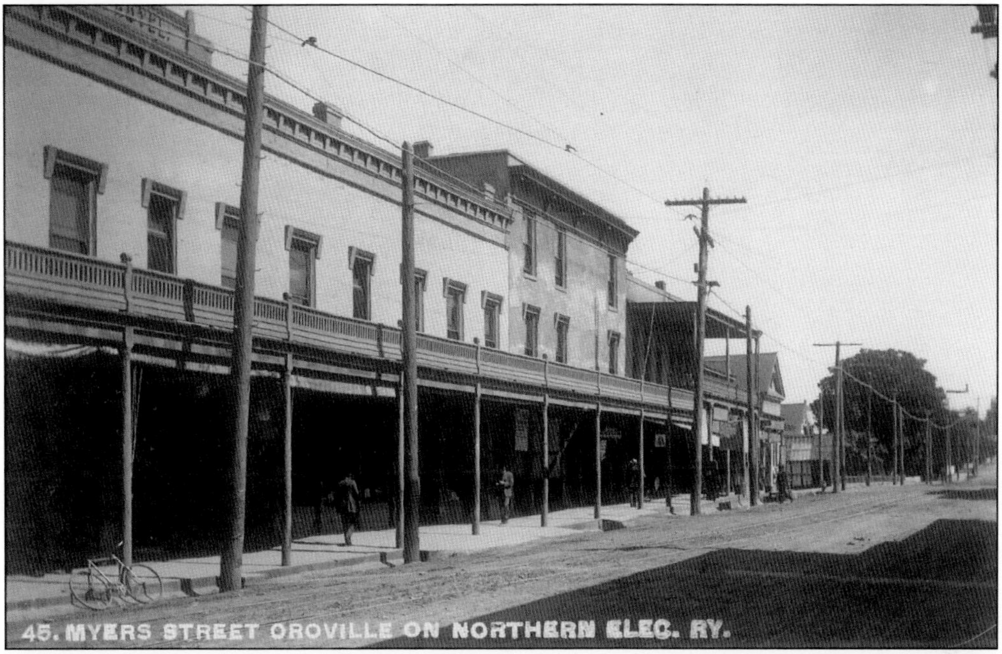

Looking up Myers Street after 1900. The refurbished Union Hotel is shown at left. Note that the streets are not yet paved.

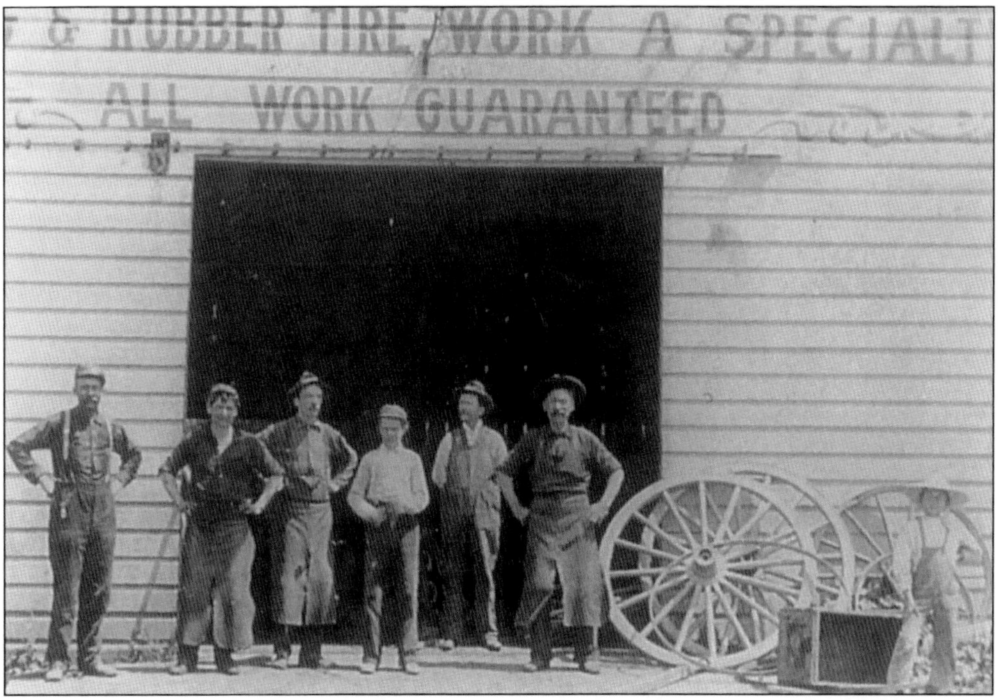

August Johnson operated a successful blacksmith shop in Oroville for many years. Standing sixth from left, with hands on hips, he also landed the largest sturgeon ever caught in the Feather River. His son Ray Johnson later became a state senator, authoring legislation permitting historic structures no longer wanted by public agencies to be deeded to non-profit societies.

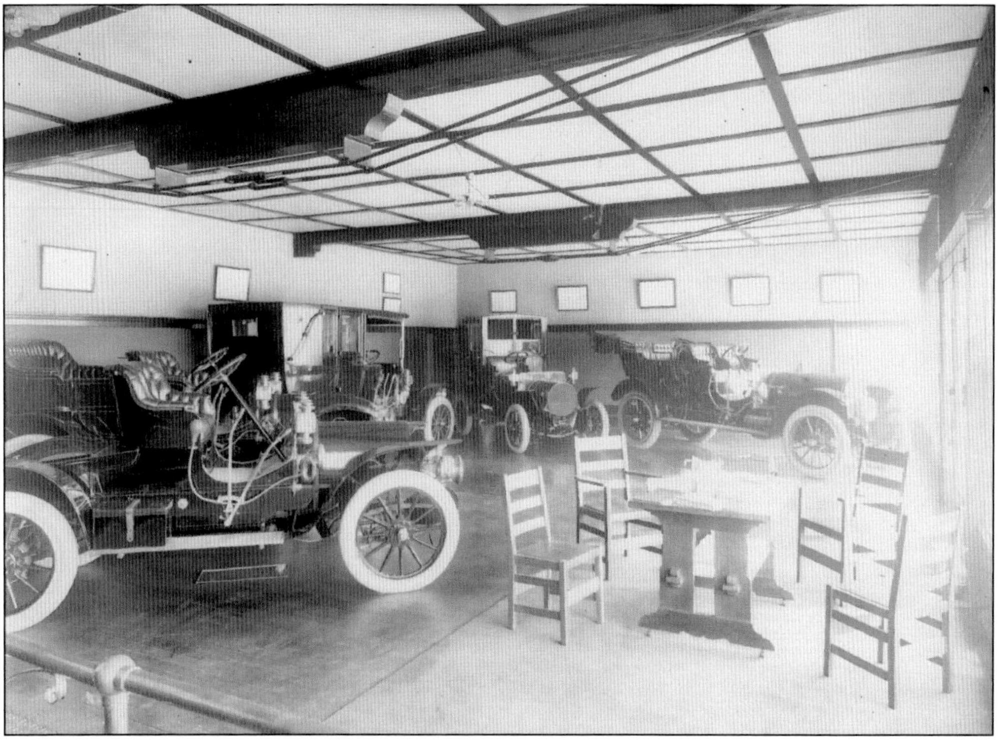

Advent of the horseless carriage changed everyone's lives, including those in Oroville. Shown above is a new car sales showroom in Oroville around 1910.

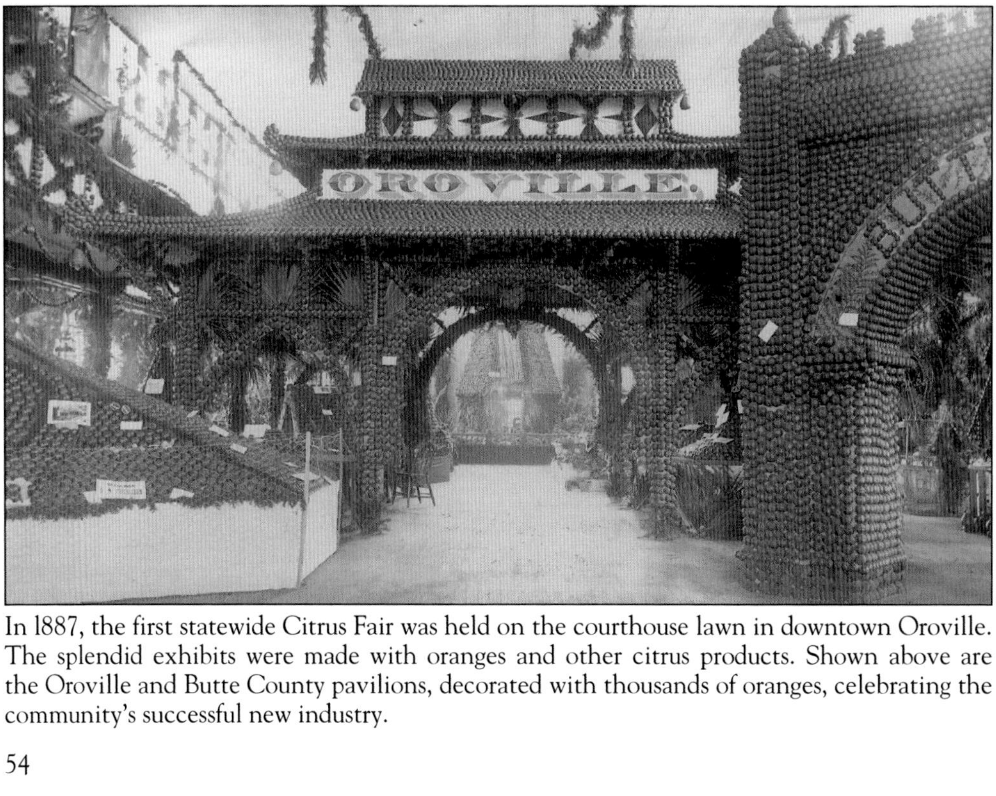

In 1887, the first statewide Citrus Fair was held on the courthouse lawn in downtown Oroville. The splendid exhibits were made with oranges and other citrus products. Shown above are the Oroville and Butte County pavilions, decorated with thousands of oranges, celebrating the community's successful new industry.

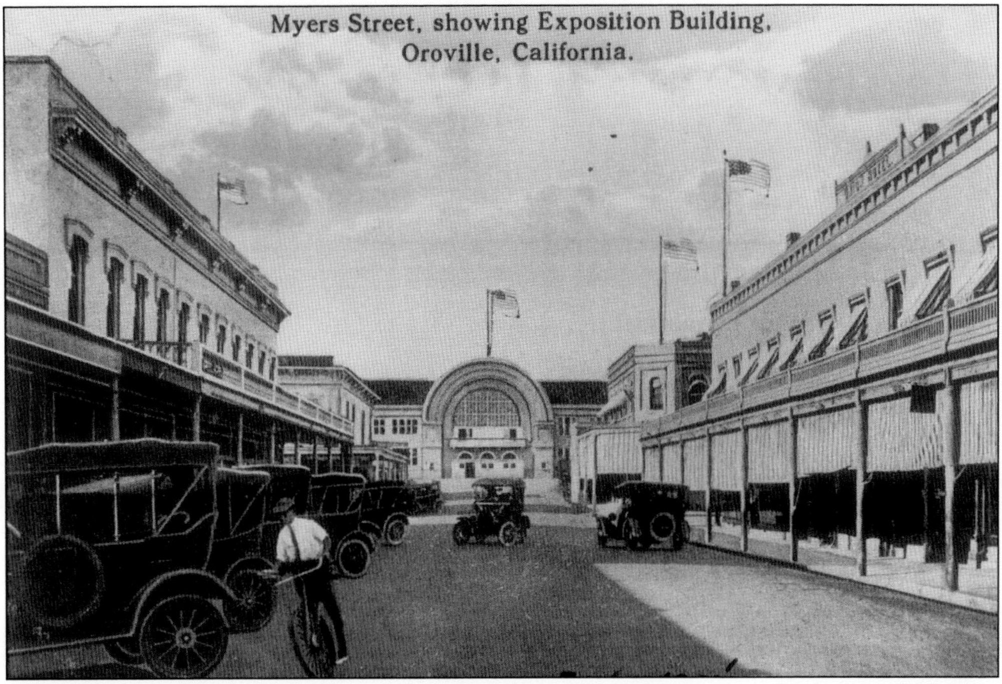

So popular was the Citrus Fair over the years that, when olives were added, Oroville built a grand exposition building at the foot of Myers Street overlooking the river. The structure serves today as the Oroville Municipal Auditorium.

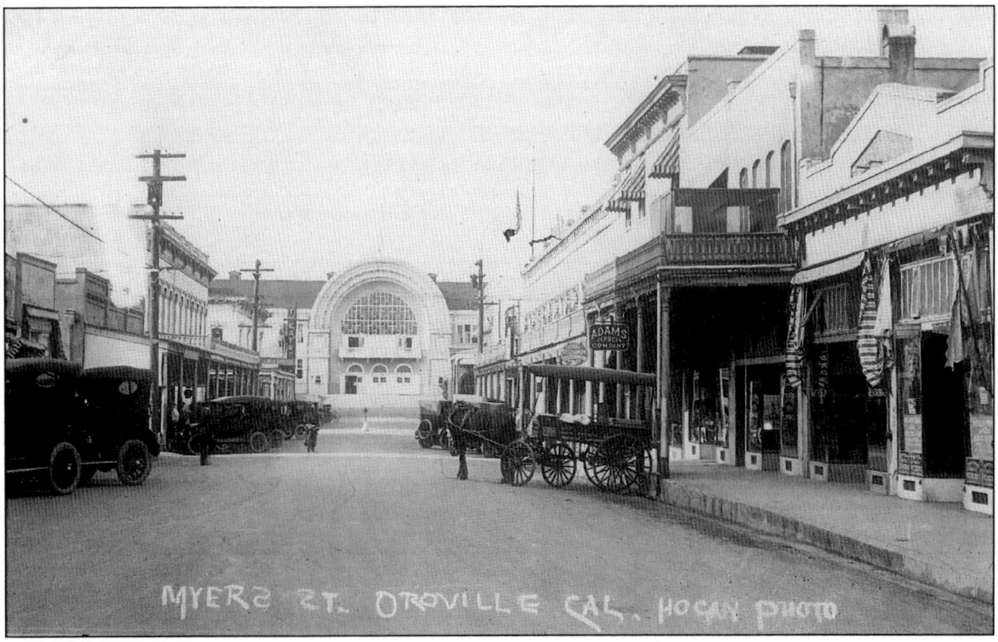

J.H. Hogan took this picture of Myers Street and the new Exposition Building a few years after it was constructed. Note that wagons had not yet gone completely out of fashion.

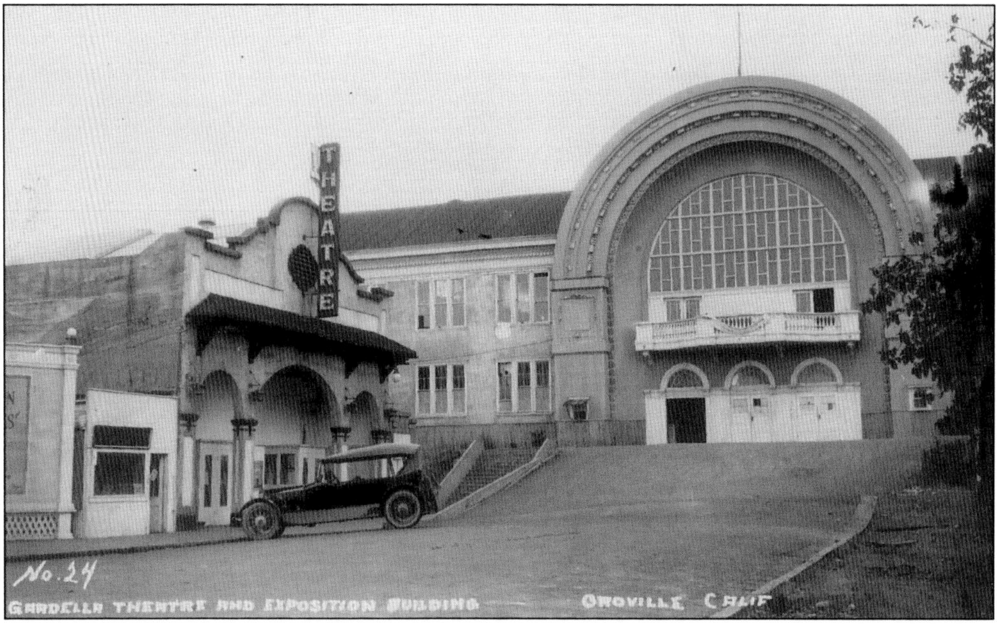

Lawrence Gardella erected the Gardella Theatre next to the Exposition Building with money he made dredging gold from his truck farm at the edge of town. It was a vaudeville theater for many years. Harriet Jacoby played the piano there for silent movies before moving to San Francisco to play at the Orpheum Theatre.

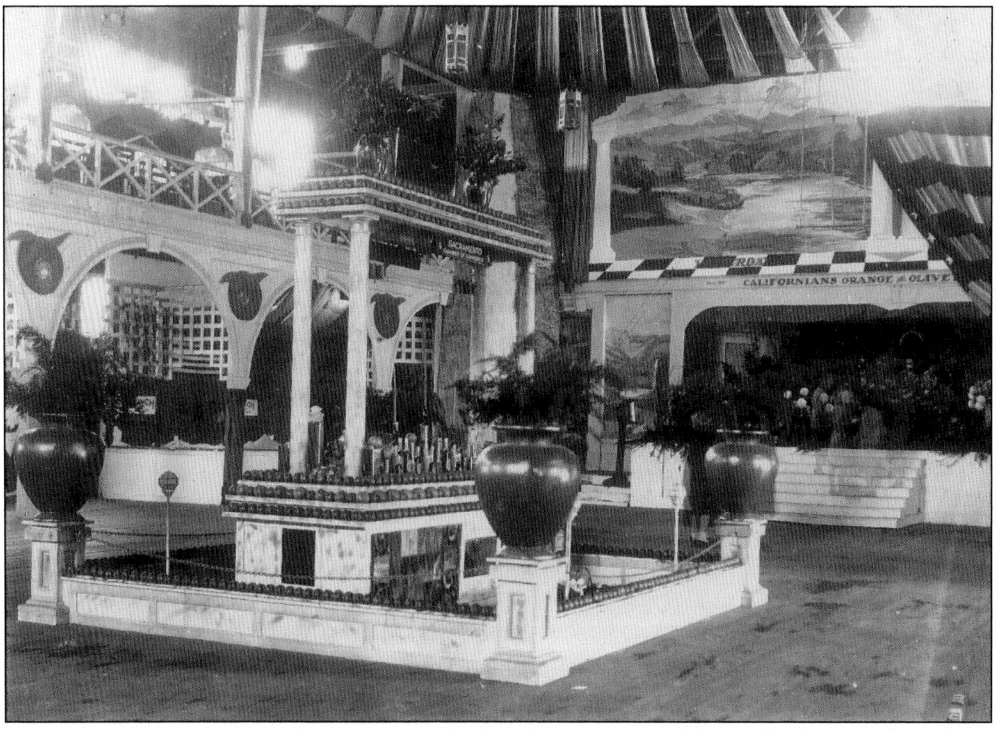

Here is an interior view of the Orange and Olive Exposition Building. The huge arch in front was originally painted the colors of a rainbow.

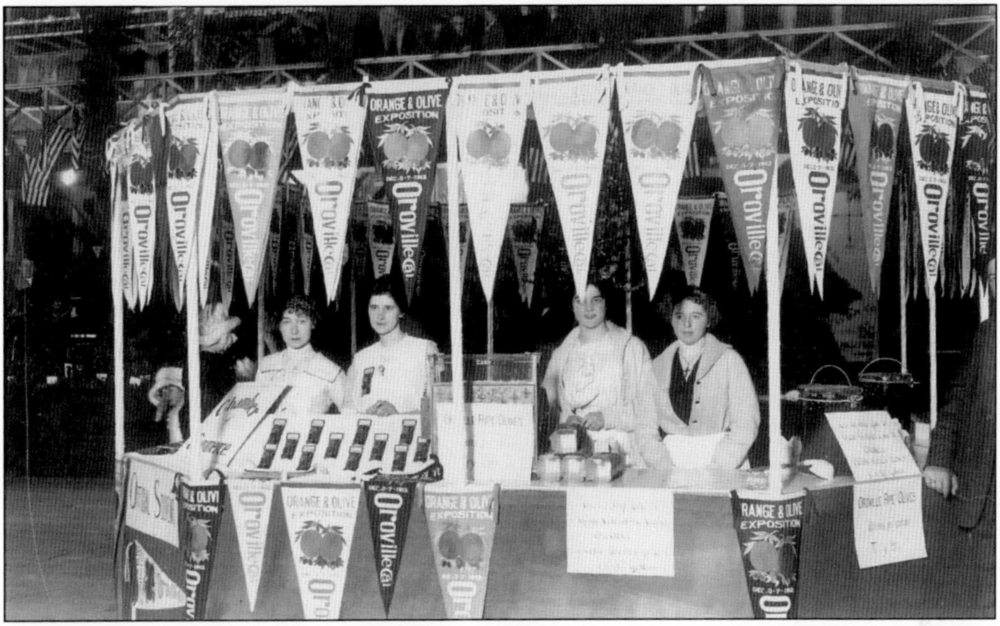

This postcard shows local ladies peddling banners at one of the annual Orange and Olive Expositions.

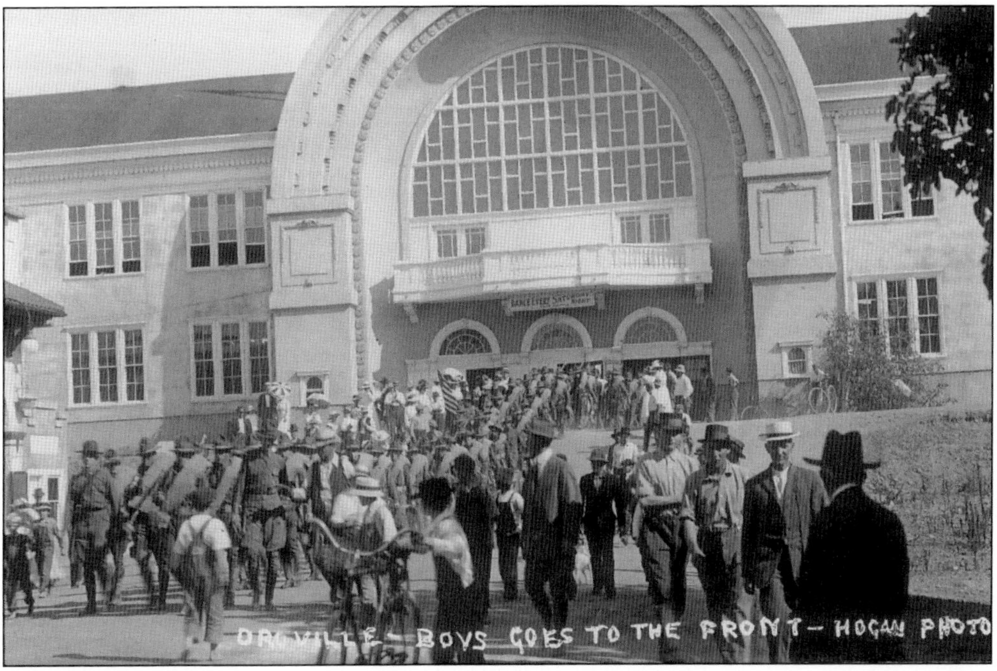

Oroville boys are shown marching off to war after the U.S. joined the European conflict in 1917.

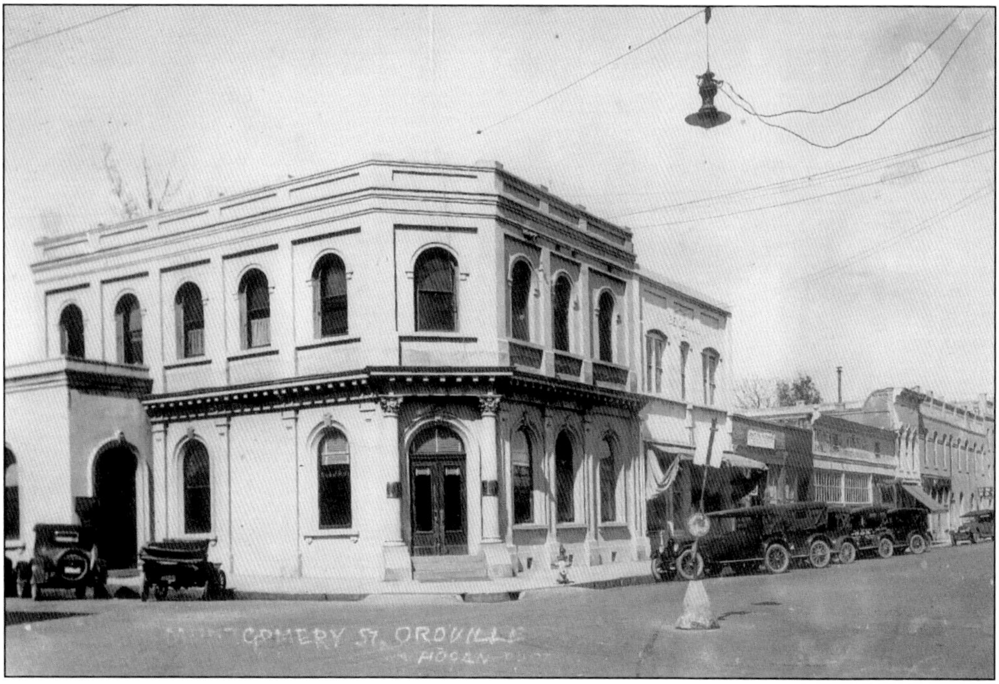

Rideout-Smith Bank, successors to the first bank in Oroville, added a second floor to its building in later years. After the Bank of Italy acquired the Rideout chain, the building was replaced altogether by a new one.

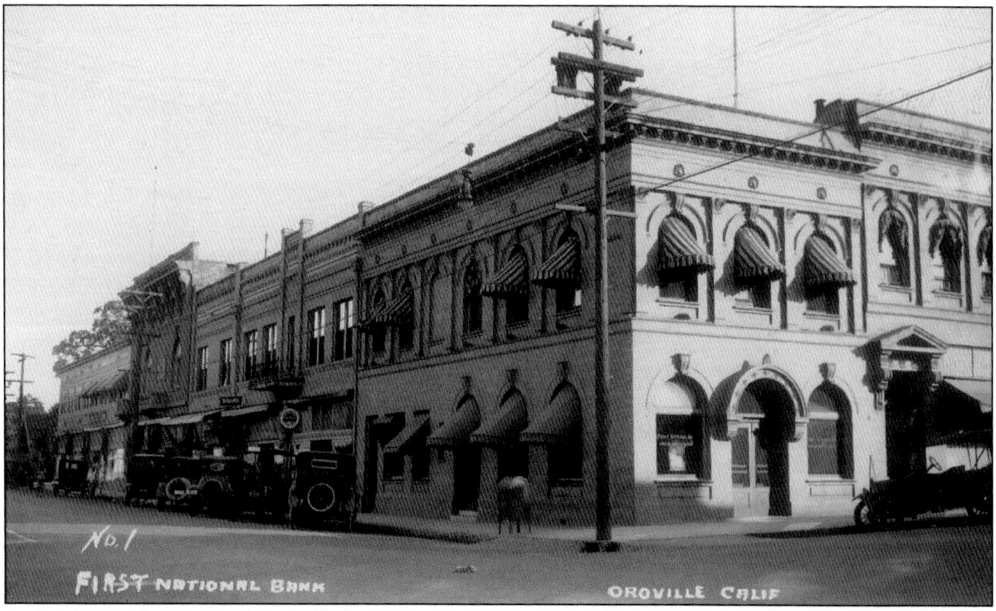

In the 1890s, the Bank of Oroville became the First National Bank and erected this stately building on the corner of Bird and Myers Streets. Although considerably altered, the structure still stands. Shown at left is the Sutherland Hotel, Masonic Hall, and City of Paris department store.

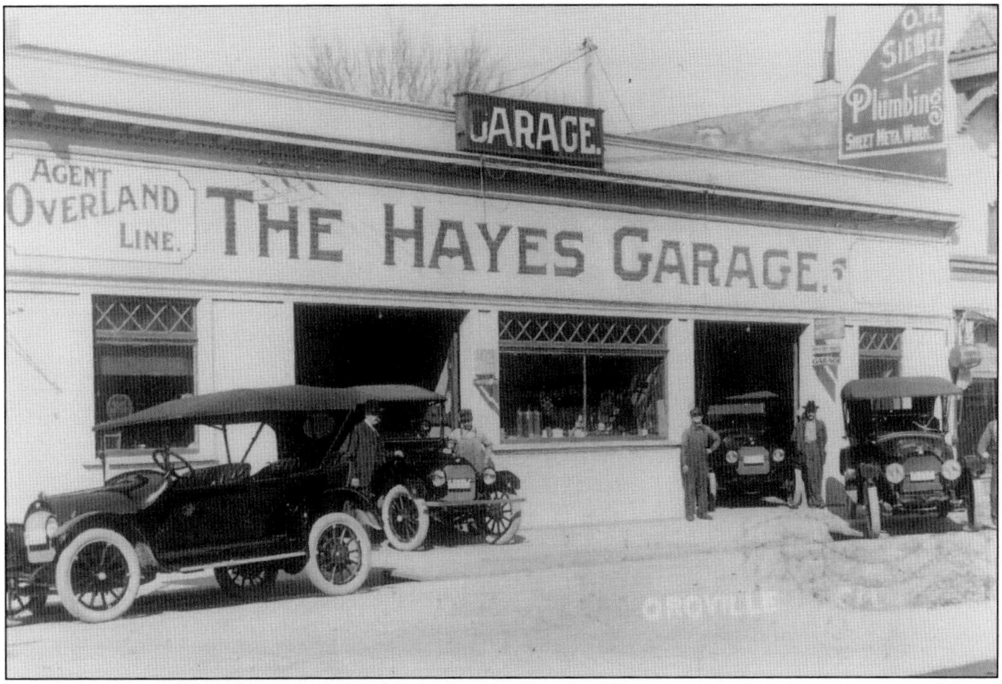

In 1914, Victor Hayes took over the blacksmith shop his father owned on Montgomery Street and built a new garage where he sold Willys Overland and Studebaker cars for many years. It later became Blanchard's Pontiac.

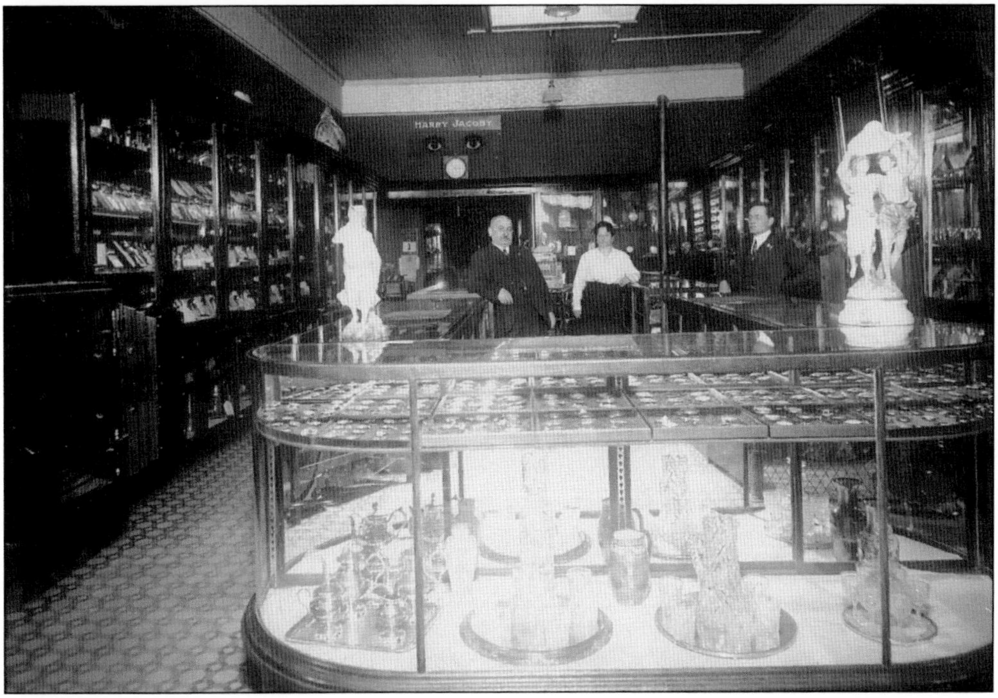

Interior view of Jacoby's Jewelry Store located on Montgomery Street between Huntoon and Myers Streets. Shown here are: Harry Jacoby, Harriet Jacoby, and employee Mr. Reading.

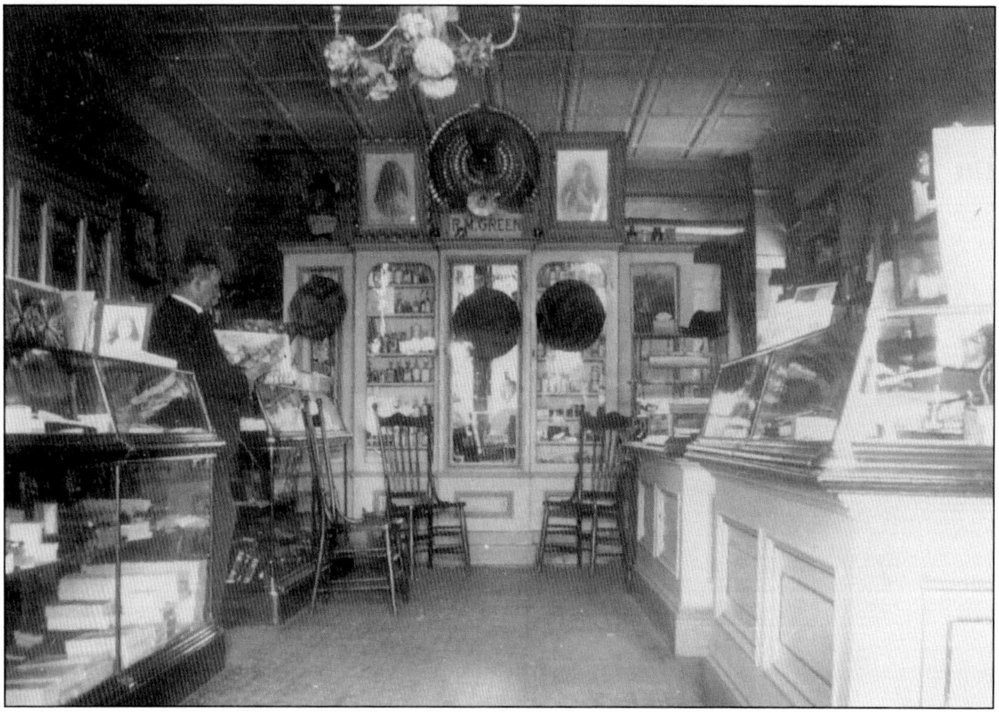

Interior of Green's Drug Store on the corner of Huntoon and Bird Streets. Green, standing at left, pioneered a pine sap liniment and was a founder of the Bank of Oroville, now a branch of Bank of the West.

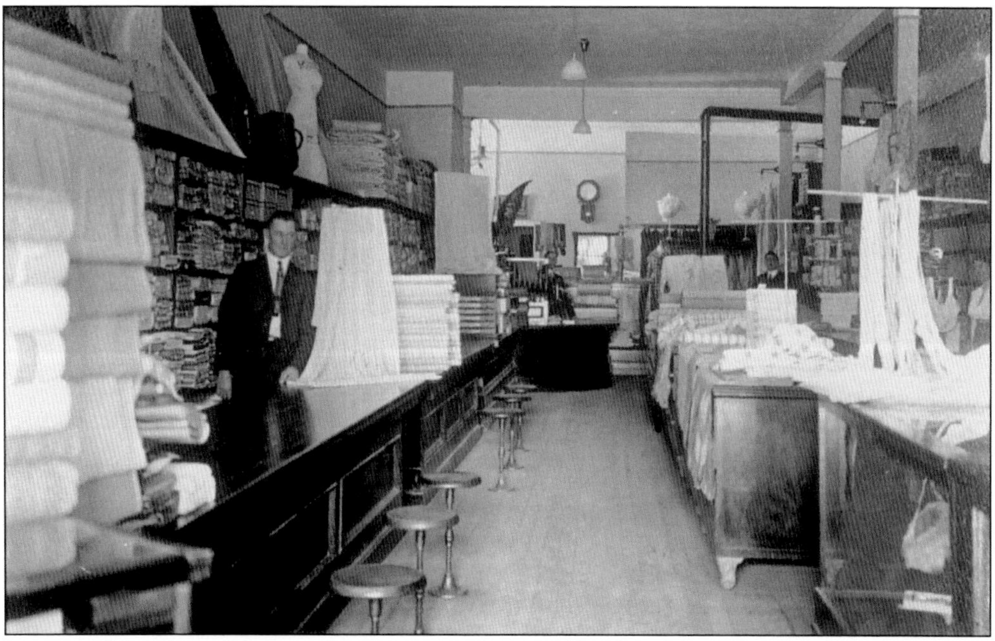

Interior of the Henn Store on the corner of Myers and Bird Streets in 1917. "Ripley's Believe It or Not" made Henn famous when it printed that Oroville educator "Jay Partridge lives in the Henn House on Bird Street next to the Feather River!"

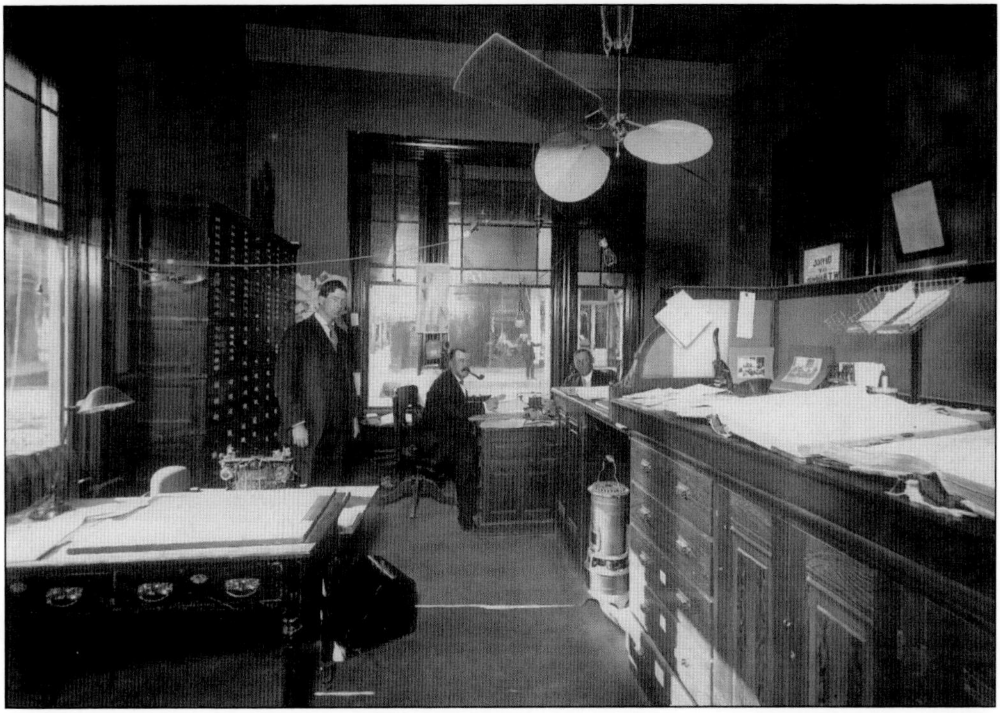

Interior view of the Butte County Title Company in 1908. Shown, left to right, are Bert and W. T. Baldwin. The firm was founded in 1877.

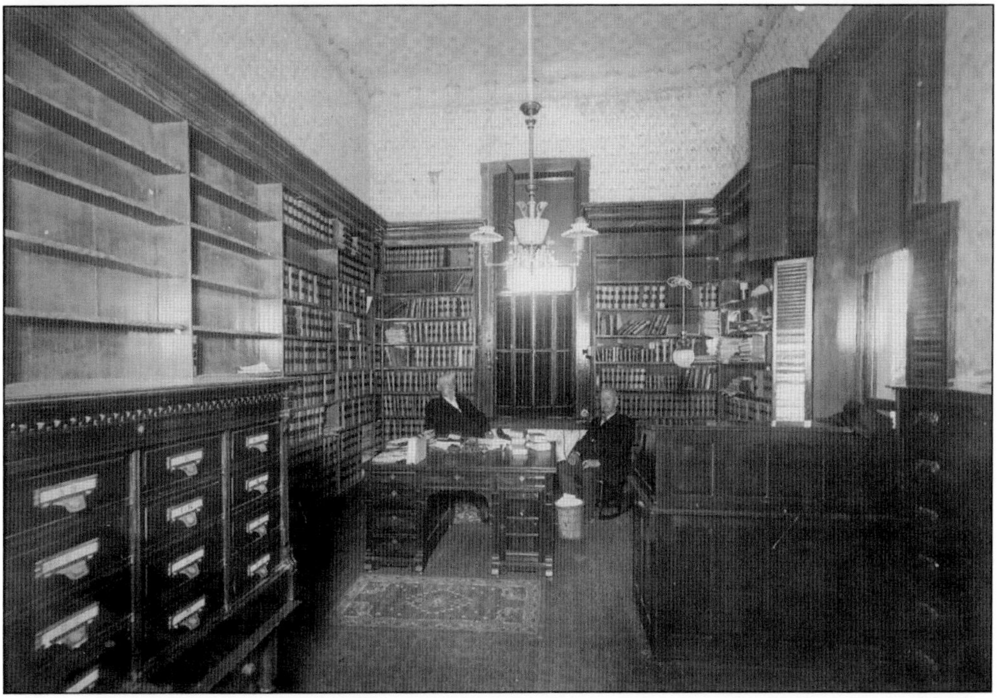

Offices of Judge John C. Gray in the upstairs of the old courthouse in downtown Oroville. The large courtroom adjoining was used from 1856 to 1975.

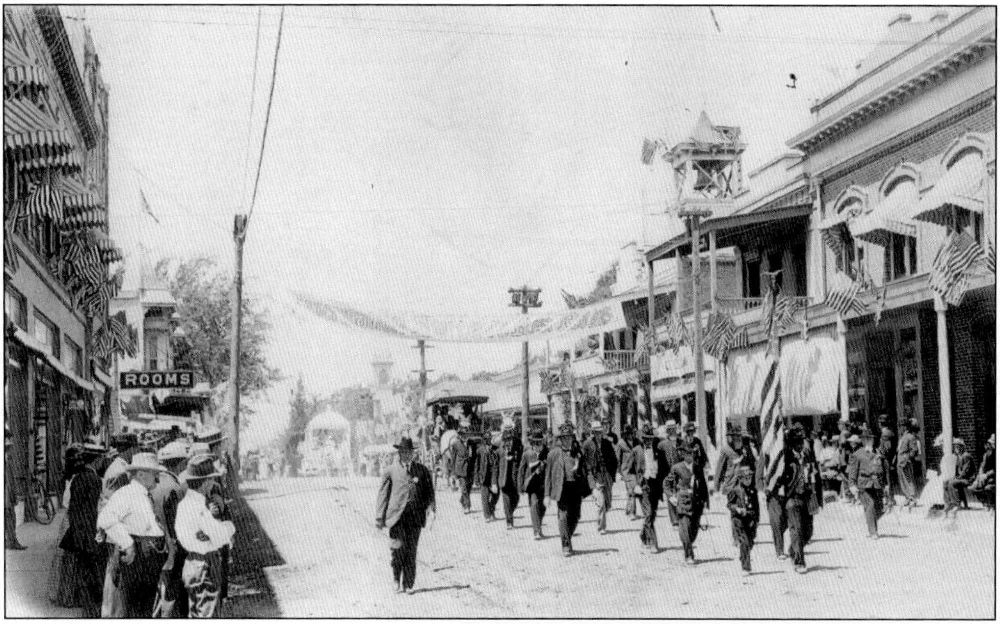

Civil War veterans march proudly down Bird Street during one of Oroville's many parades. The local organization was named after General W. T. Sherman, who was a California pioneer and visited Butte County with President Hayes in 1880. Note the belfry on the fire house at right.

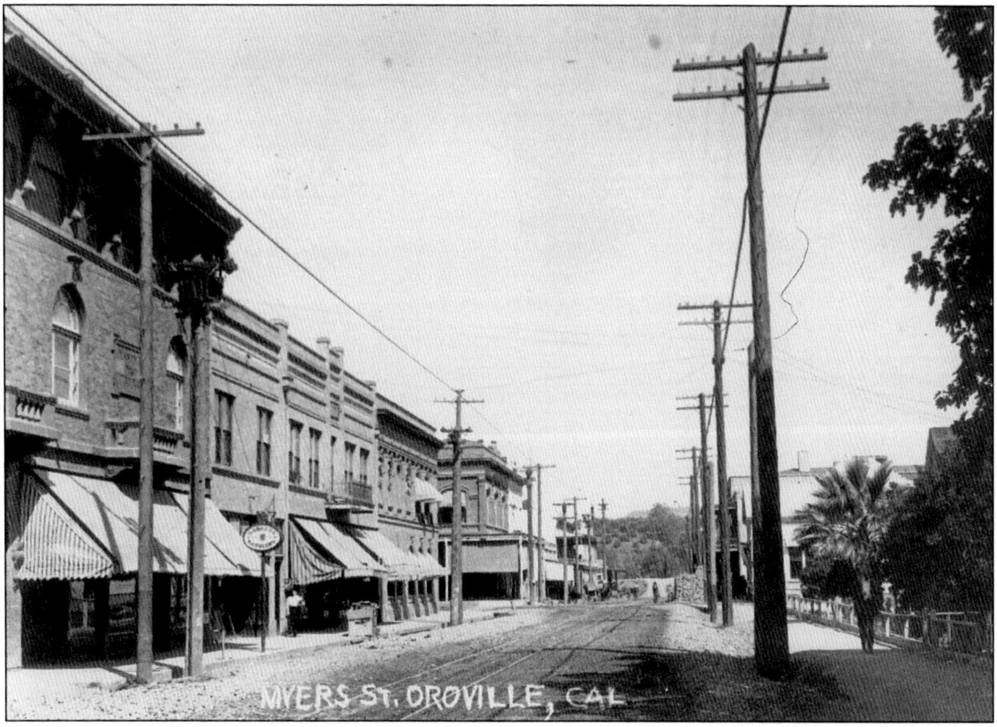

Looking down Myers Street after Northern Electric tracks were laid in 1905, several years before the Exposition Building was erected at the foot of Myers Street in 1912. A new Masonic Hall is at far left.

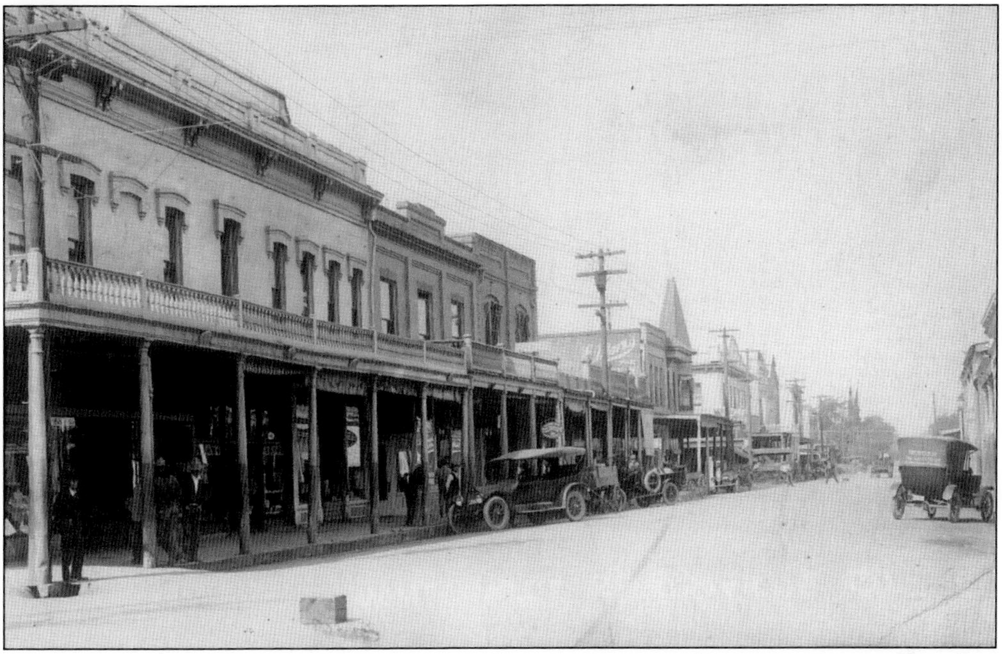

View of the south side of Montgomery Street between Myers and Huntoon Streets was taken around 1918. Historic Washington Block is shown at left. The pointed roof at the end of the block is on the Hecker Building.

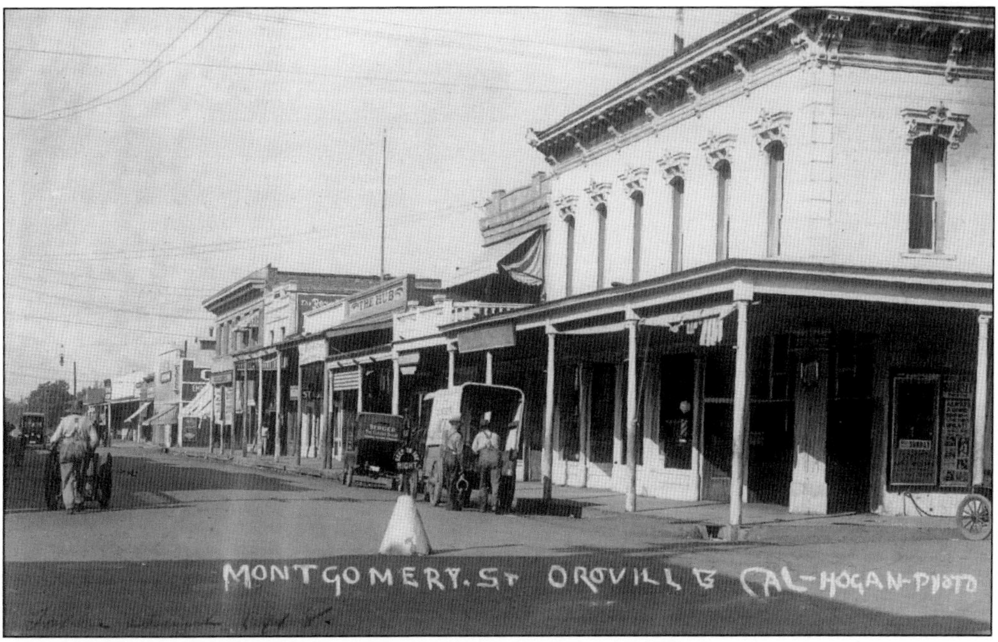

The opposite side of Montgomery Street between Myers and Huntoon Streets the same year shows the Perkins Building in foreground.

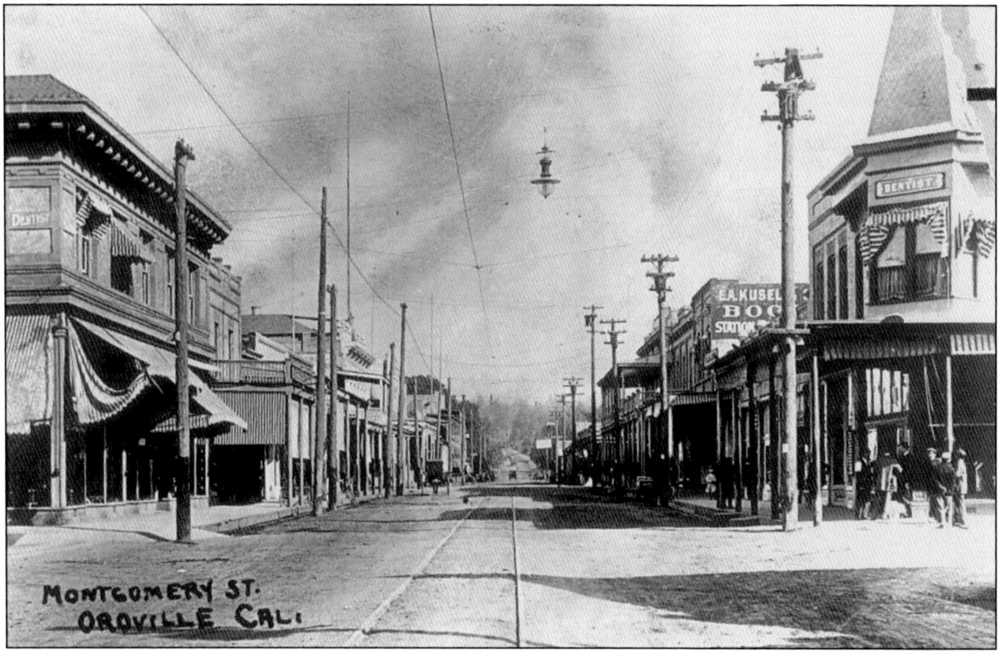

Looking east on Montgomery Street from the corner of Huntoon Street shows a handsome two-story building that housed the J.C. Penney Store for a time. Hecker Shoe Store is on the corner at right. Tracks of the Northern Electric Railway may be seen in the center of the street.

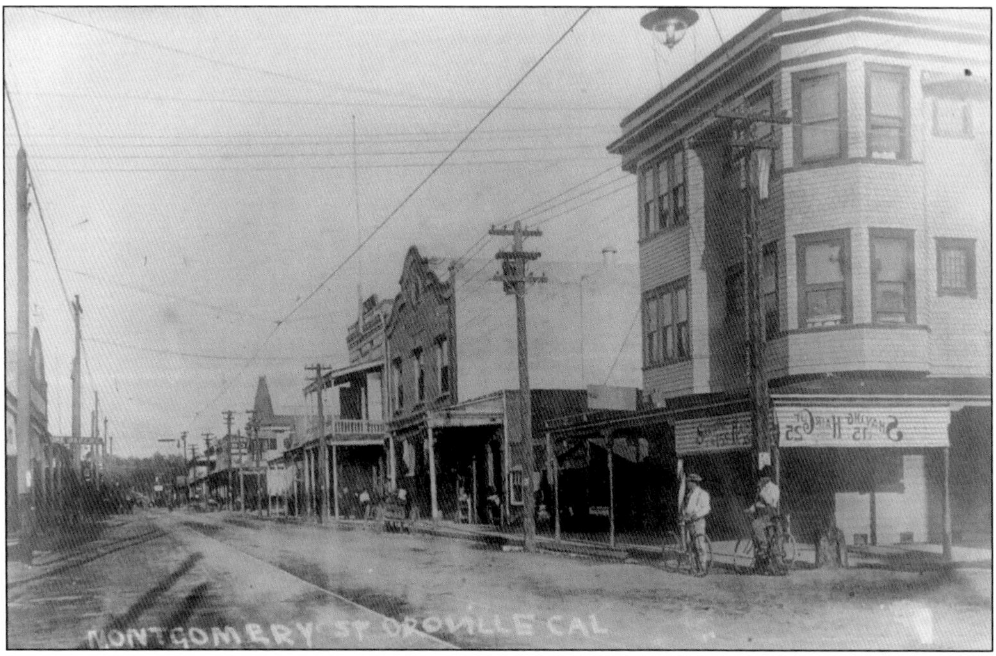

Looking east on Montgomery Street from the corner of Lincoln Street. Sturgeon Hotel is in the foreground with two-story Braden and Odd Fellows buildings further up the block. A barber shop on the corner advertised a shave for 15¢ and a haircut for 25¢.

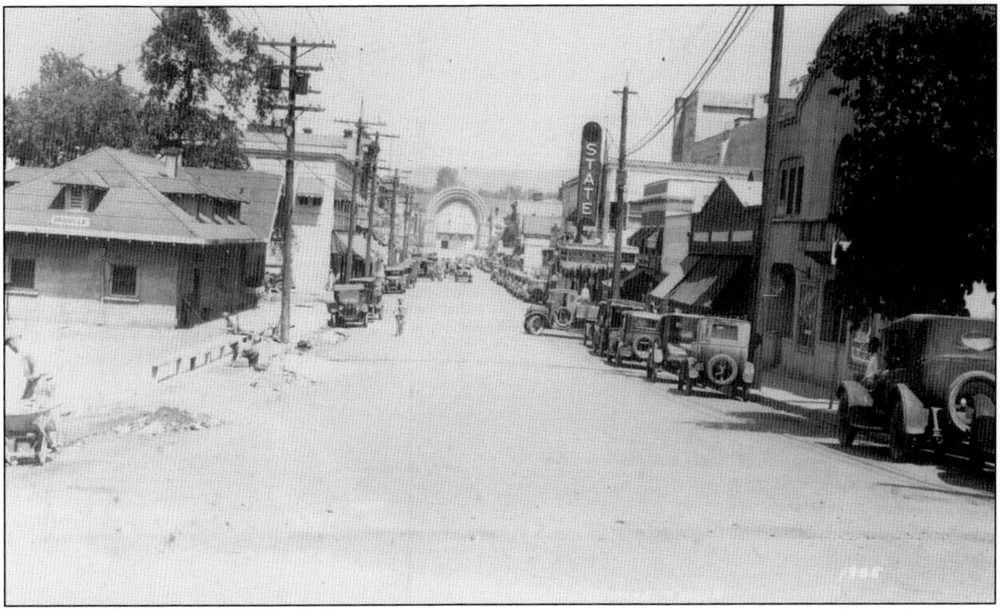

Looking down Myers Street in the 1930s shows the Rex Theatre on the right and the Northern Electric Depot at left. The recently-constructed State Theatre soon became the leading showhouse in town. It is now owned by the City of Oroville and used for various community functions.

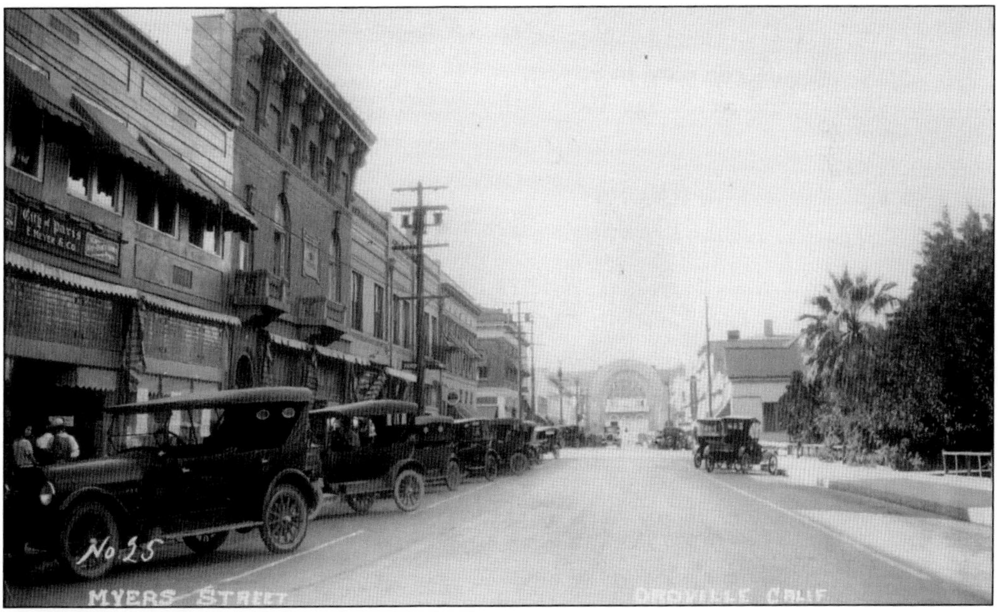

Shown above is Myers Street just prior to construction of the new State Theatre on land occupied by residences at the right. City of Paris, founded by E. Meyer, is at far left. The elaborate electric sign on the corner of the building has been retained as a landmark, even though the firm is no longer in business.

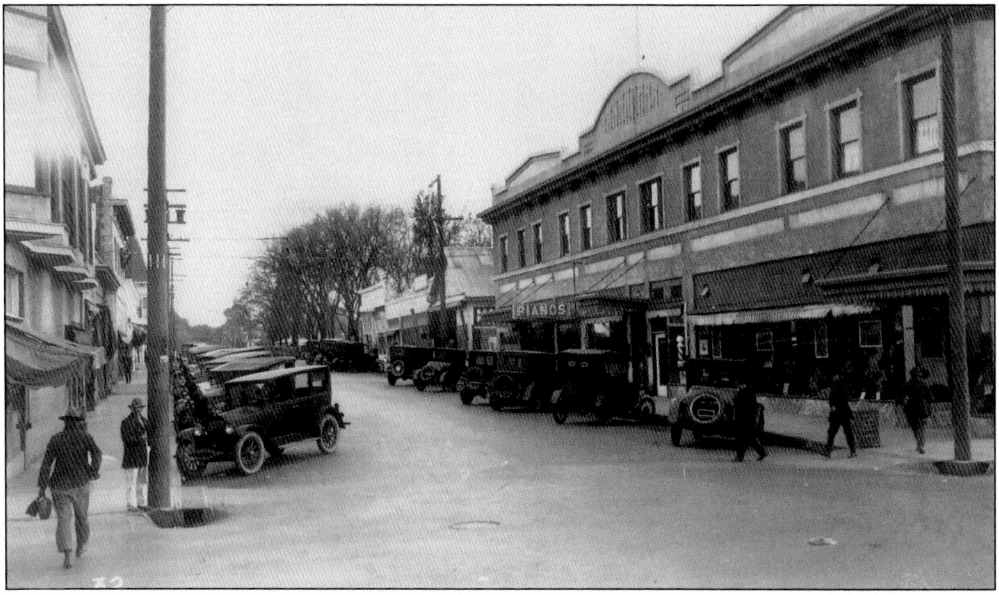

Besides the Gardella Theatre, Lawrence Gardella erected the impressive Gardella Building on the southwest corner of Huntoon and Montgomery Streets. Clothing merchants Mike Stiller and Walter W. Reece shared the building along with the U.S. Post Office. Several apartments still occupy the second floor.

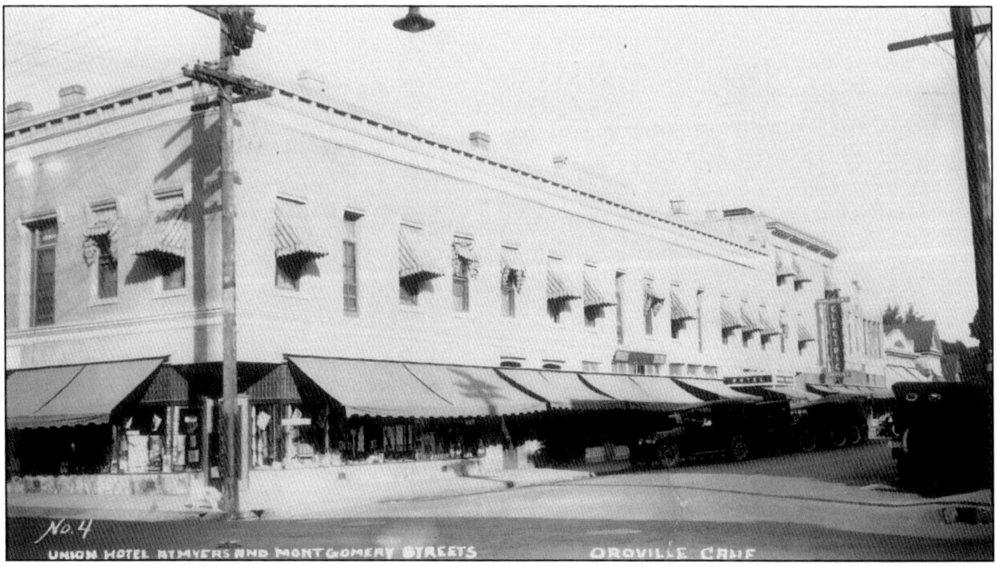

The facade of the Union Hotel facing Myers Street in the 1930s is shown after modern glass windows and retractable awnings were installed. Vertical sign at far right advertises Dahlmeier Electric Supplies.

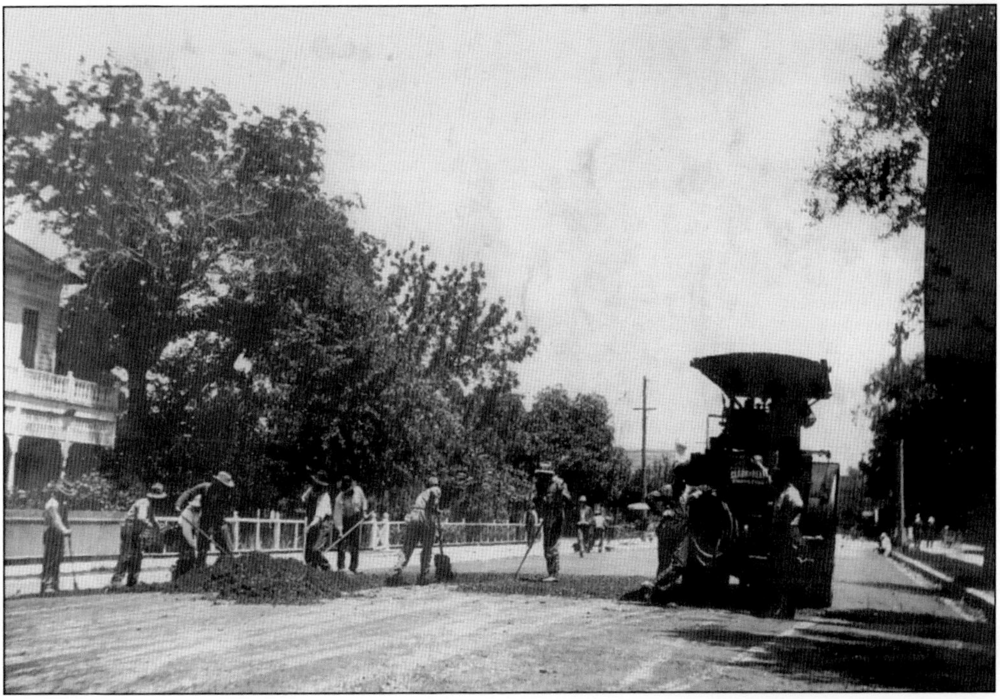

A photo taken in 1914 shows men and equipment busy paving Oroville's streets. Workers spread the asphalt by hand while the tractor waits to press it down. Note the beautiful trees the townspeople preserved at their residences, many of which survive to this day.

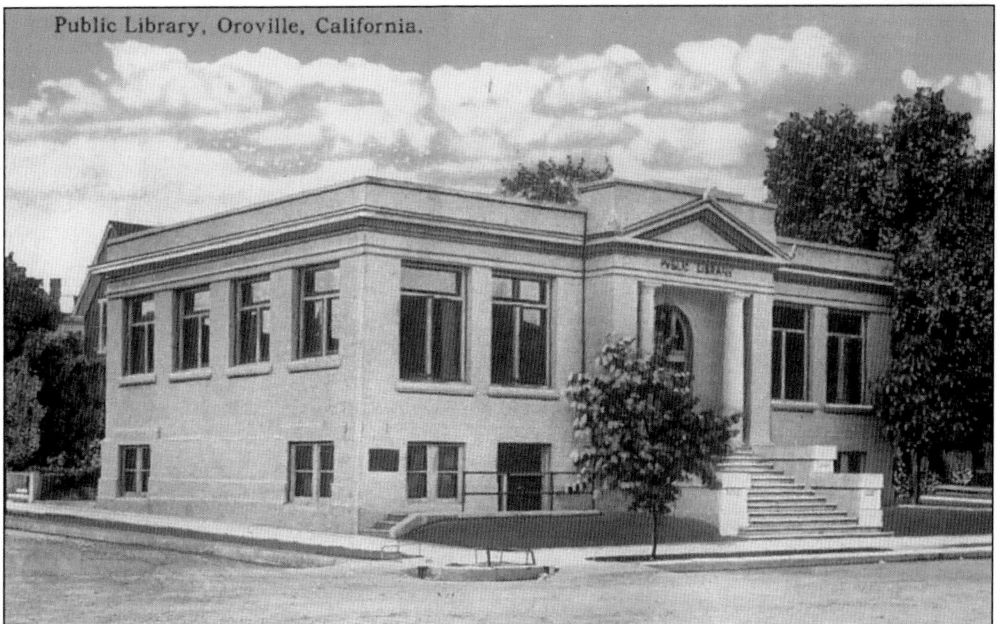

The Carnegie Memorial Library was a handsome addition to the town's architecture when constructed in 1912. Although succeeded by a larger facility, the building is still maintained by the city for other civic purposes.

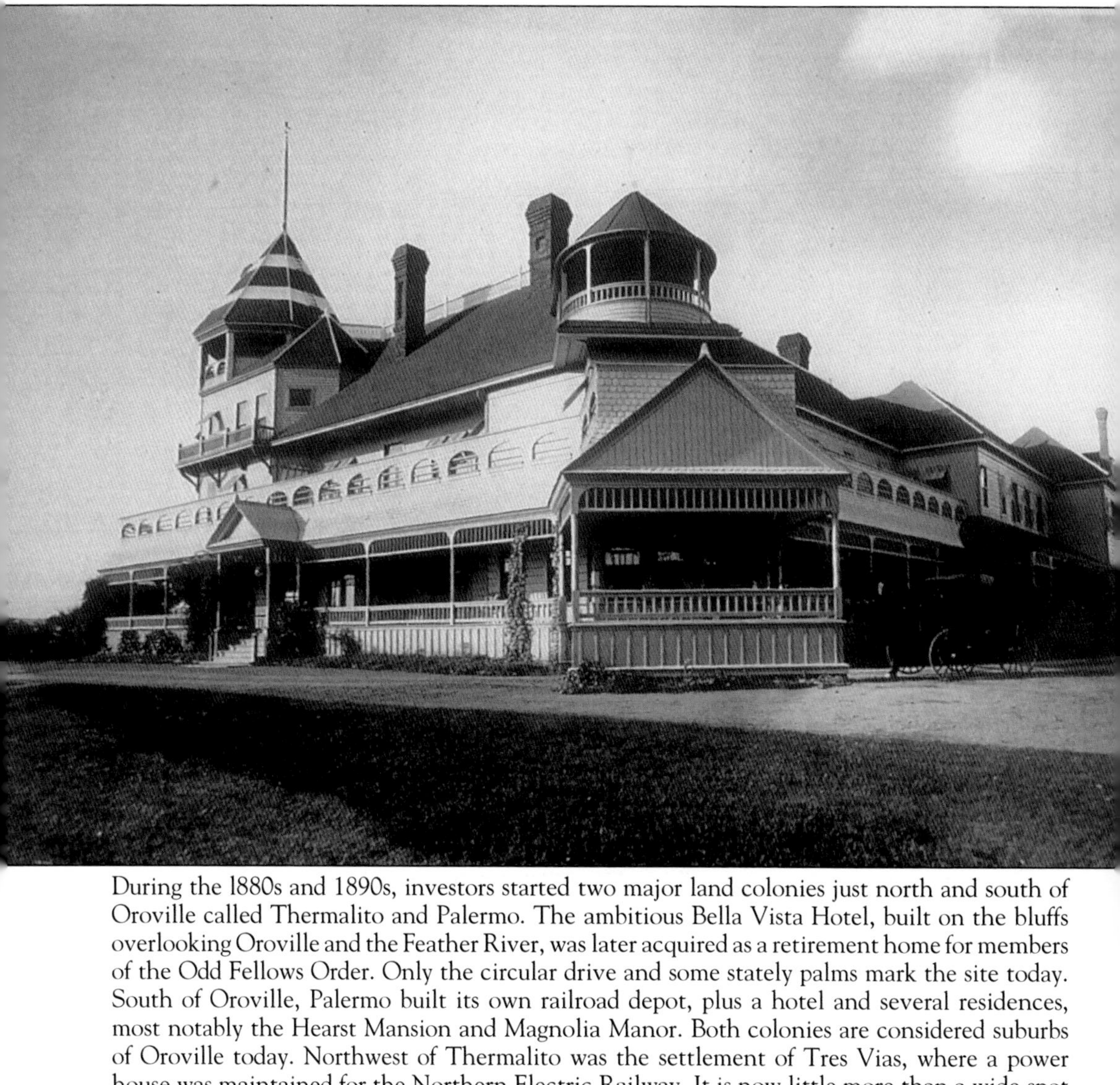

During the 1880s and 1890s, investors started two major land colonies just north and south of Oroville called Thermalito and Palermo. The ambitious Bella Vista Hotel, built on the bluffs overlooking Oroville and the Feather River, was later acquired as a retirement home for members of the Odd Fellows Order. Only the circular drive and some stately palms mark the site today. South of Oroville, Palermo built its own railroad depot, plus a hotel and several residences, most notably the Hearst Mansion and Magnolia Manor. Both colonies are considered suburbs of Oroville today. Northwest of Thermalito was the settlement of Tres Vias, where a power house was maintained for the Northern Electric Railway. It is now little more than a wide spot in the road. West of Oroville later developed the community of Richvale, with its profitable rice-growing enterprise.

Four

Home Sweet Homes

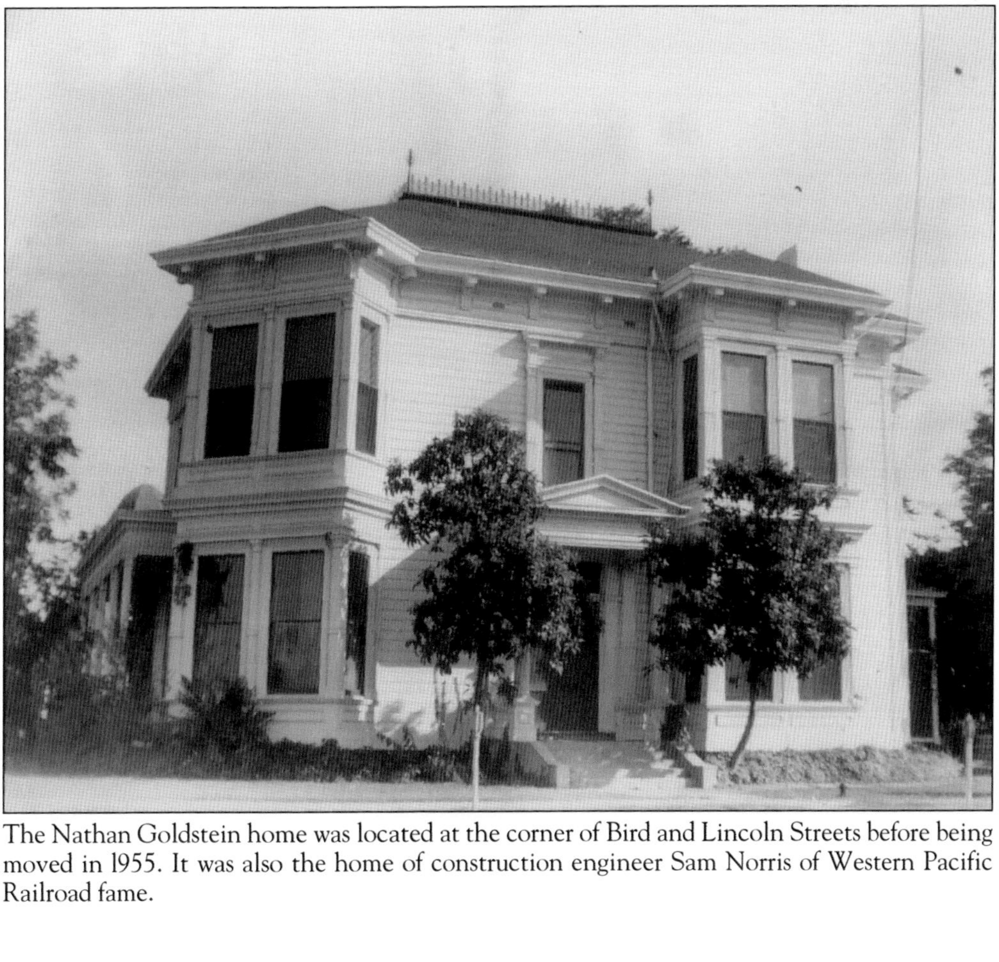

The Nathan Goldstein home was located at the corner of Bird and Lincoln Streets before being moved in 1955. It was also the home of construction engineer Sam Norris of Western Pacific Railroad fame.

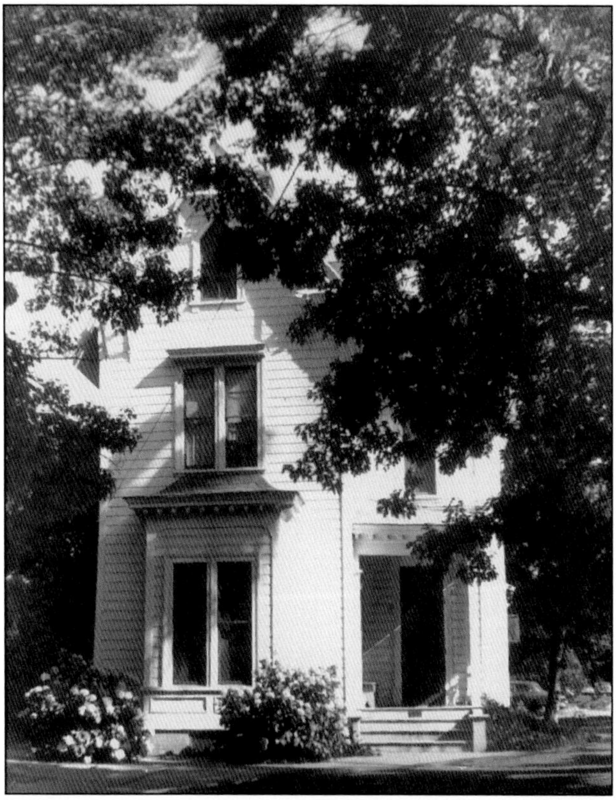

The home of John C. Gray on Bird Street was restored in 2001. Gray was principal of the Oroville Grammar School before becoming county judge.

Home of Judge John C. Gray as it appeared in Wells & Chambers *History of Butte County*, 1882.

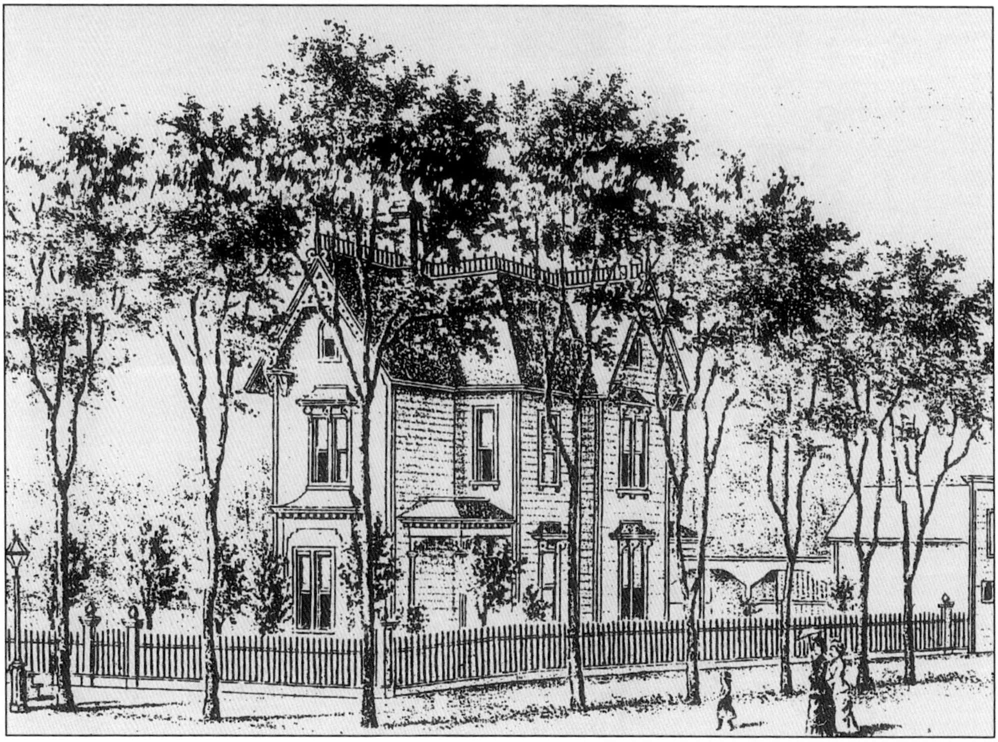

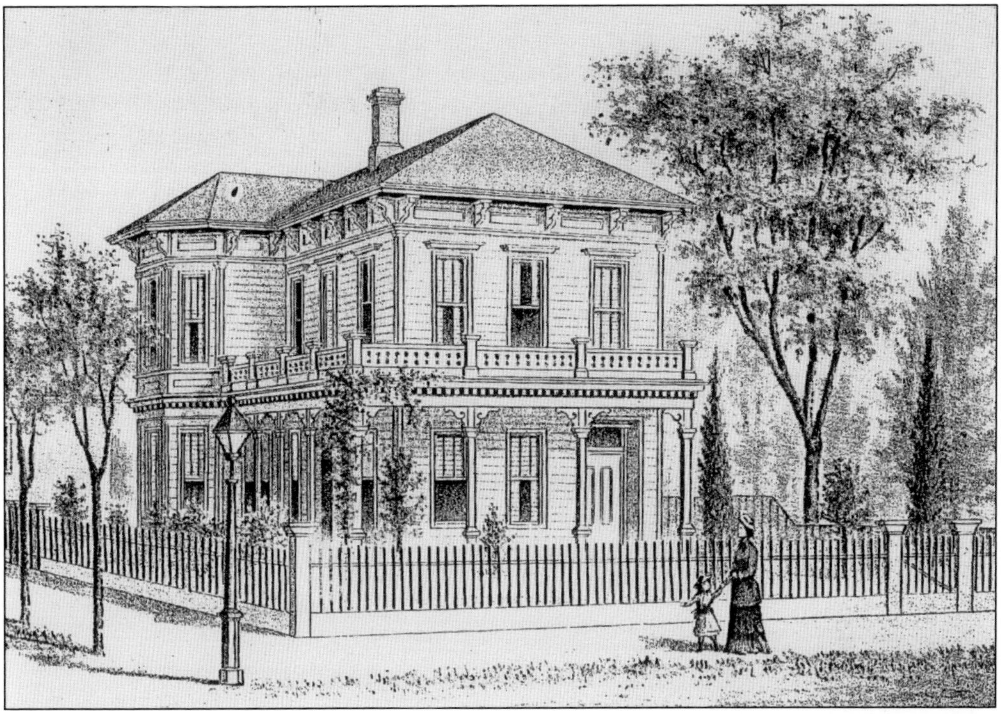

The residence of Dr. James Green stood on the corner of Montgomery and Pine Streets. The Congregational Church has a stained glass window in memory of the Green family.

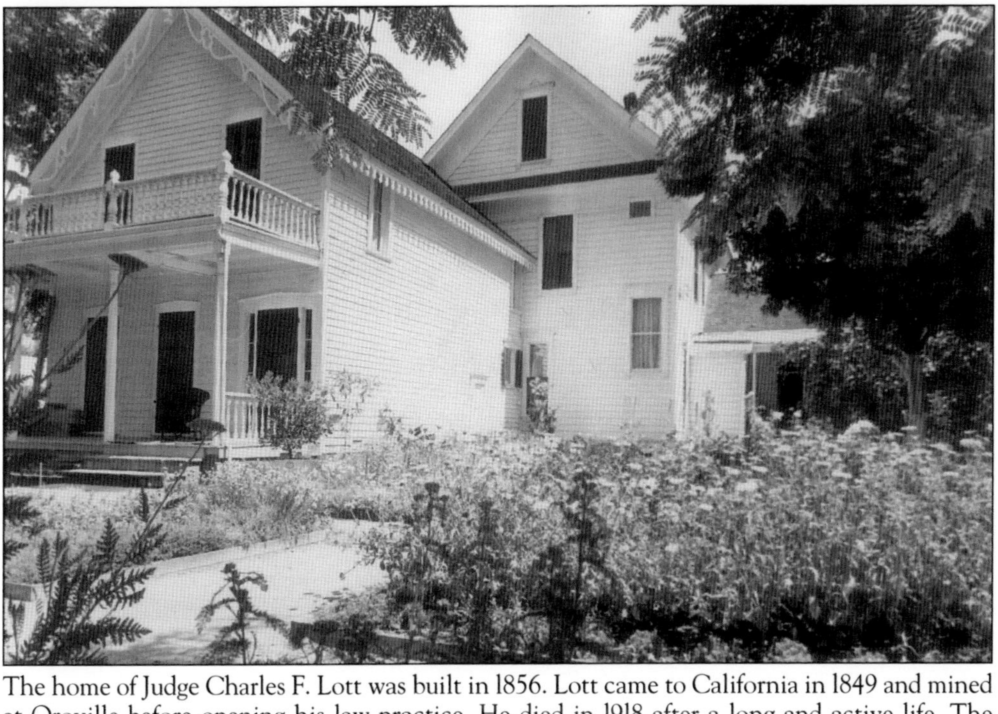

The home of Judge Charles F. Lott was built in 1856. Lott came to California in 1849 and mined at Oroville before opening his law practice. He died in 1918 after a long and active life. The home is now part of a city park.

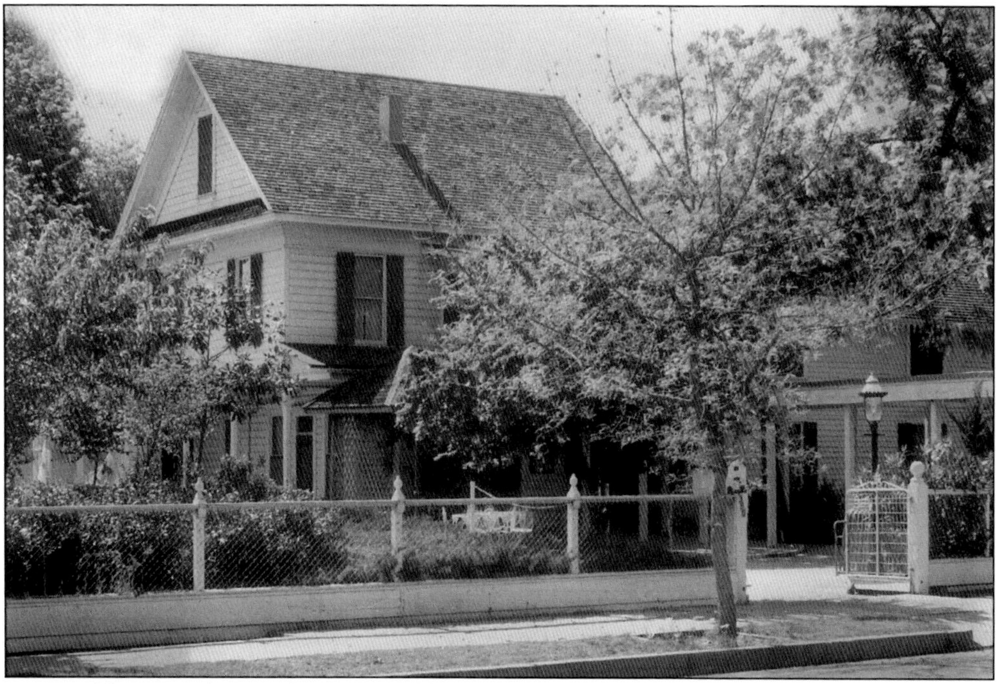

A rear addition to the Lott home was added during the 1880s. The home site occupies an entire city block complete with its original well and furnishings.

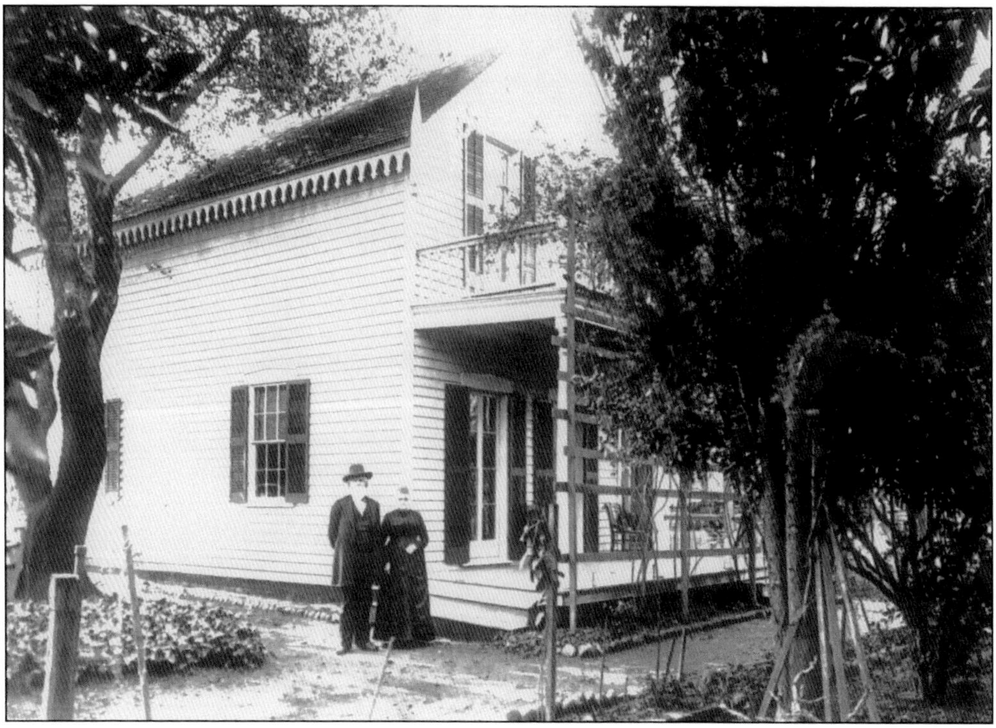

Judge Lott and his wife are shown standing in the garden by their home around 1900. The home is the oldest still standing in Oroville.

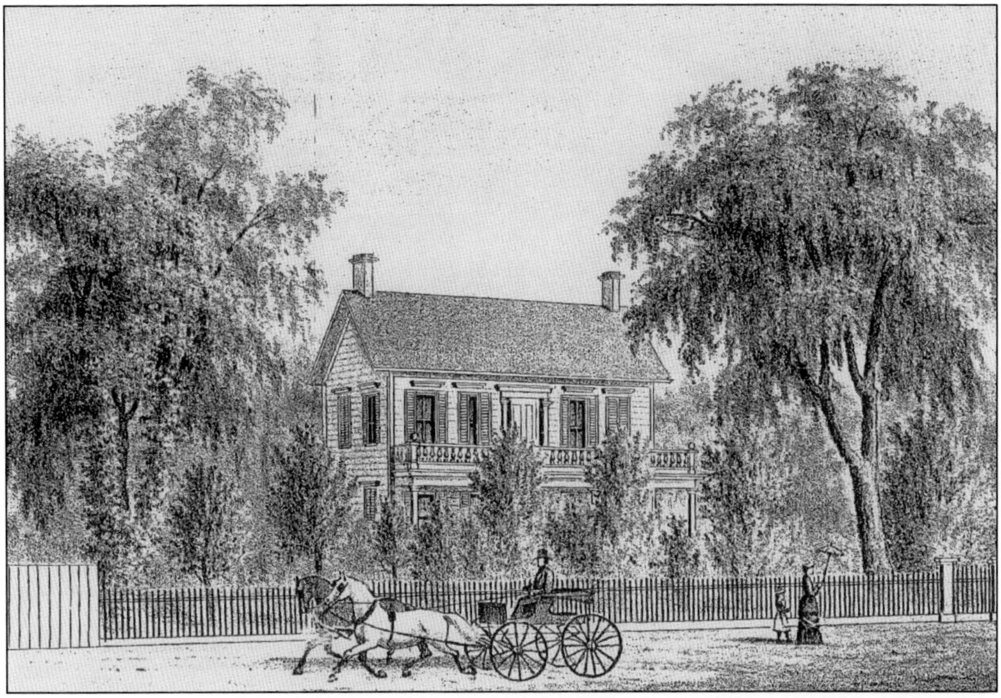

The residence of Sheriff Leon Freer stood at the corner of Montgomery Street and Second Avenue, replaced by a home erected by Elsworth Meyer and later occupied by Dr. Raymond Kilduff.

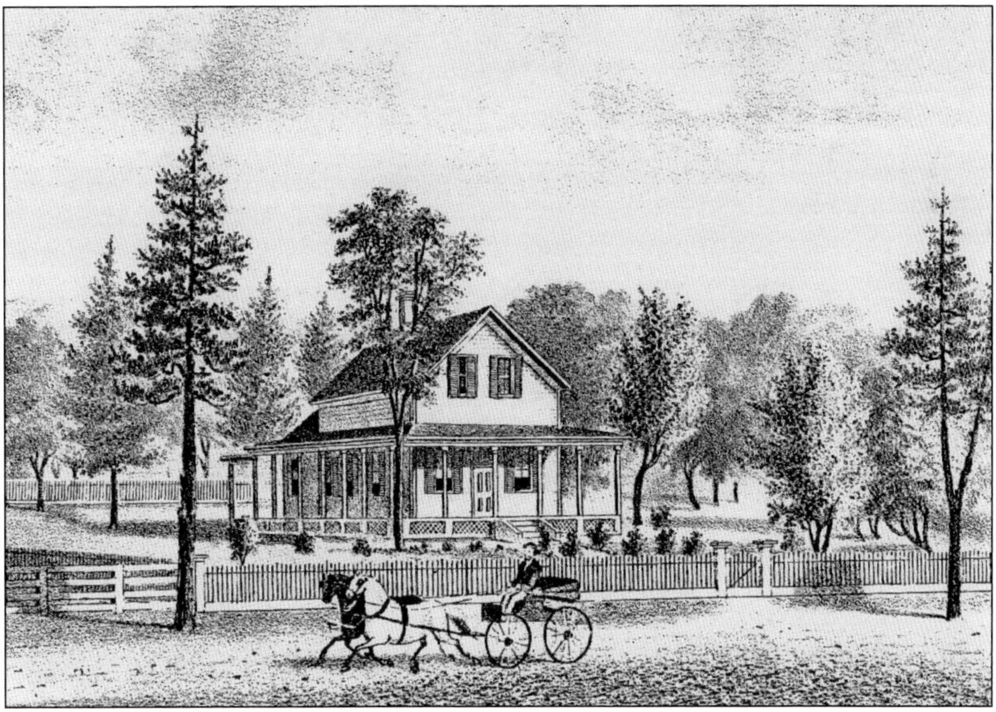

The home of the Smith brothers on Table Mountain near Oregon City was a landmark for over a century before burning down a few years ago. The brothers are buried side by side across the road.

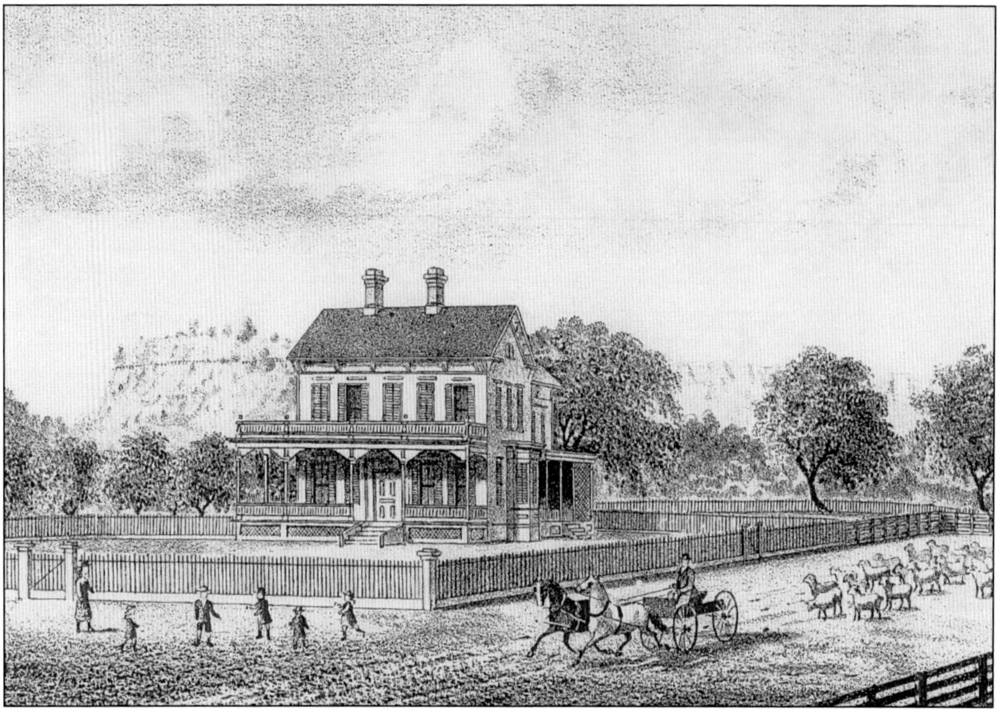

The elegant home of William and Robert Campbell on Table Mountain Ranch just north of Oroville was a showplace for many years. It had several marble fireplaces and was located at the base of Table Mountain.

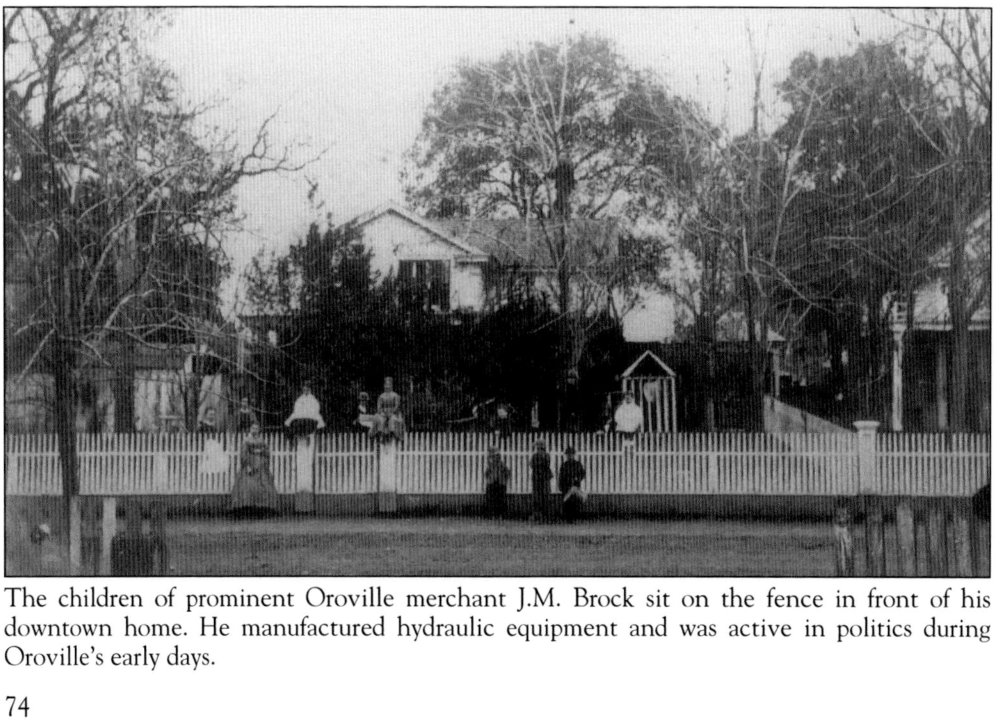

The children of prominent Oroville merchant J.M. Brock sit on the fence in front of his downtown home. He manufactured hydraulic equipment and was active in politics during Oroville's early days.

The stately home of bootmaker Fred Hecker stands on the corner of Bird and Pine Streets, erected in the 1880s. The original iron fence was located and re-installed by the late Sam Girdler, who purchased the home from Mr. Hecker's daughter, Alice. She continued to run her father's store at the corner of Huntoon and Montgomery Streets for many years.

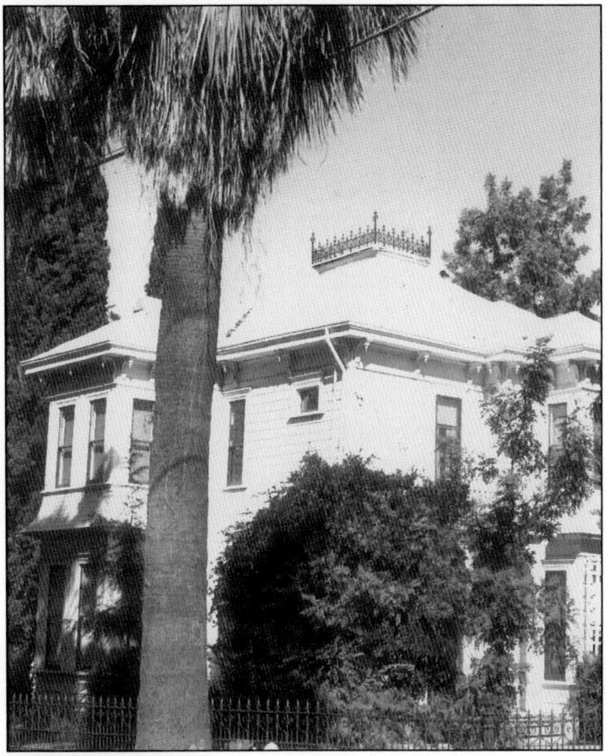

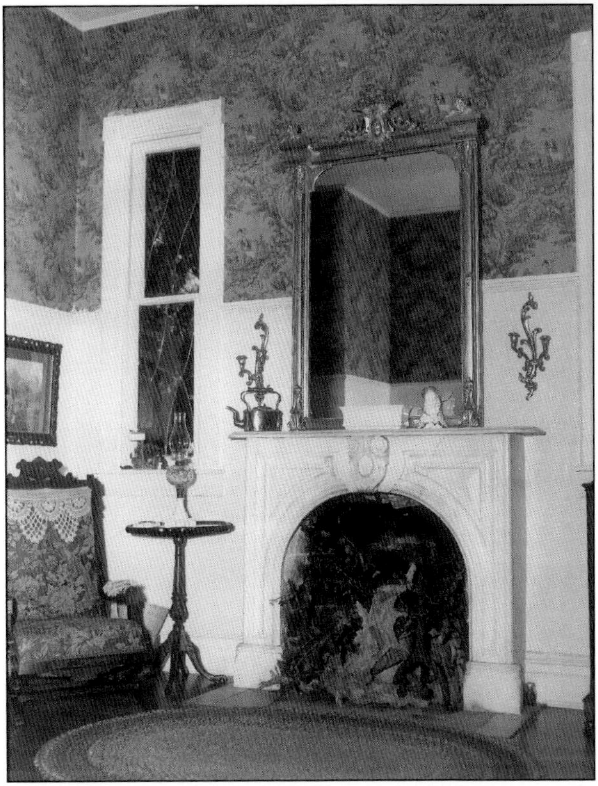

This interior view of the Hecker living room was taken by the author while Alice Hecker resided there. It still contains the original marble fireplace and gold leaf mirror, plus gas lights which are lit on special occasions.

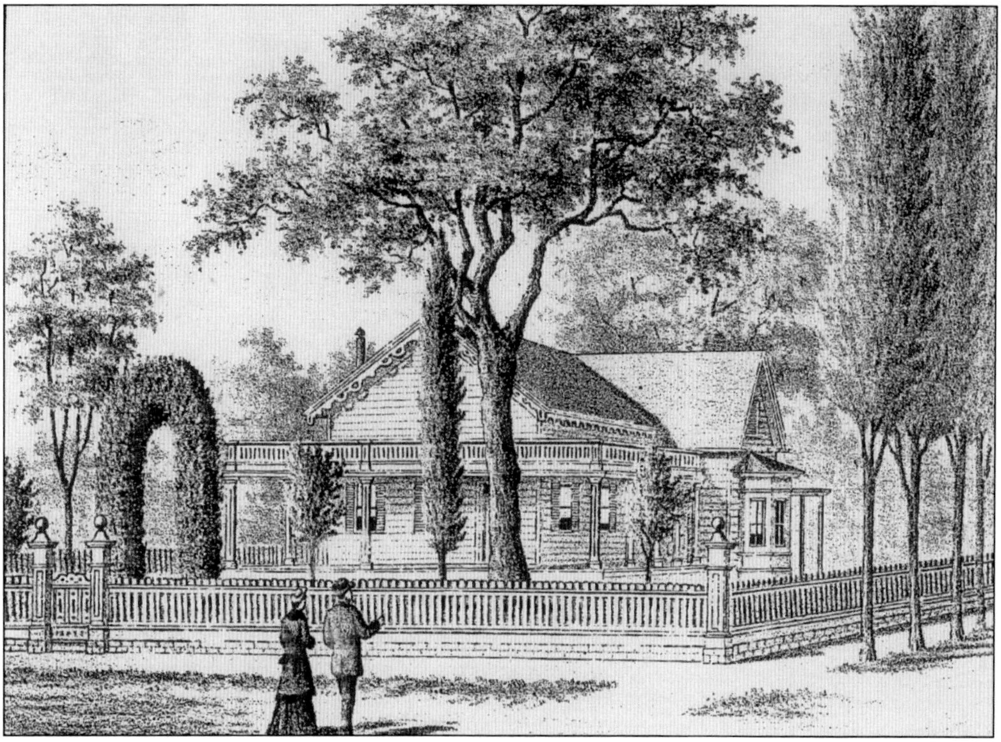

The residence of George C. Perkins on the corner of Robinson and Lincoln Streets was originally one story tall. When this engraving was made in 1882, it was the home of the governor's brother, David.

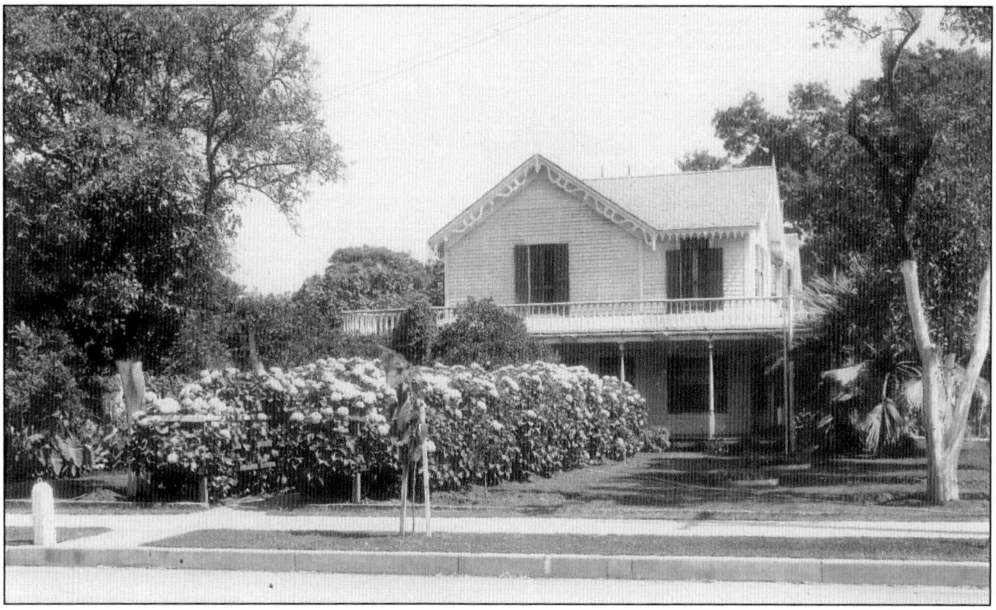

Like several homes in Oroville, a second floor was added, as shown in this 1912 photo taken by William Leeson, who also lived in the house. The marble fireplace and French doors were salvaged by the author when the home was torn down to make room for the Bidwell Title Company.

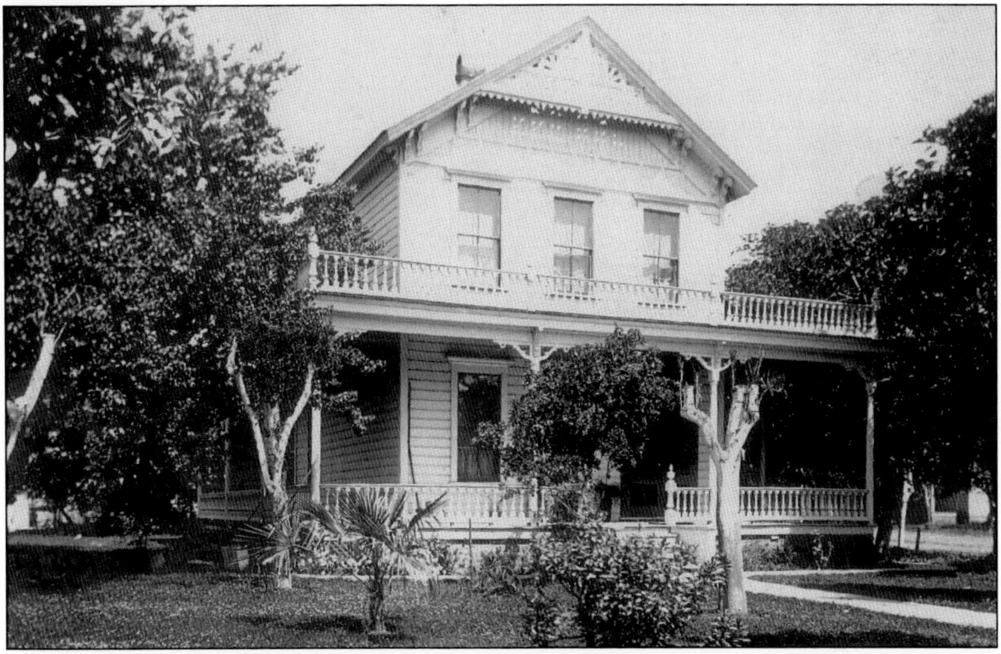

This photo of the author's home on Montgomery Street was taken around 1900. It was erected for the widow Rosina Sheehan in 1878 and was subsequently occupied for many years by the John Tuhey family. It was purchased and restored by the author and his wife in 1961.

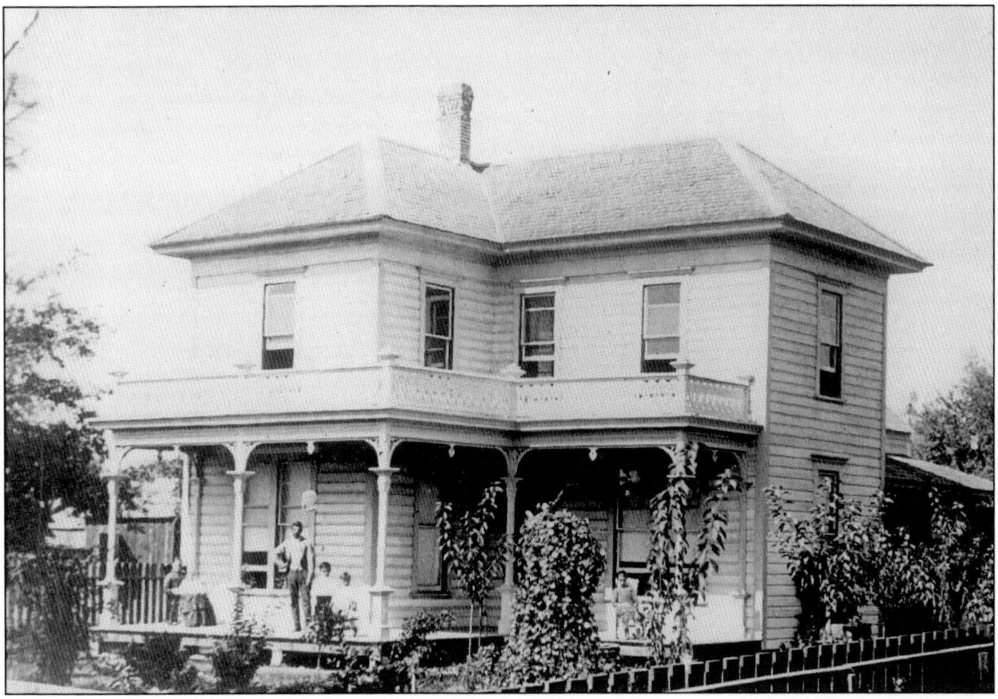

Directly across the street from the Lott home stands the Henry Rowe house, later occupied by Judge Patrick Hundley, who replaced the portico with massive columns, installed a second chimney, and added a bay window on the side.

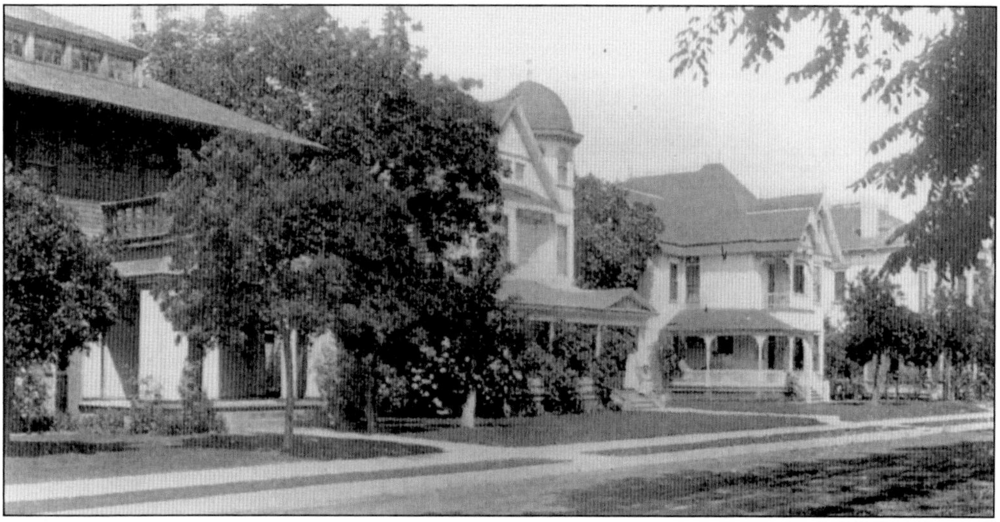

A view of the block on Lincoln Street opposite the Courthouse Plaza around 1920 shows, left to right, the Ehmann, Sparks, Holub, and Goldstein homes. The Sparks and Goldstein homes were later moved.

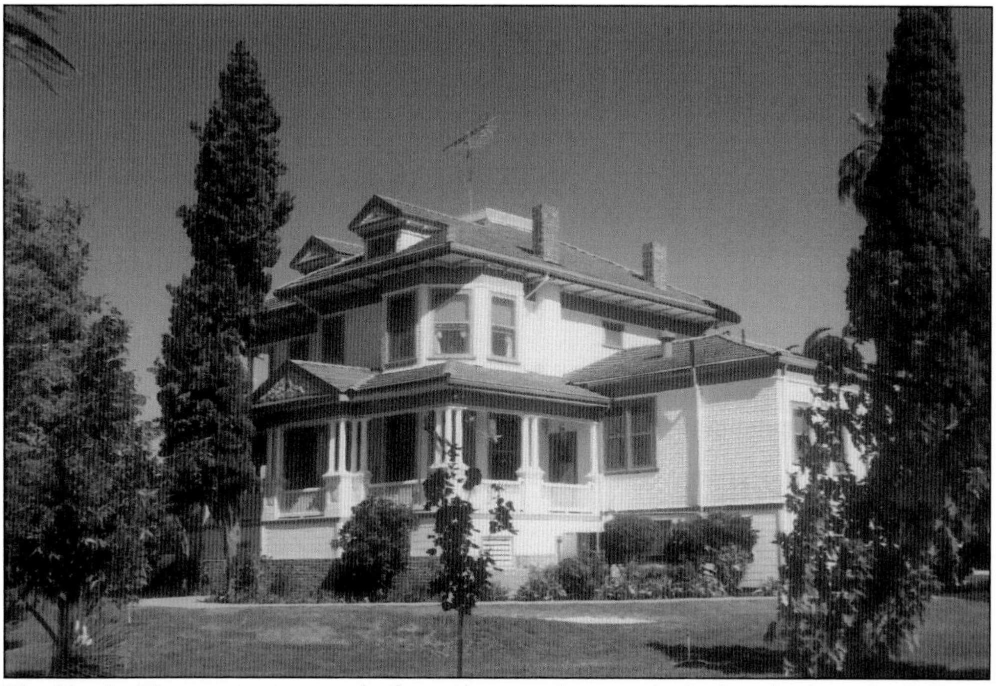

The Phoebe Hearst mansion was built on the sprawling ranch she bought from the Palermo Land Colony in 1888. Mining mogul Wendell Hammon later occupied the home and planted much of the acreage with orange groves. On occasion, the home has been open to the public.

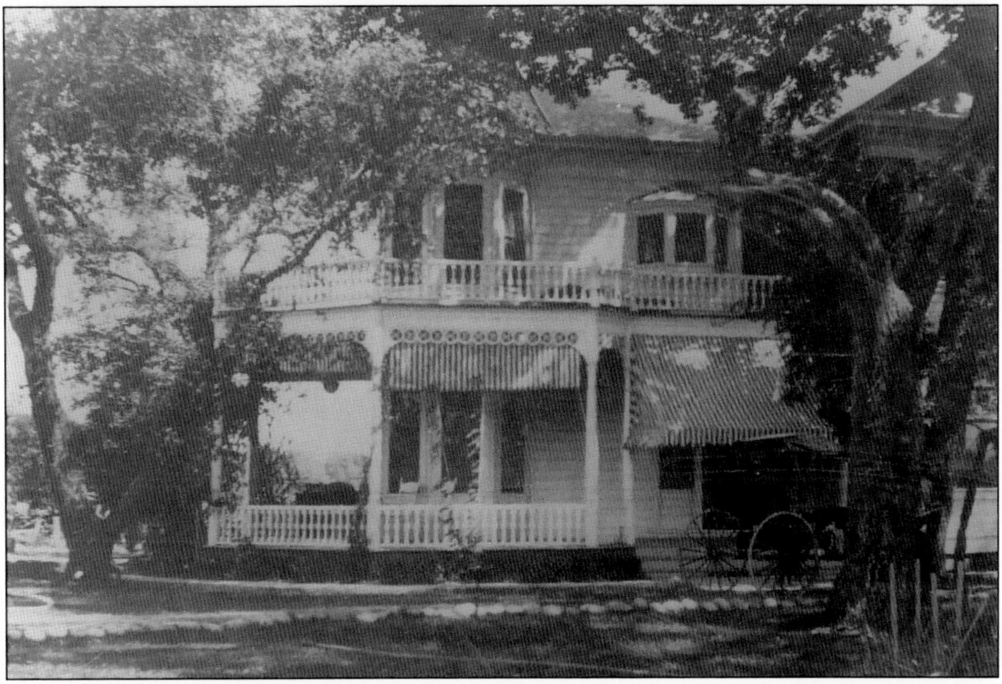

The elegant home of Charles Leggett once stood near the intersection of Oro Dam Boulevard and Fifth Avenue. The Leggett family later dredged its marginal farm land for the gold that lay beneath. The site is now occupied by several businesses.

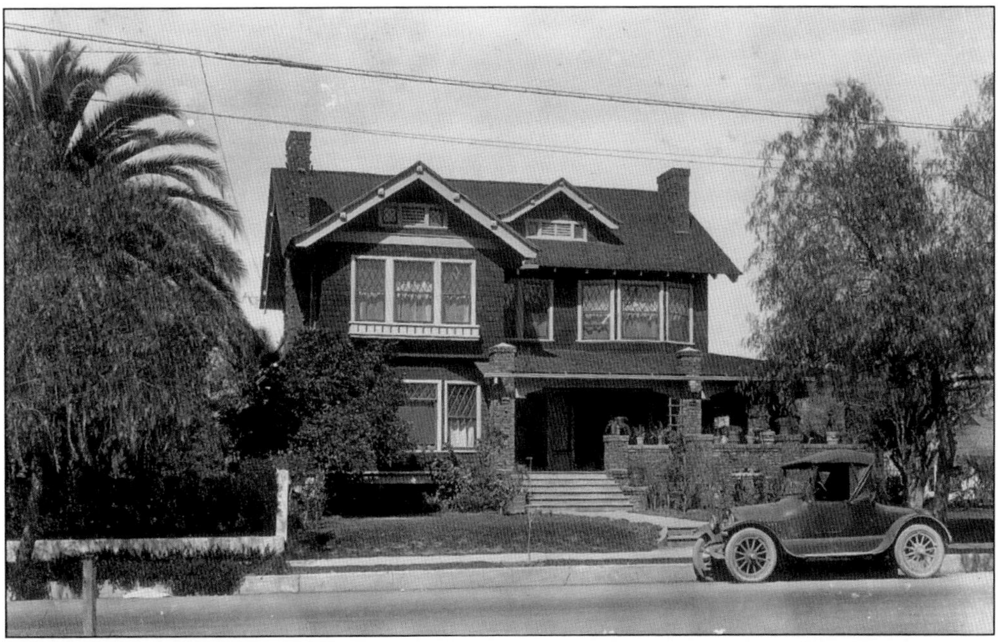

The J.E. Sangster home on the corner of Montgomery Street and First Avenue was built in 1914. Reminiscent of a later era in the history of Oroville, it became the home of Fred Huntington. Next door, the Arthur McDermott home was built in 1856 and later expanded by lumberman A.H. Land.

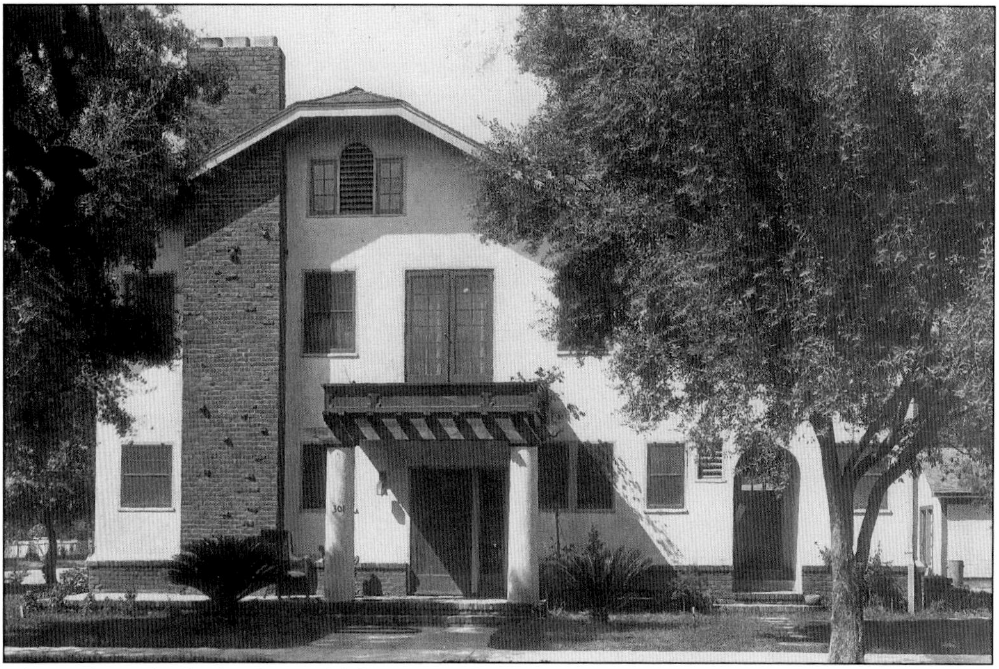

Ed Steadman built this beautiful home on the corner of Bird Street and Second Avenue. It was later embellished by attorney Paul Minasian and his wife Jean, both of whom played rolls preserving Oroville's history.

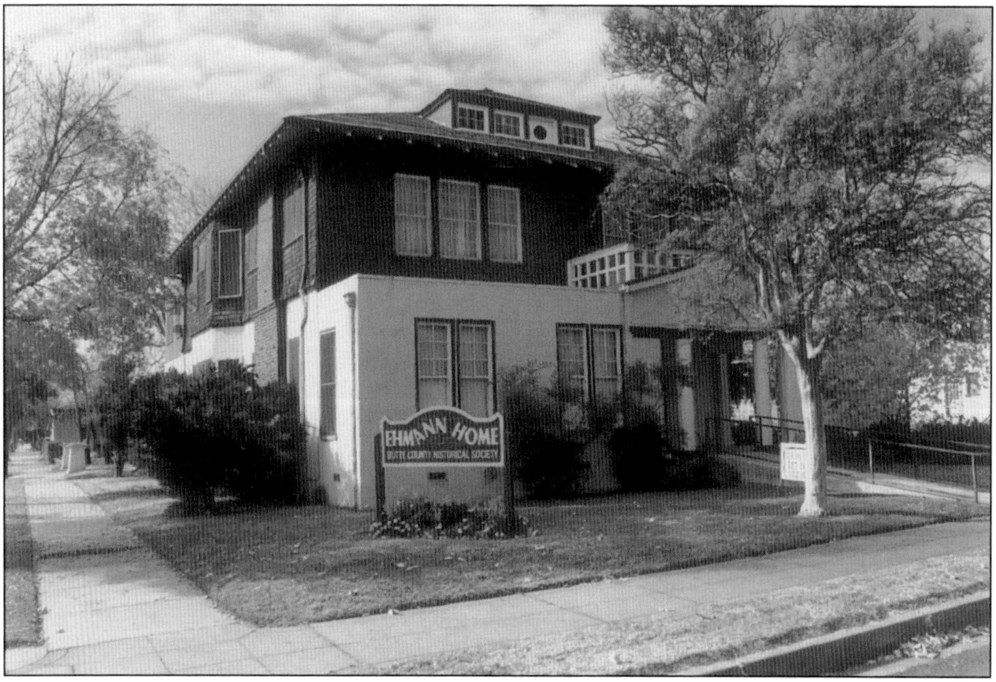

Erected in 1911, the same year Ishi was "captured," the home of Mayor Edwin Ehmann and his famous mother Freda is now maintained by the Butte County Historical Society. The Society also maintains a museum, the Oregon City School, and the historic Bangor Community Church.

Five

FAITH AND EDUCATION

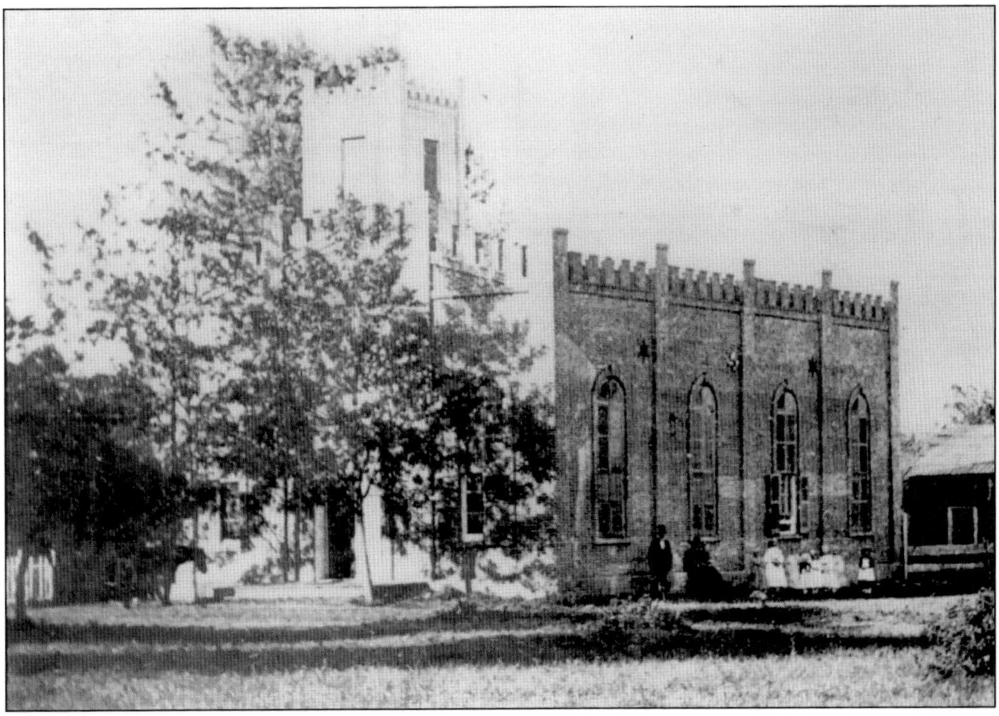

The first church in Oroville was built by Congregational minister Bela N. Seymour and parishioners in 1858. Referred to as Oroville's Union Church during the Civil War, it was located at the corner of Oak and High Streets until replaced by a second structure two blocks away in 1875.

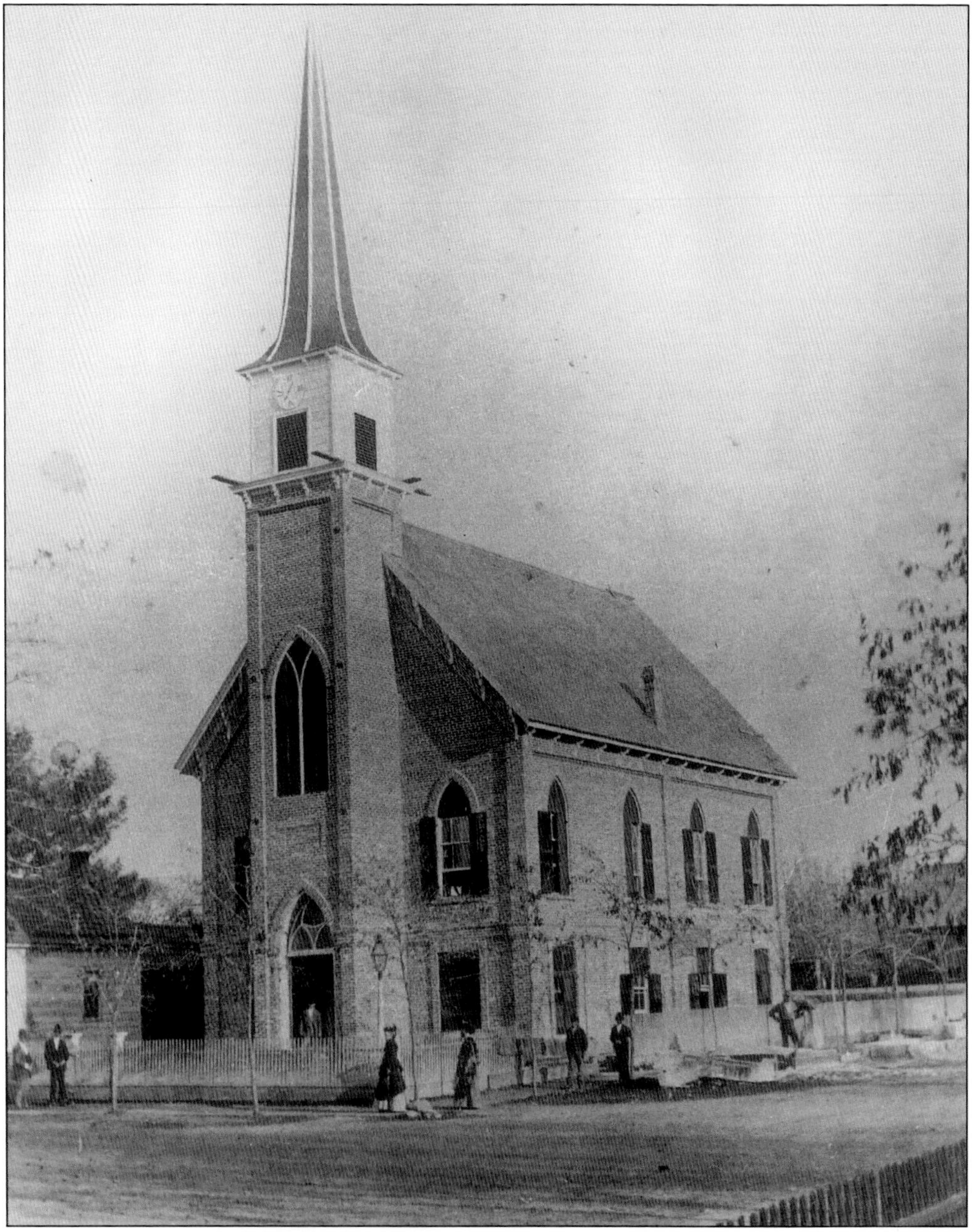

This view of the second Congregational Church was taken in 1876, shortly after it was completed at the corner of Bird and Oak Streets. Note the gas street light in front and clock at the top of the steeple. The social hall was on the first floor and the sanctuary on the second.

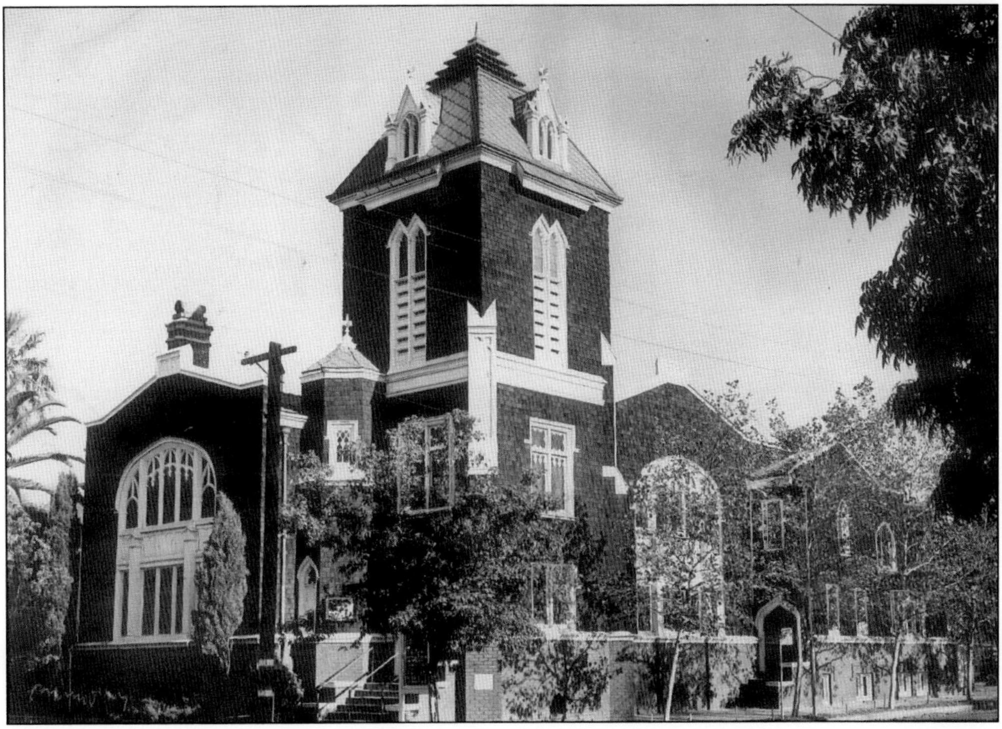

The third Congregational Church, built in 1912, contained some of the most impressive stained glass windows in northern California. A few were saved and put into the current structure following a tragic fire in 1982.

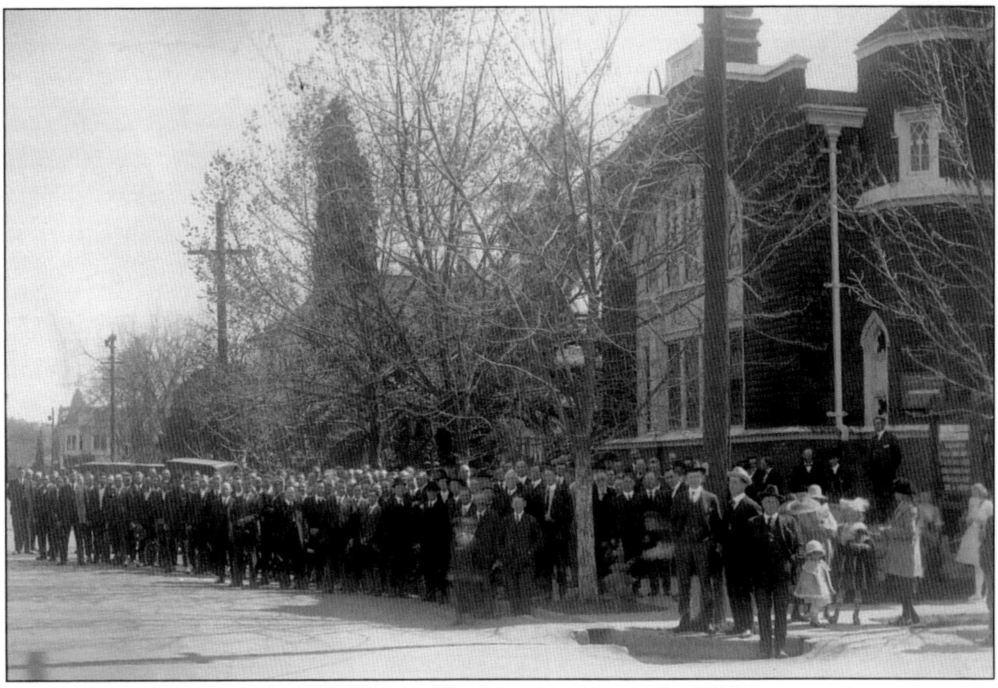

The men's Sunday school class posed for this picture taken in the 1920s.

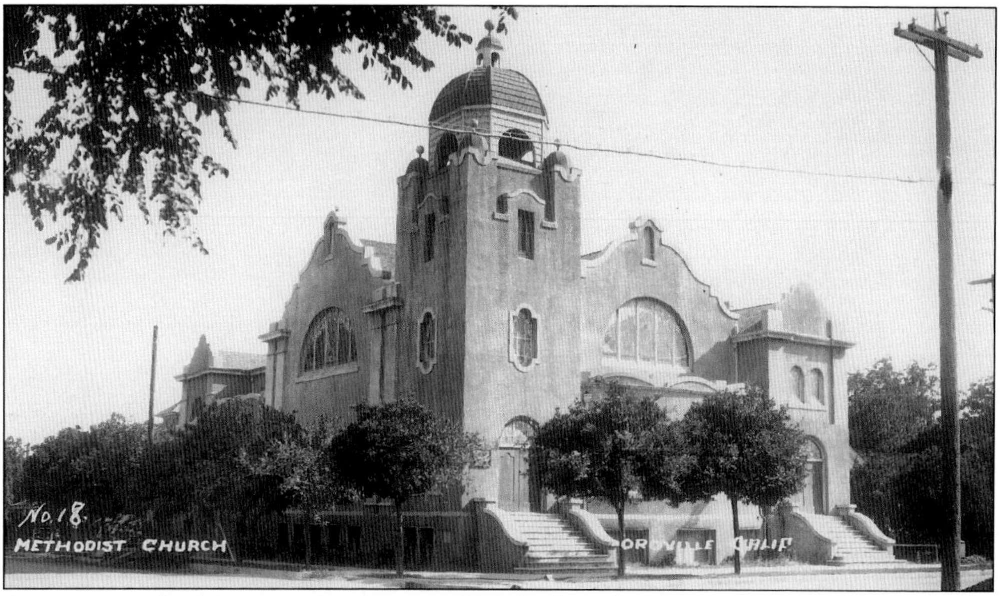

Incorporating the Mission style, the second Methodist Church was built in Oroville in 1911 at the corner of Robinson and Lincoln Streets. It stood for many years until replaced by a new structure on Acacia Avenue.

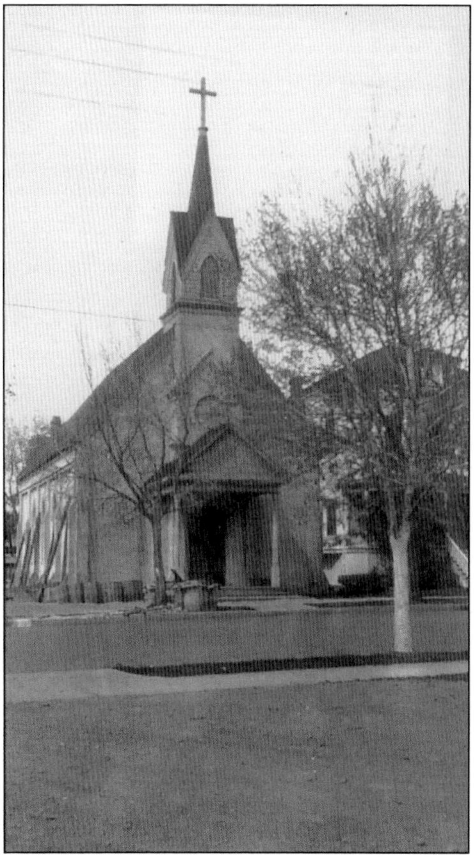

Although dating from the early days of Oroville, local Catholics did not build their own church until 1875. Shown above is the church and portion of the rectory on Bird Street, where a newer church now stands. A parochial school was added later.

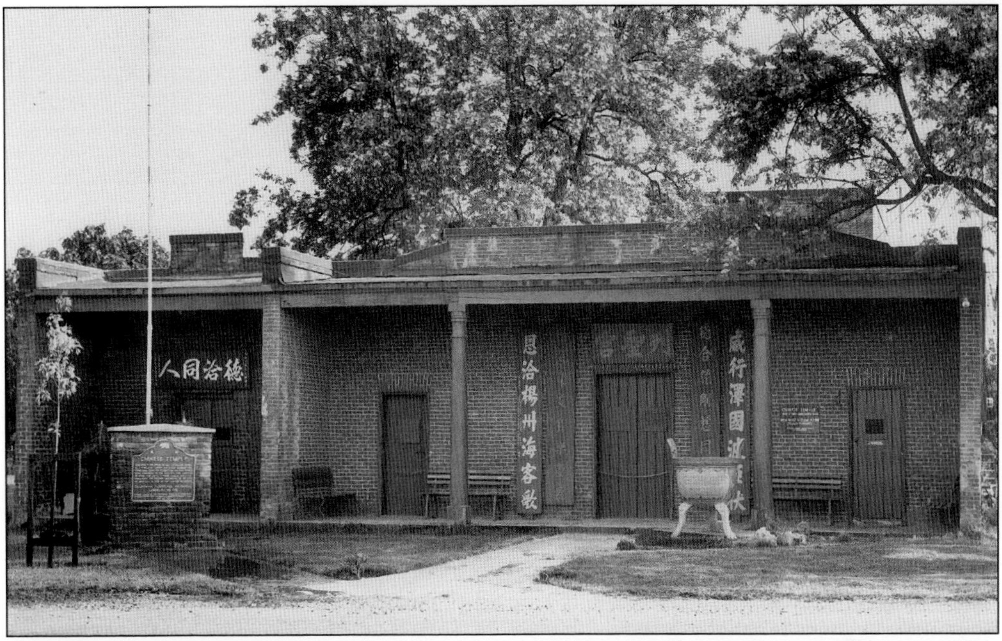

The Chinese Temple was erected in Oroville in 1863 and still contains most of its priceless furnishings. A tapestry hall has been added to display other treasures. Traditional Chinese plays were held in a theatre next door.

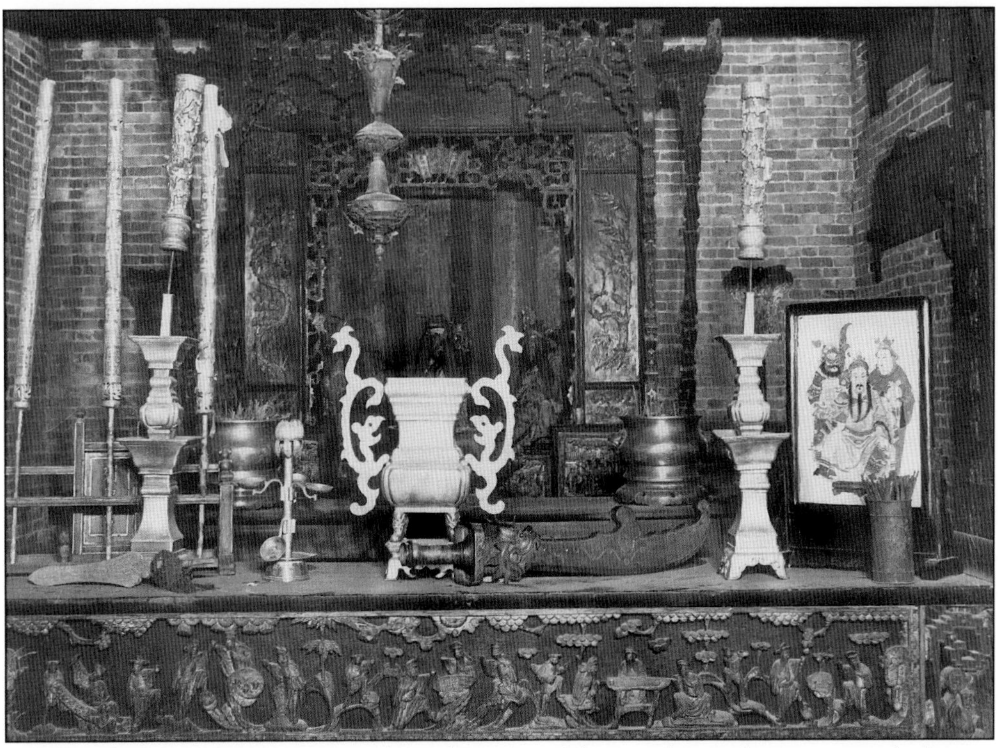

Interior view of the main sanctuary shows but a few of the wondrous religious items which were found in the temple before it reopened in 1949.

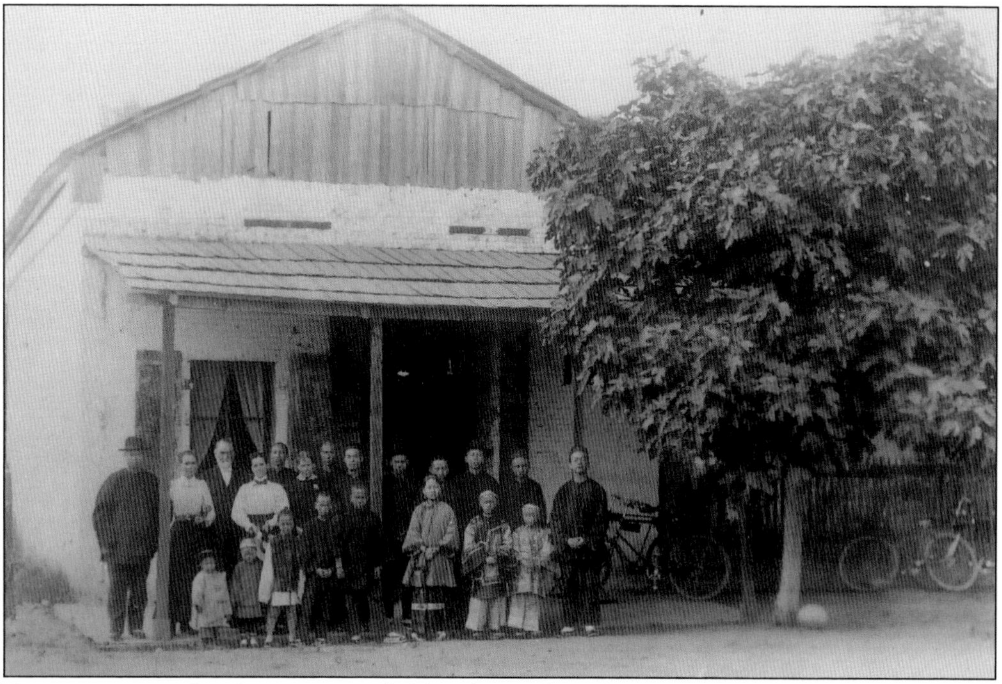

For many years the Congregational Church conducted a mission in Chinatown to teach residents English and the American culture. Shown third from the left is Rev. William Pond, who organized missions to various Chinese settlements in California.

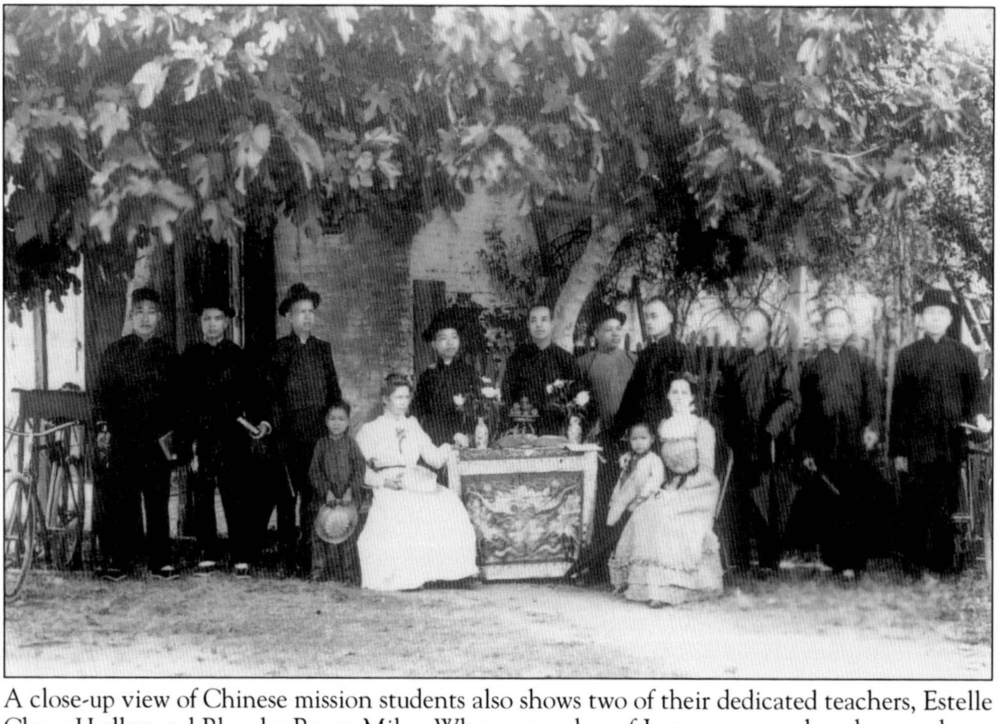

A close-up view of Chinese mission students also shows two of their dedicated teachers, Estelle Chase Hadley and Blanche Reece Miles. When a number of Japanese moved to the area later, they were also enrolled at the mission.

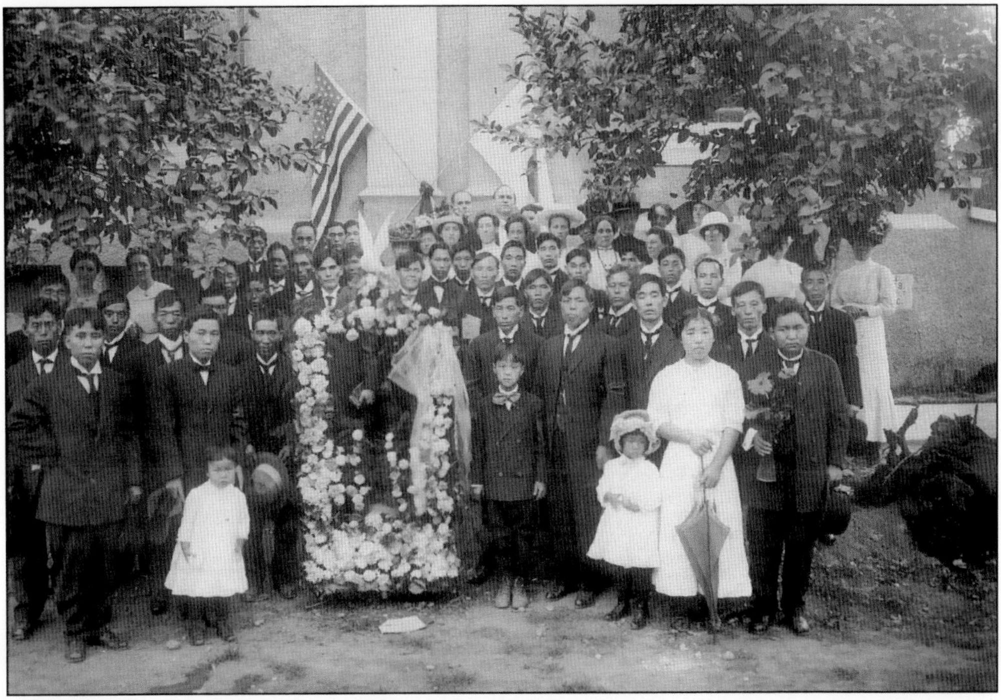

After the turn of the century, many Japanese migrated to the area, starting farms and businesses. Shown here are several Japanese Christians who gathered for a service in memory of Emperor Hirohito's father. The Methodist Church is in the background.

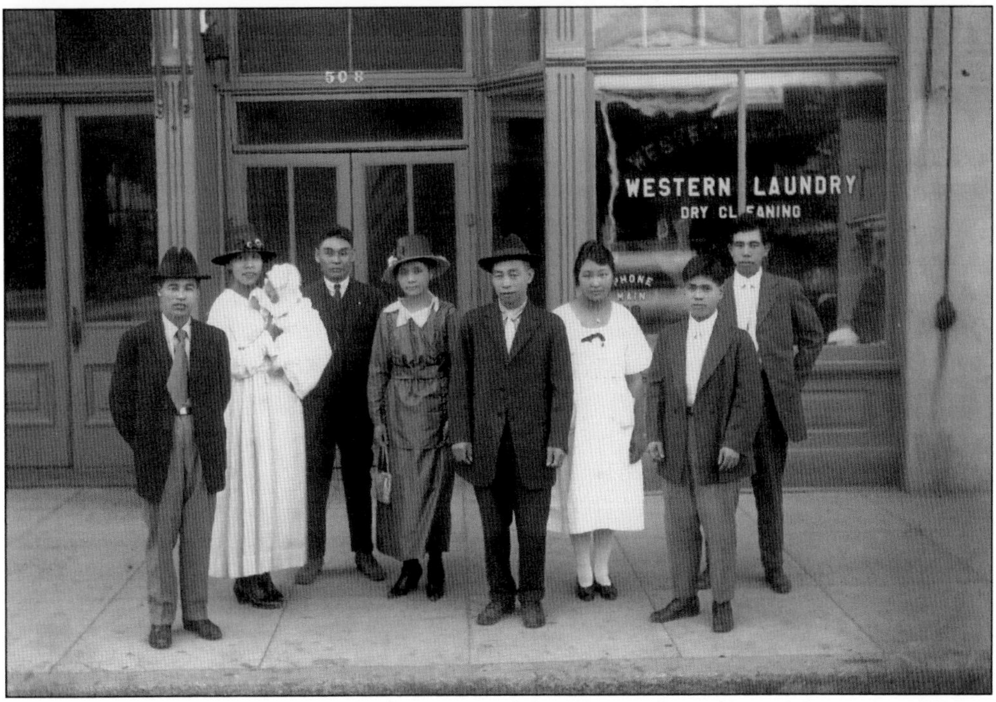

Shown above is the Japanese family that operated the Western Laundry on Montgomery Street. Others worked on the gold dredgers or developed farms south of town.

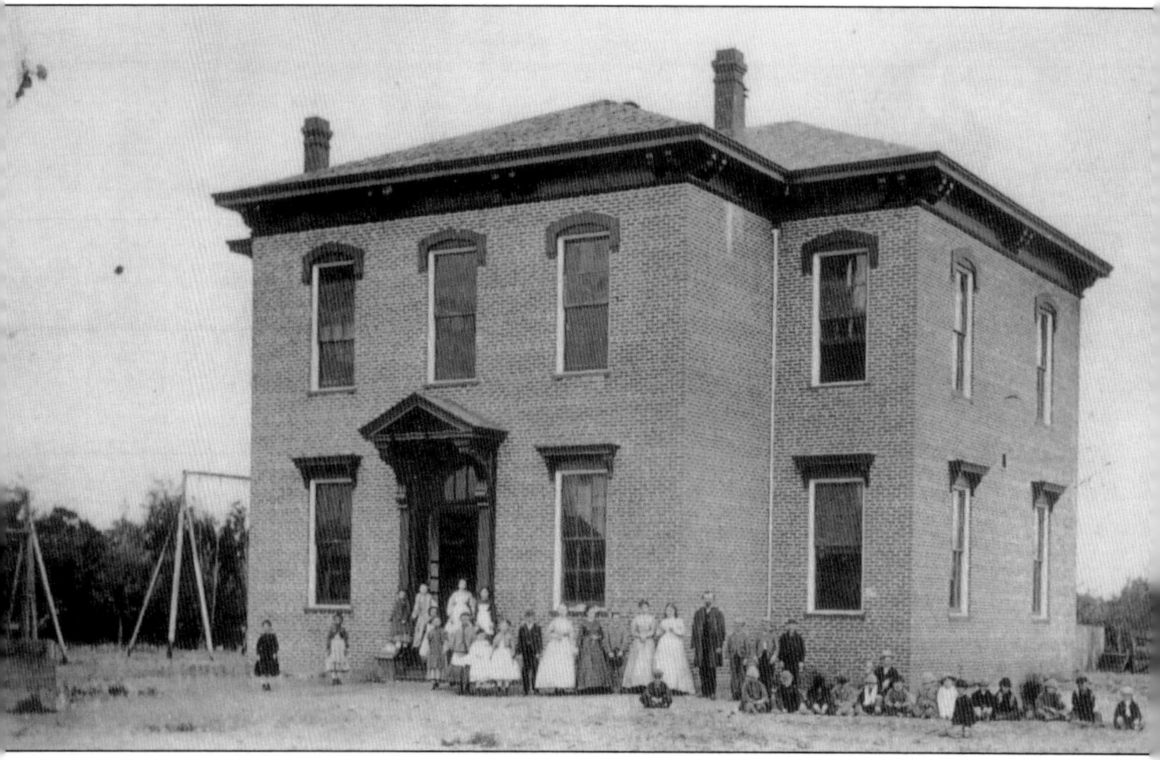

The first grammar school in Oroville was built on Bird Street in the 1870s. Over the years it would be periodically expanded with new additions to the front and rear. A modern school now occupies the same site.

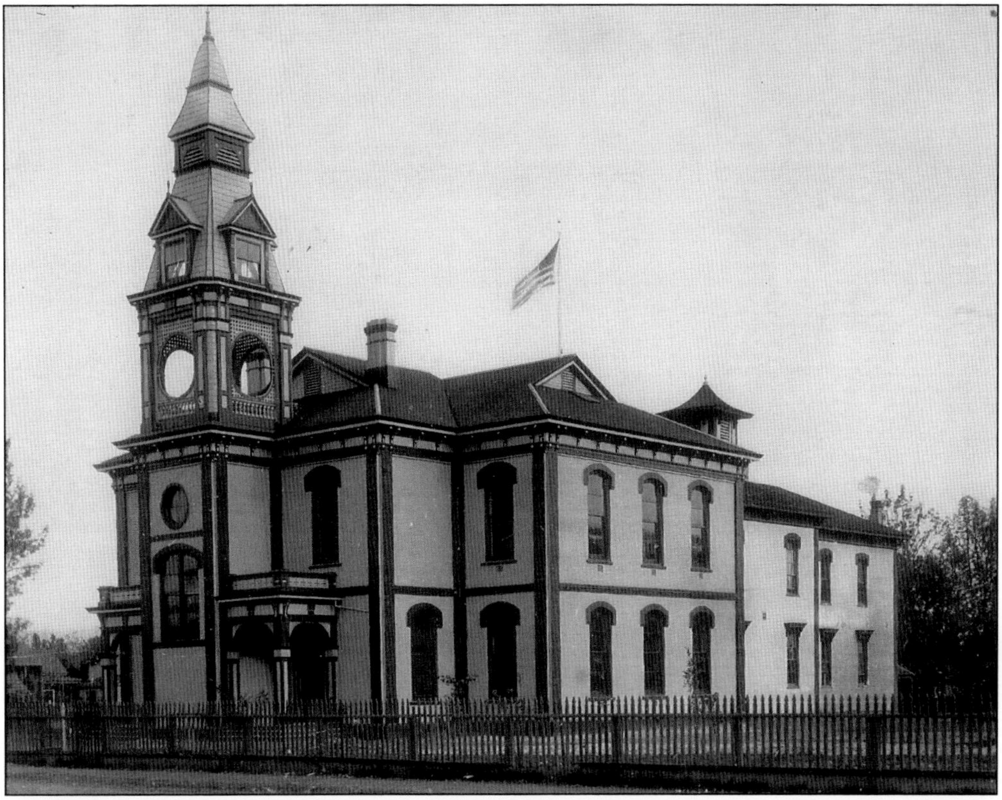

In 1892, Oroville's first high school was combined with the grammar school when this impressive structure was added in front of the original building. The high school would meet here until a separate school was erected a couple blocks away.

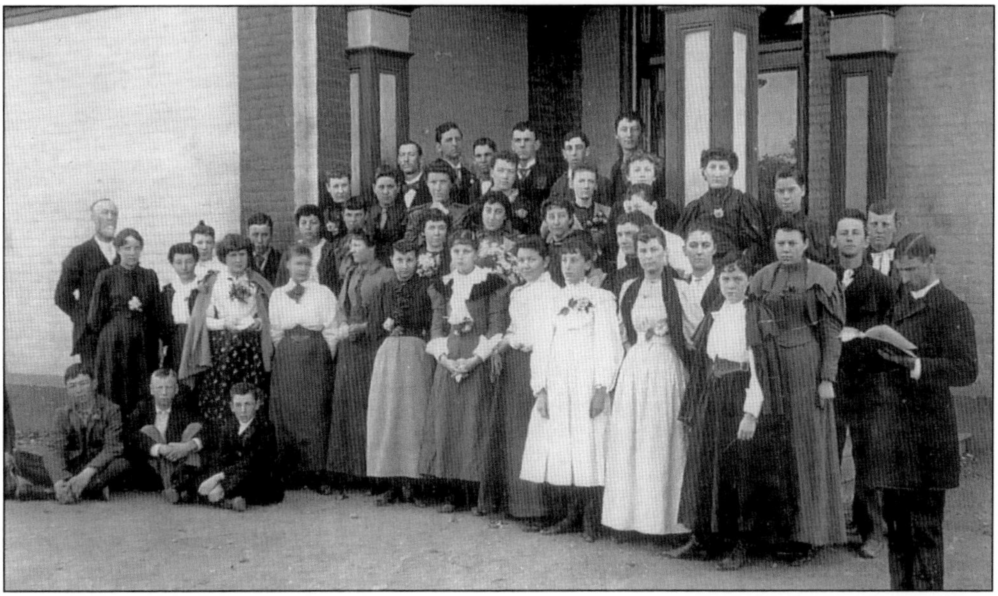

Shown here are students of the high school in 1896. Looking on from either side are trustee H.T. Batchelder, far left, and principal J.A. Snell, far right.

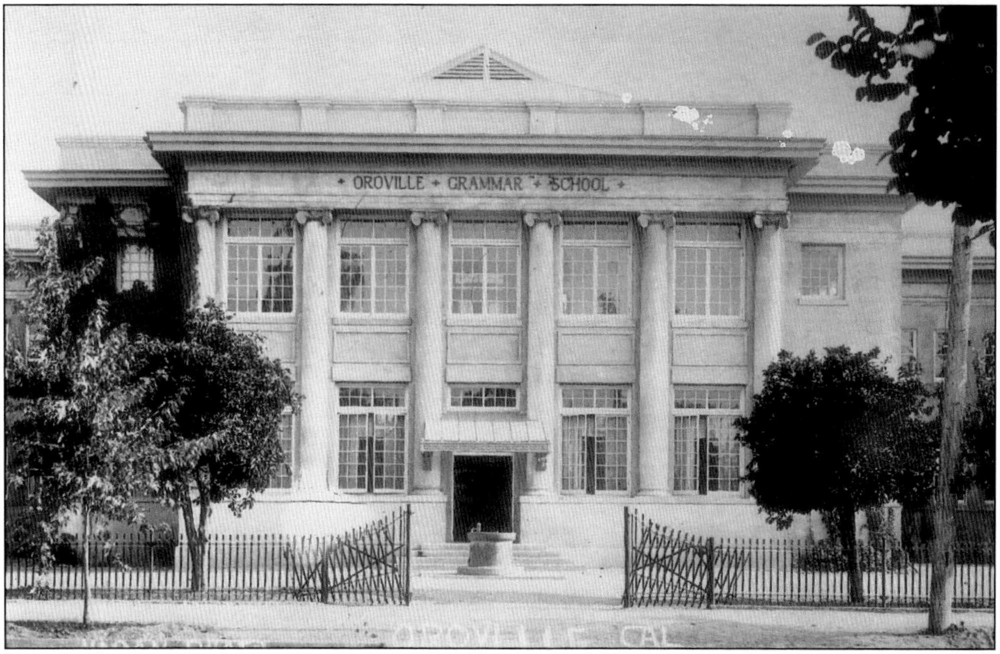

In 1912, a brand new grammar school was erected, incorporating a portion of the old school behind the new Roman facade. Although not damaged by an earthquake caused by the filling of the Oroville Dam in 1975, trustees decided to demolish the grand edifice and build a smaller school.

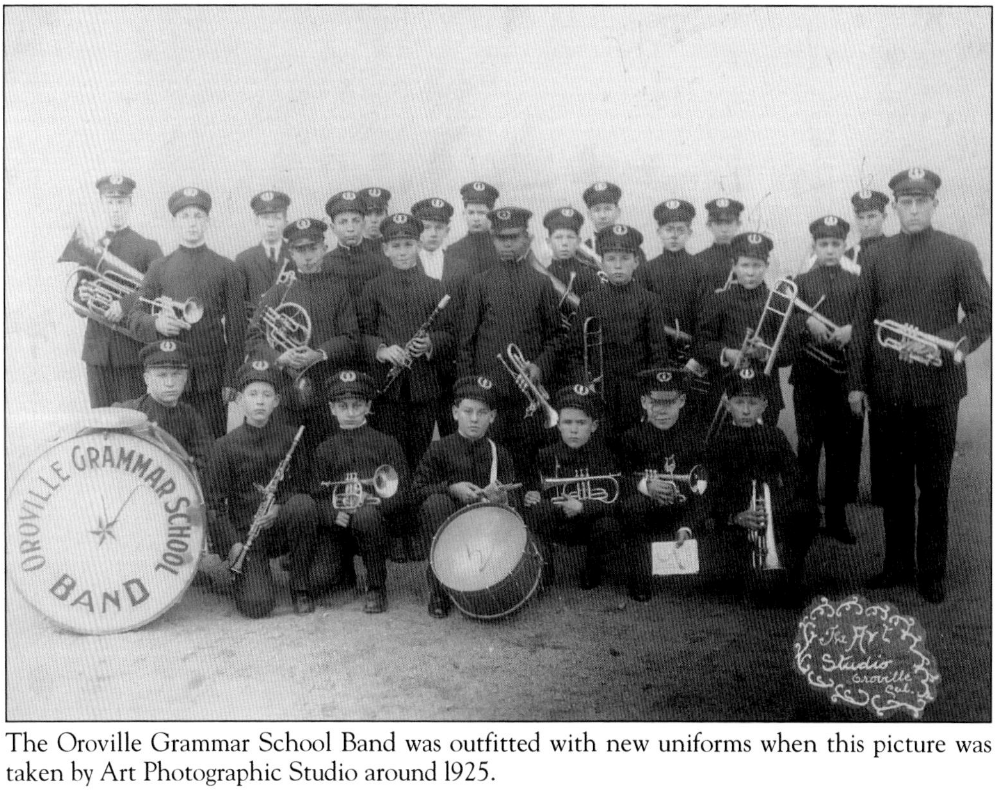

The Oroville Grammar School Band was outfitted with new uniforms when this picture was taken by Art Photographic Studio around 1925.

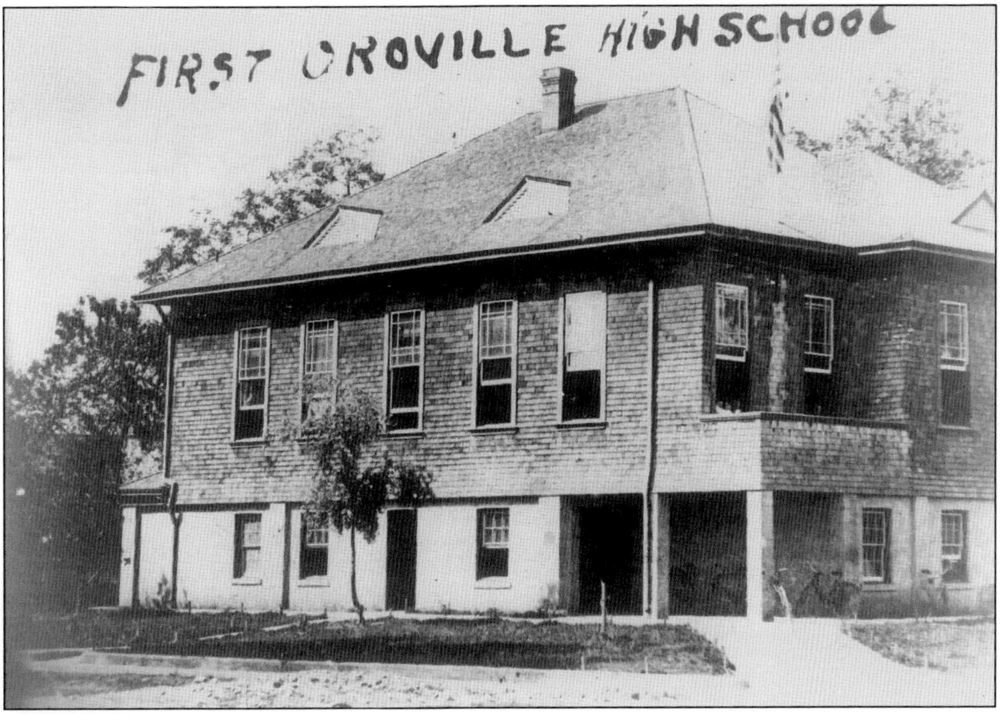

Oroville's first separate high school building was erected at the corner of Robinson Street and Second Avenue in 1904.

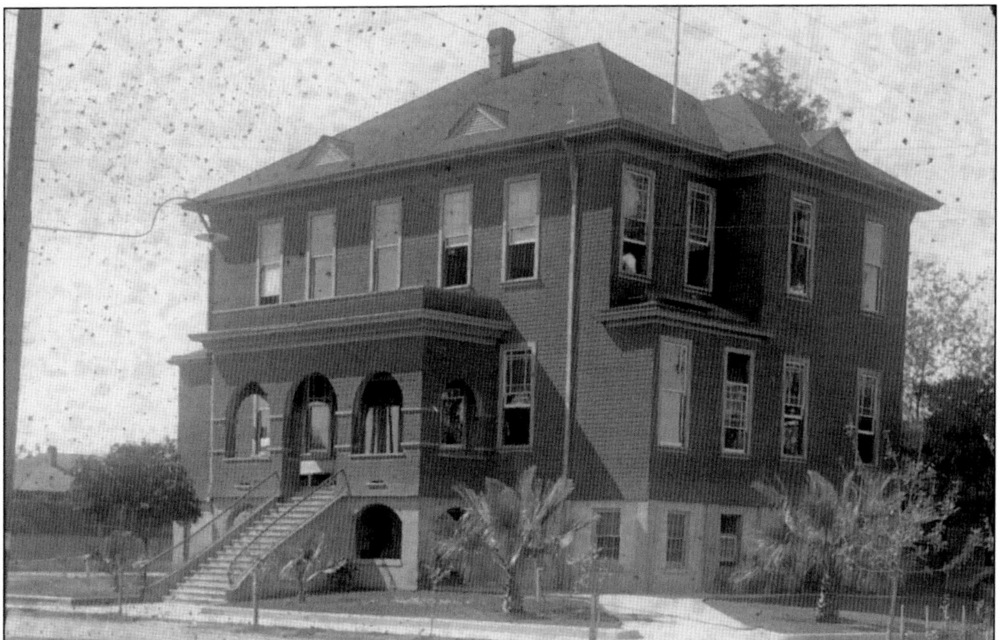

Soon the new high school was too small, so a second level was added. The school continued to operate until June of 1918 when an even larger edifice was erected on Bridge Street where the present facility is located.

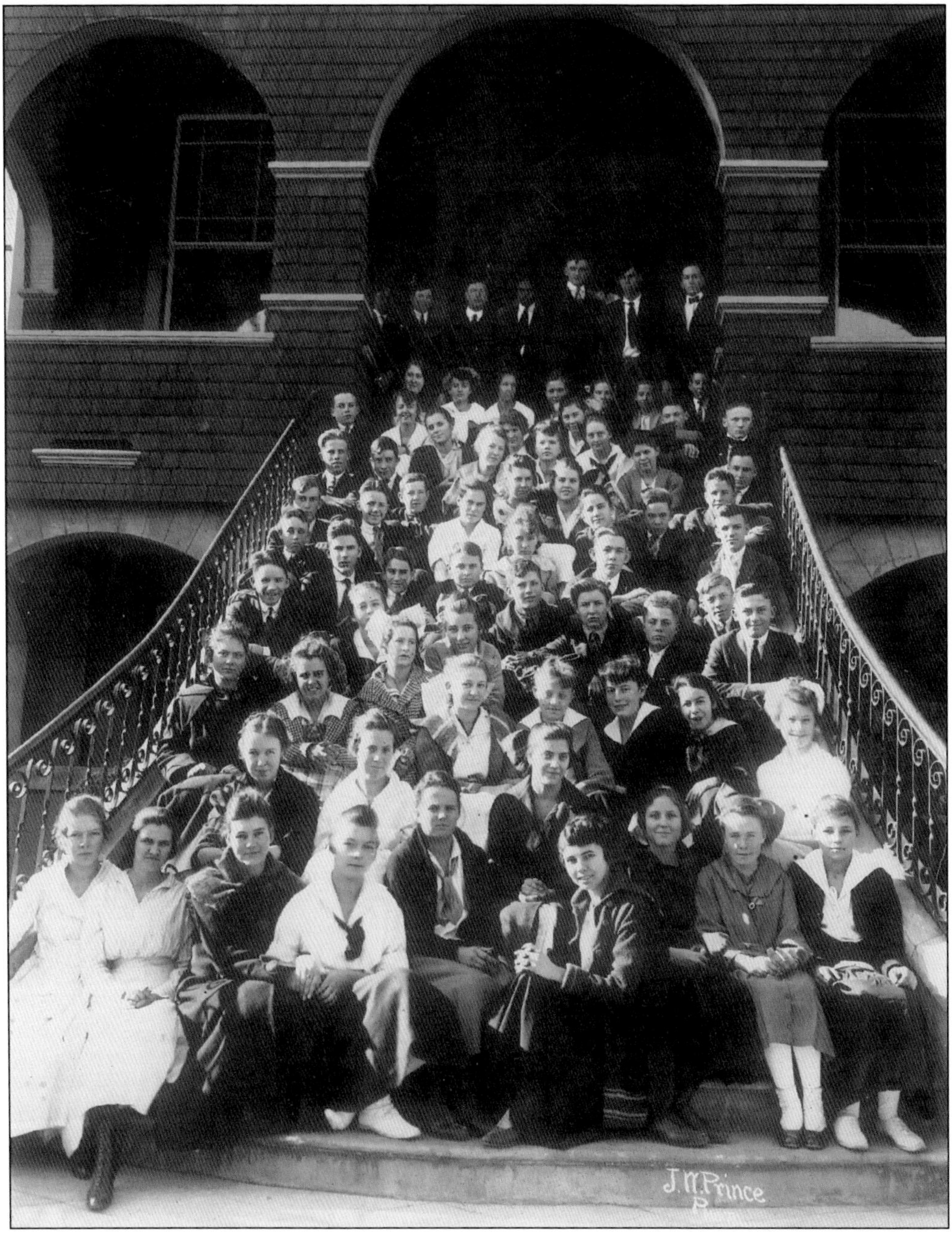

Members of the Freshman Class pose on the front steps of their high school on Robinson Street in 1917. Faculty is shown at top in background. The tallest one is James C. Nisbet, who started teaching at the school in 1916, became principal at the new high school in 1930, and was eventually appointed the first superintendent of the unified district.

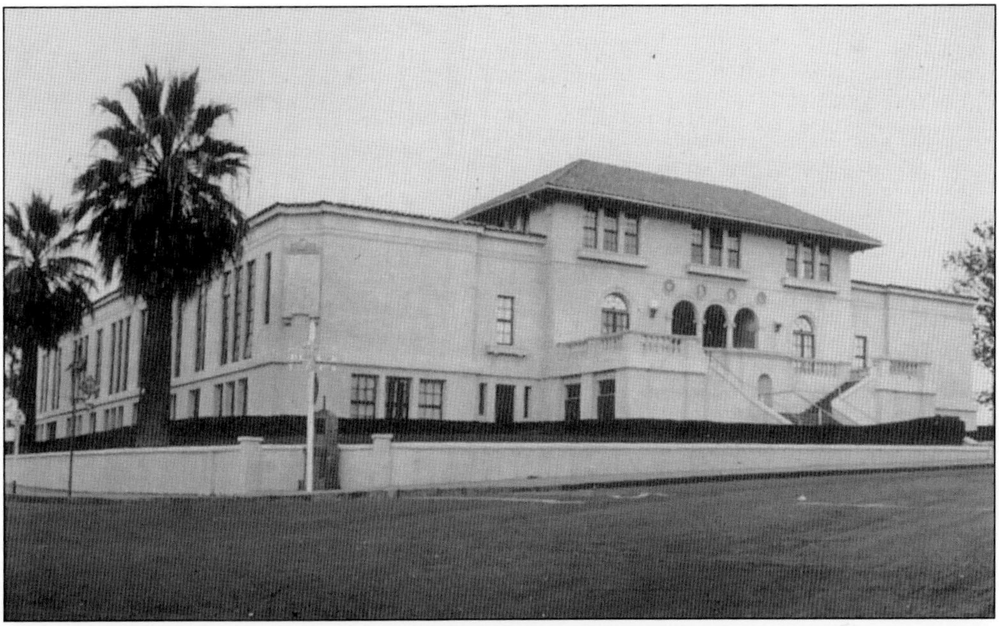

With the support of long-term trustee Major A.F. Jones, who also served in the state legislature, a brand new high school was completed in 1918. It was later replaced on the same site by a more modern but less impressive campus.

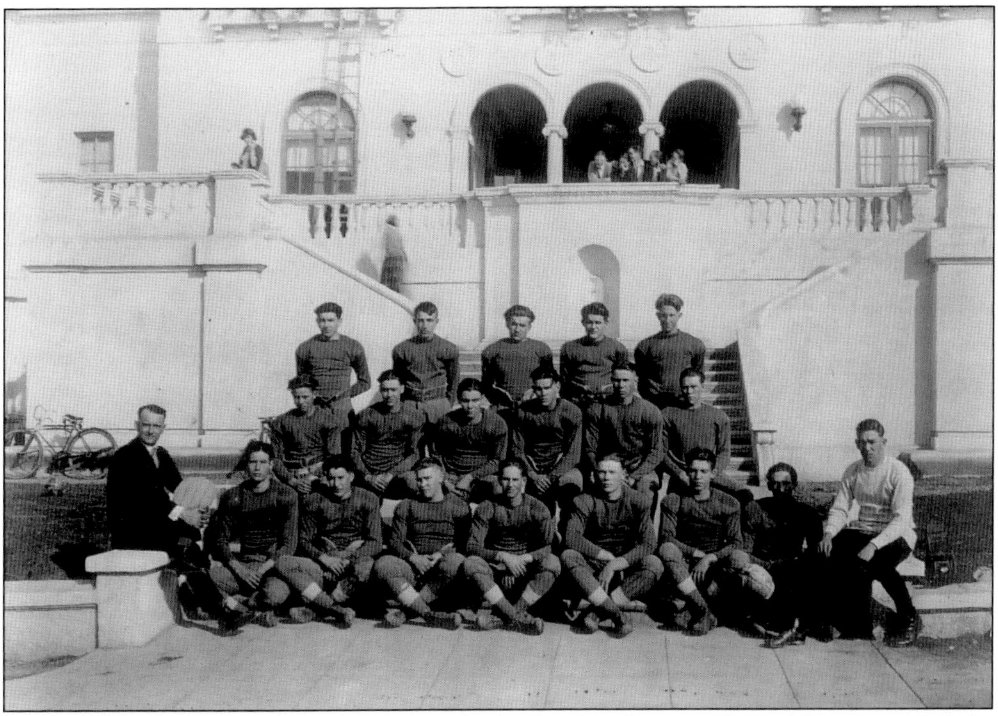

The football team poses in front of the new high school with its coach, Bud Onyett, at far left.

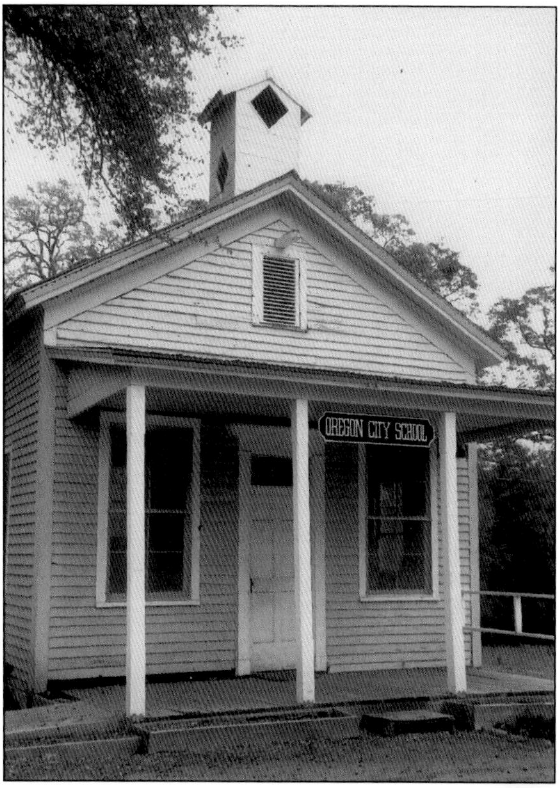

Numerous elementary schools in the area sent their graduates to the high school in Oroville. One was the quaint Oregon City school which is now maintained by the Butte County Historical Society for public functions.

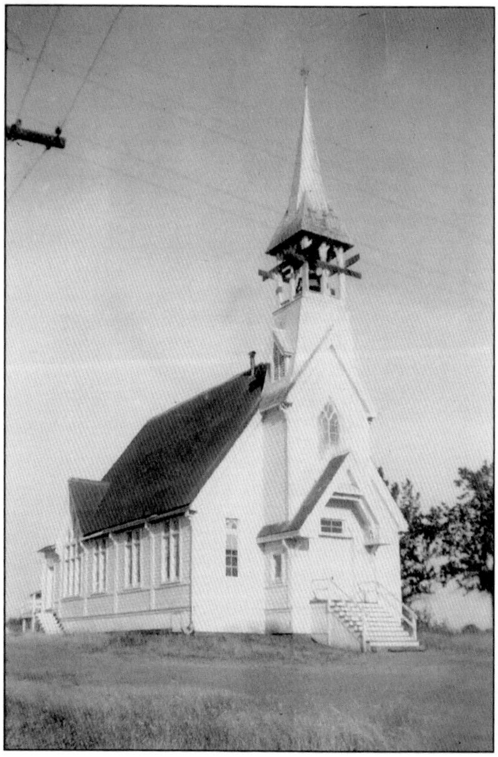

Palermo not only maintained a two-story grammar school for many years but was also proud of its community church, which students attended on Sundays for religious lessons. (The church burned in 1976.)

Six

Roads and Rails

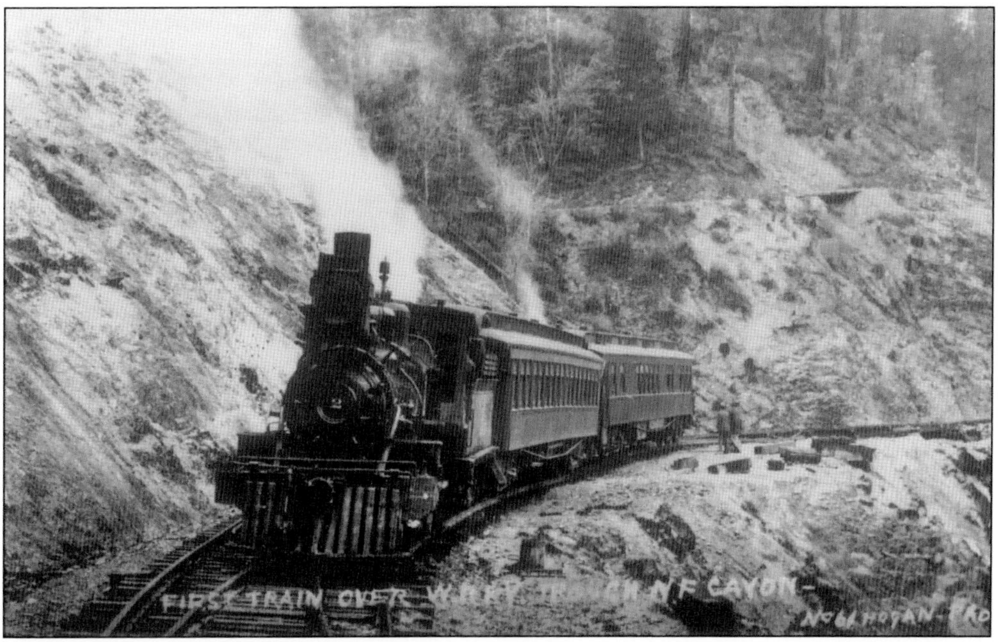

When J.H. Hogan took this picture for a postcard around 1908, he labeled it, "First train over the W.P.R.R. through the Feather River Canyon."

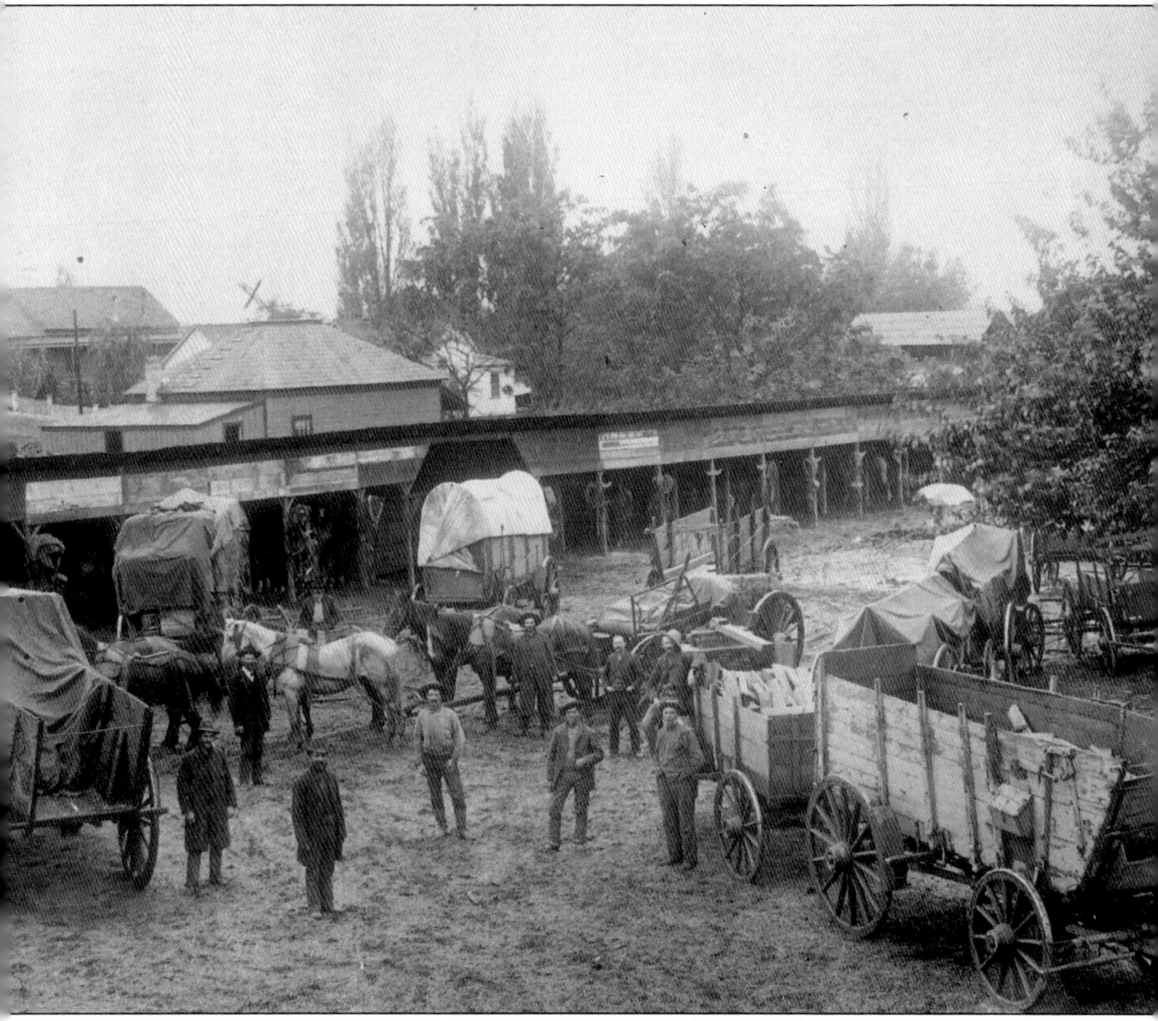

One of the largest corrals in Oroville was located near the site of the present day State Theatre. This picture was taken in 1889. Other stables were the Ohio, Fashion, and Atkins.

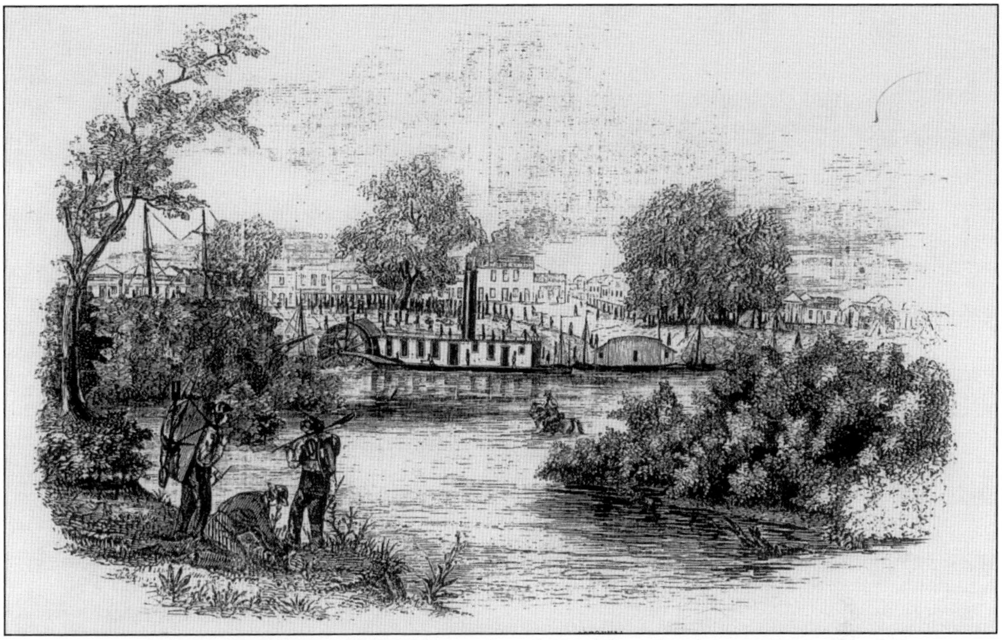

Several years before the advent of the first railroads, paddle wheel steamboats plied the waters up and down the Sacramento and Feather Rivers. The first to reach Oroville was the *Gazelle* in 1857, followed by the *Sam Soule* and the *Oroville*. (*Gleason's Pictorial*, 1852, at Marysville dock.)

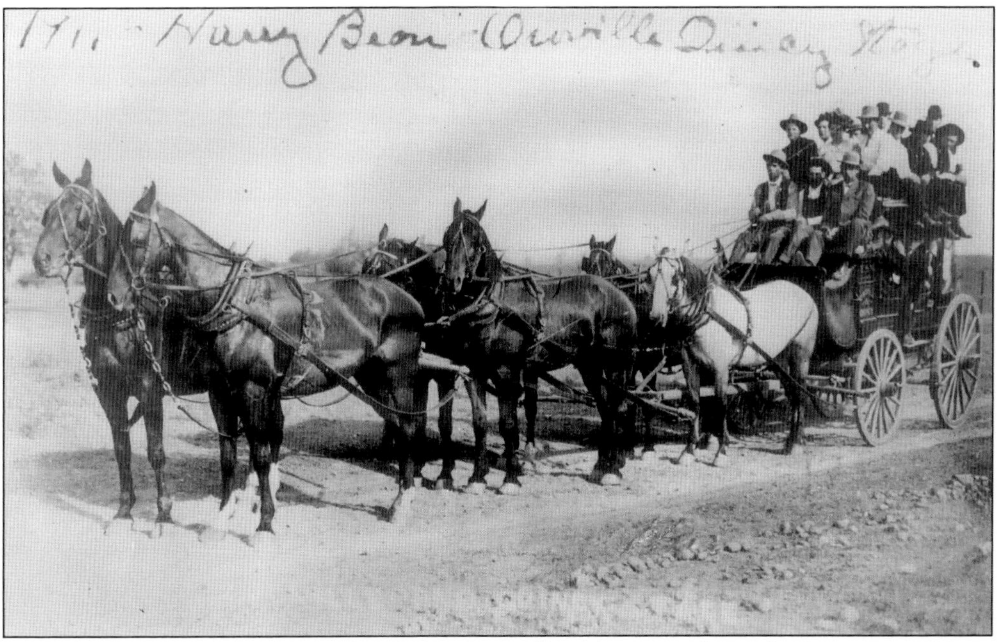

Pictured here is the last stagecoach ride from Oroville to Quincy in 1911. At the reins was Harry Bean, who enjoyed recounting the adventure during the remaining years of his life.

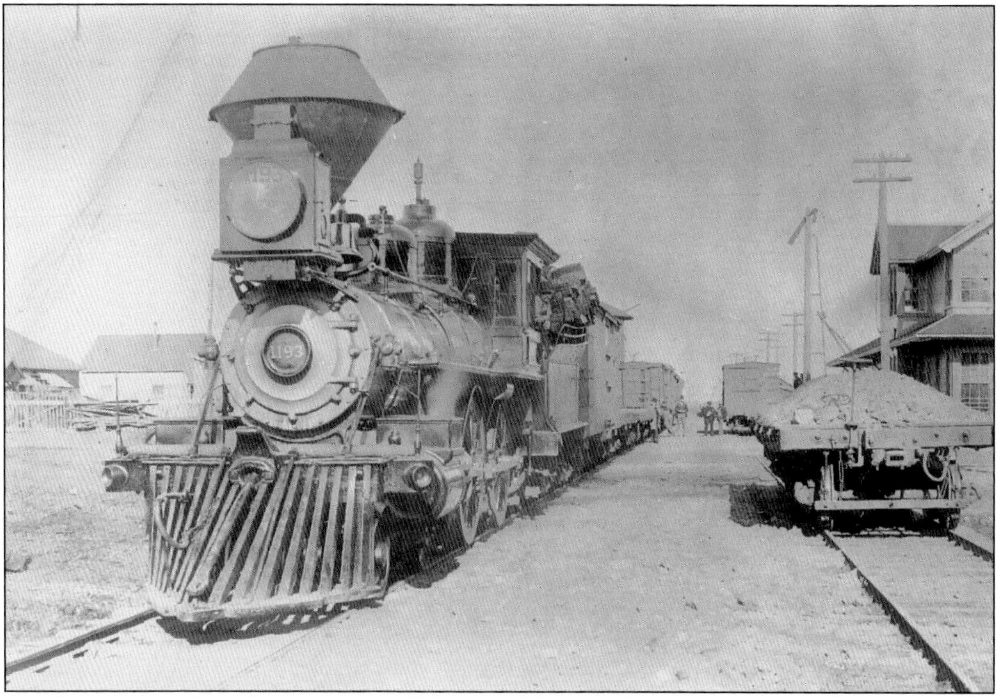

A California Northern freight train is shown stopping at Palermo on its way from Marysville to Oroville. The line was completed by A.J. Binney in 1864, the fourth railroad to be constructed in California.

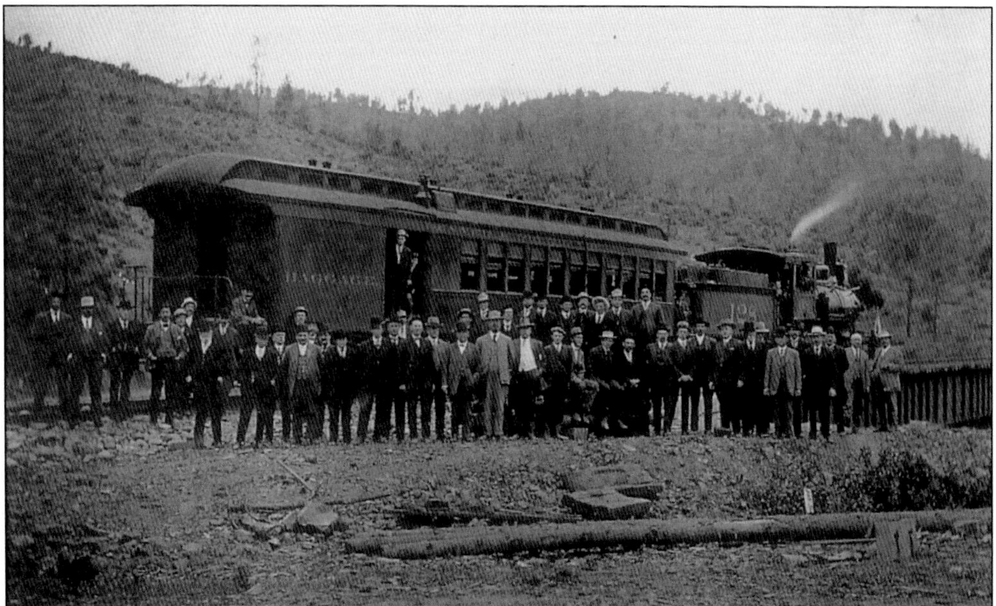

The last spike of the Western Pacific Railroad was driven at the Spanish Creek Bridge on November 11, 1909. Shown here is an excursion train that went some distance from Oroville up the line in 1908. Passengers dismounted for this portrait at Bidwell landing.

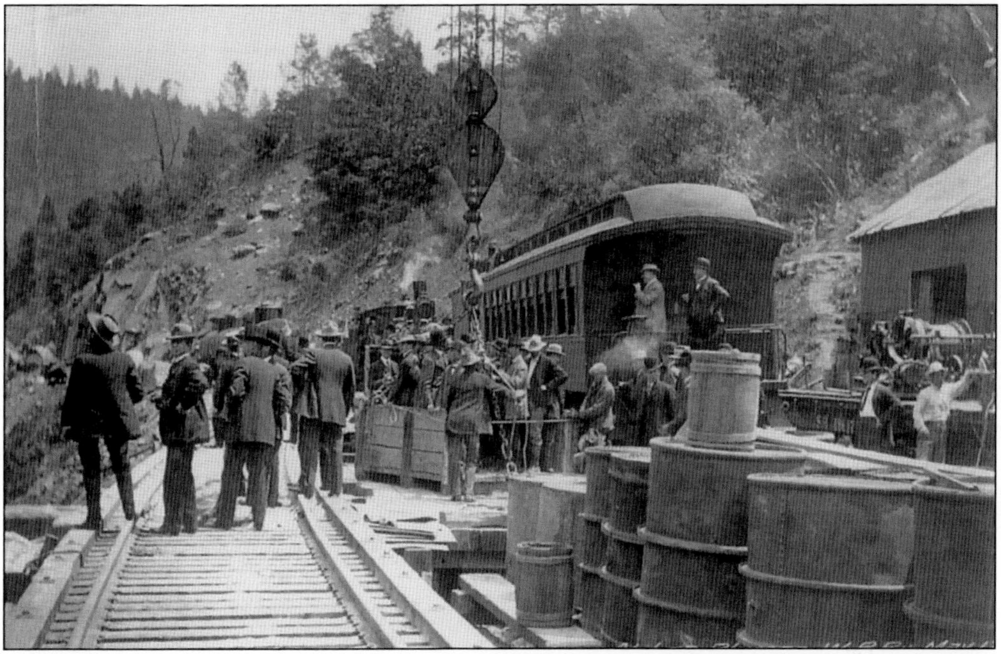

Passengers debarked the train again to inspect work being done at Las Plumas in the Feather River Canyon.

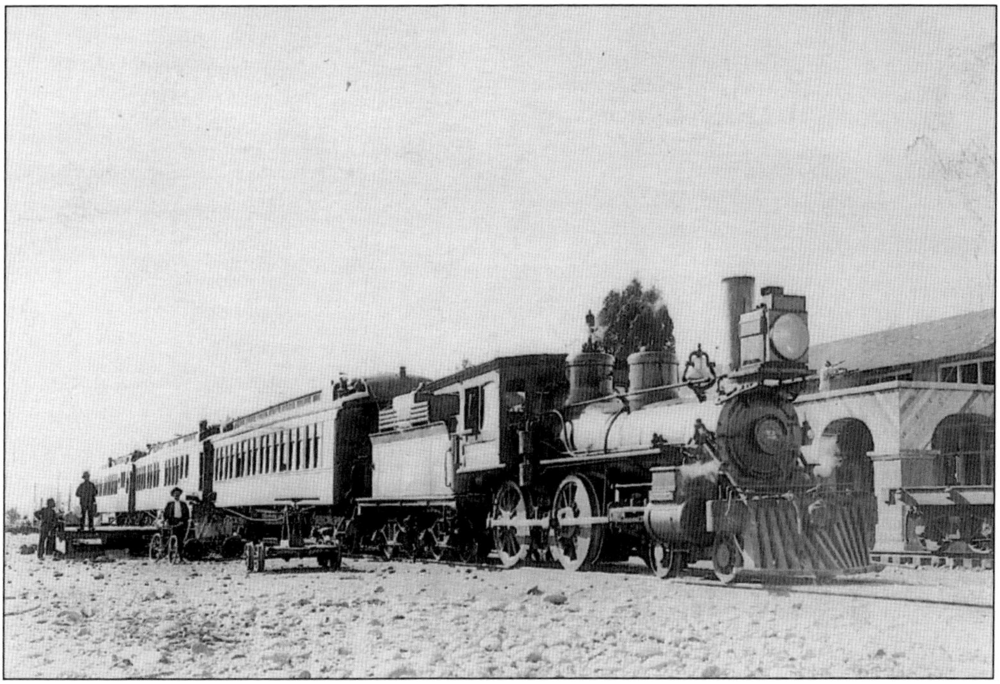

The first train from Oroville to Salt Lake City, terminus of the W.P.R.R., is shown preparing to depart after taking on passengers at the new depot. The first train arrived from Salt Lake City on August 22, 1910.

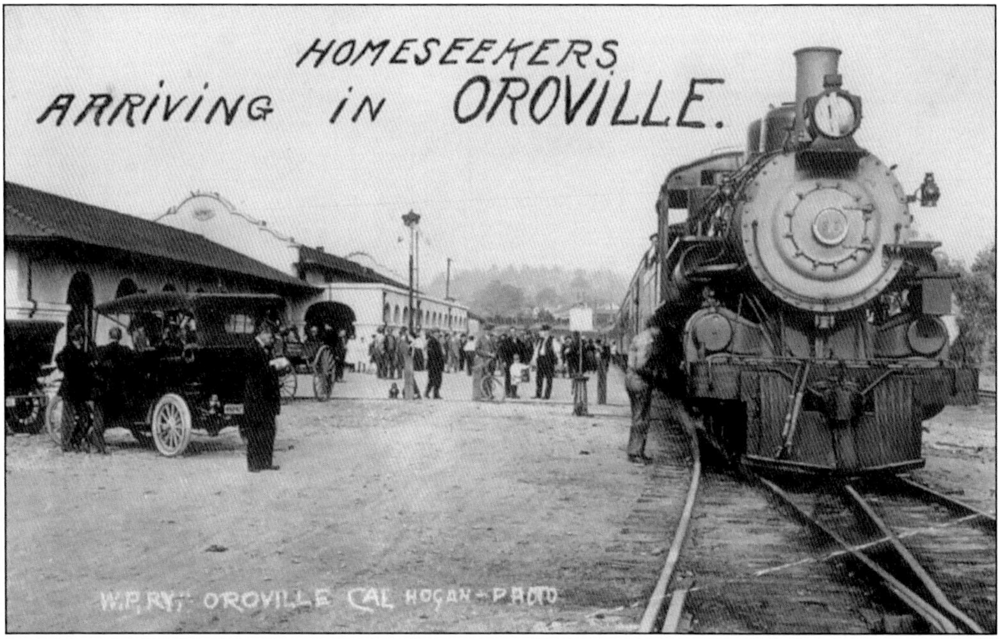

A postcard circulated to lure "homeseekers" to Oroville around 1915 shows the train at Oroville depot before heading south.

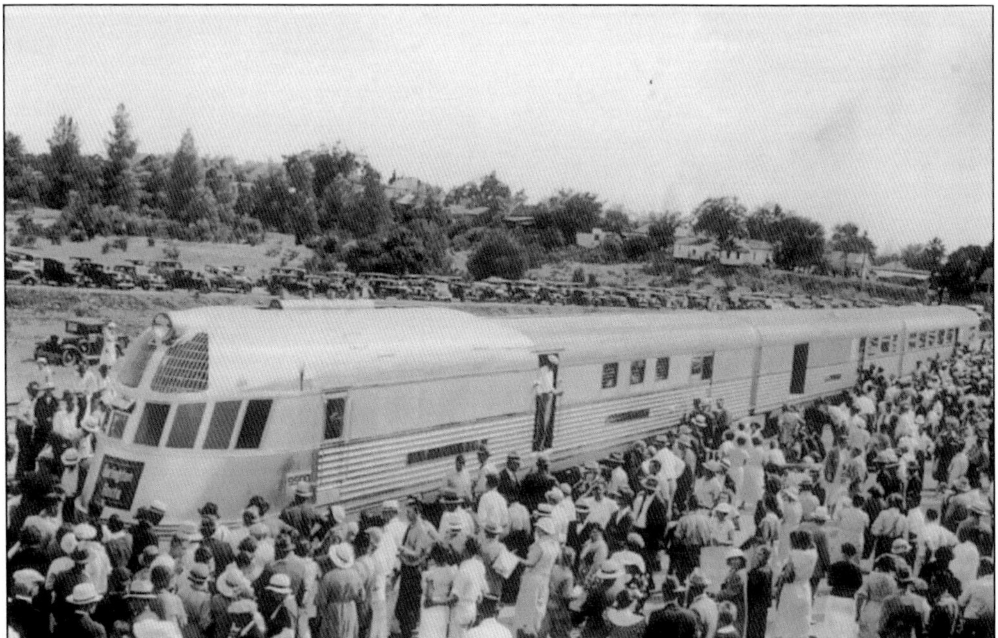
On June 25, 1934, one of the first modern trains in the nation stopped at Oroville on its way east. It would be several years before the sleek California Zephyr made regular runs through the canyon.

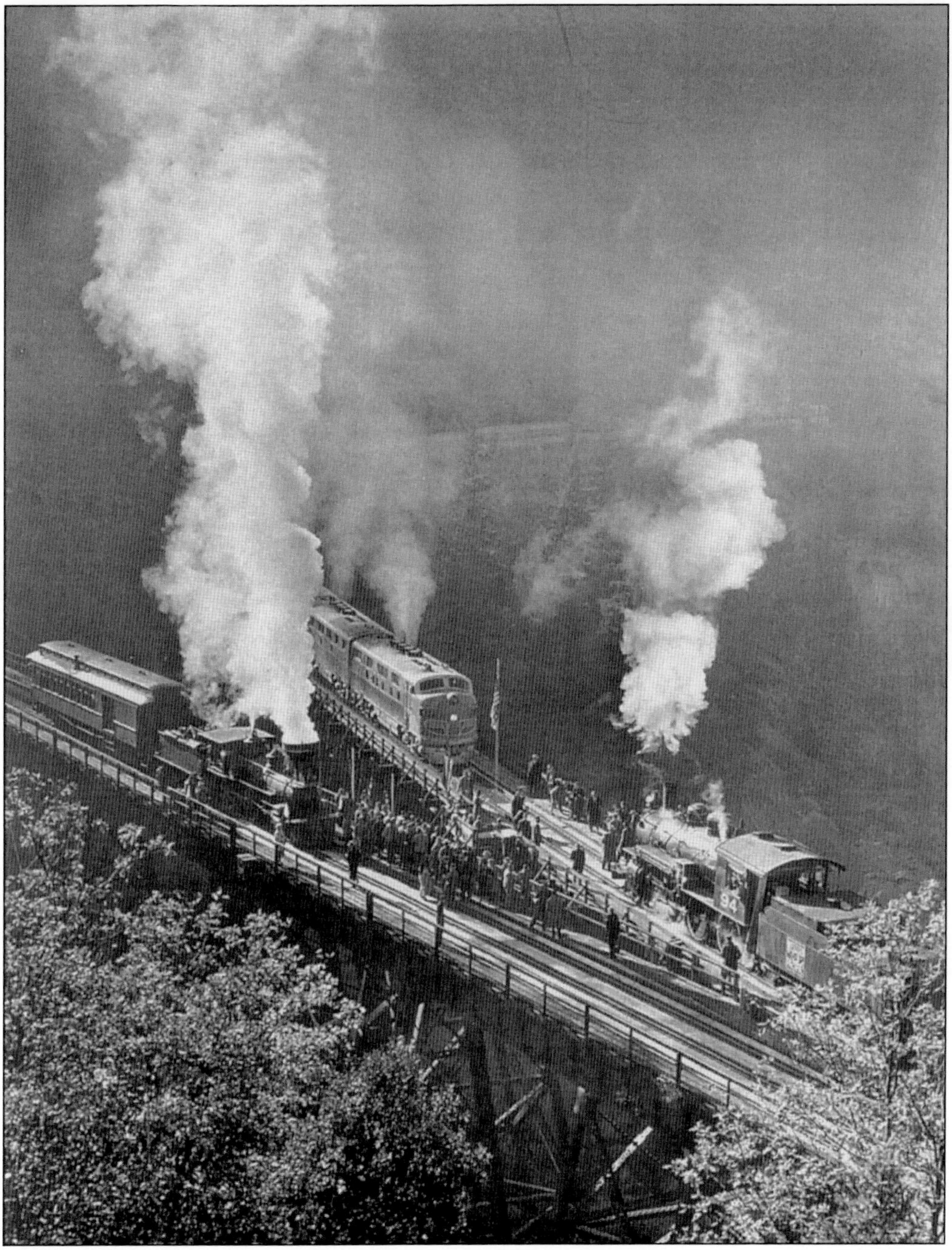

Celebrating the 50th anniversary of the beginning of the W.P.R.R., in 1949 officials had trains from three different eras meet on the Spanish Creek Bridge where the last spike was driven. Other festivities were held in Oakland, Oroville, and other stops along the line. Today, the railroad is part of the vast Union Pacific network, headquartered in Omaha, Nebraska.

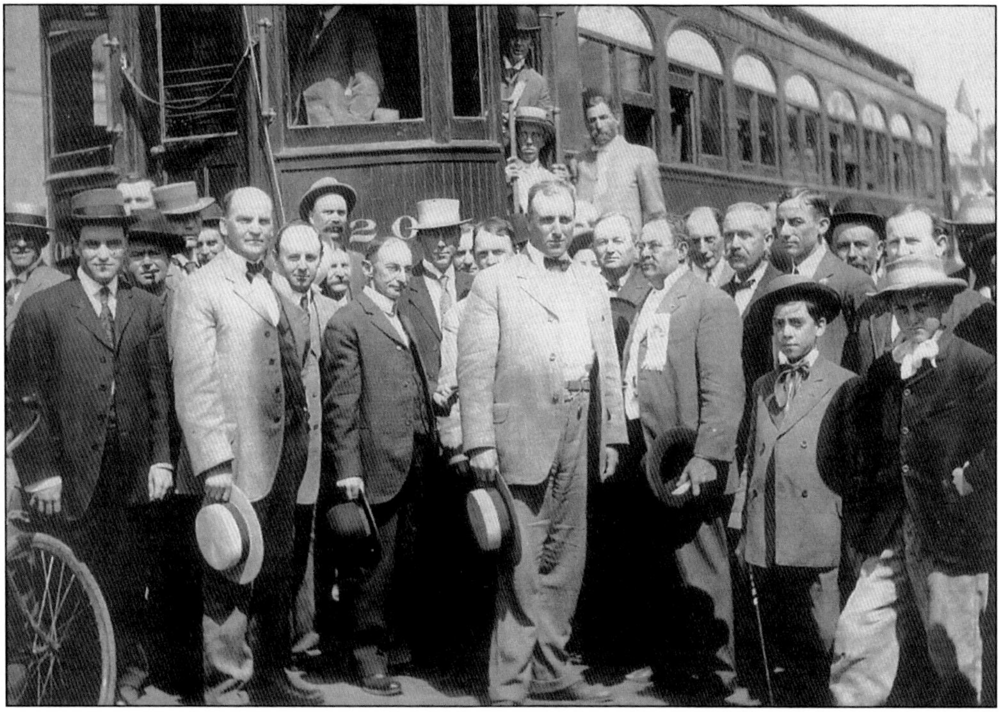

Prominent townspeople in Oroville welcome the arrival of the first Northern Electric train from Chico to Oroville in 1906. Operated by electricity, it was considered a railway far ahead of its time. It eventually was extended to Sacramento and Berkeley with branches to Woodland and Colusa. After a flood destroyed the bridge across the Feather River in 1935, it ceased service to Oroville and eventually was abandoned altogether.

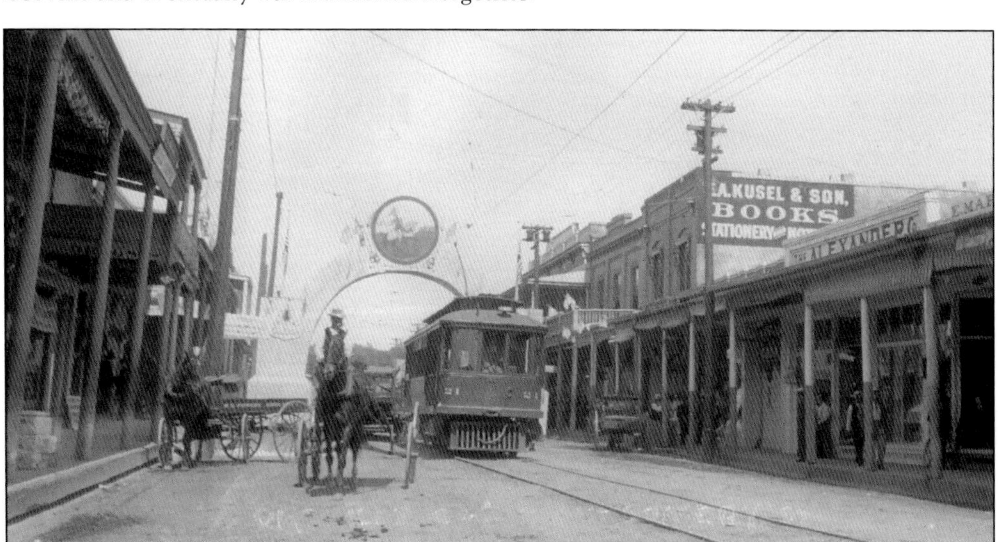

This view is of the Northern Electric going down the center of Montgomery Street just after making its turn on Myers Street. The Kusel Building at right was built by pioneer photographer E.A. Kusel, whose son, Eli became a prominent local surgeon. The arch was erected in 1913 for a second Native Sons convention.

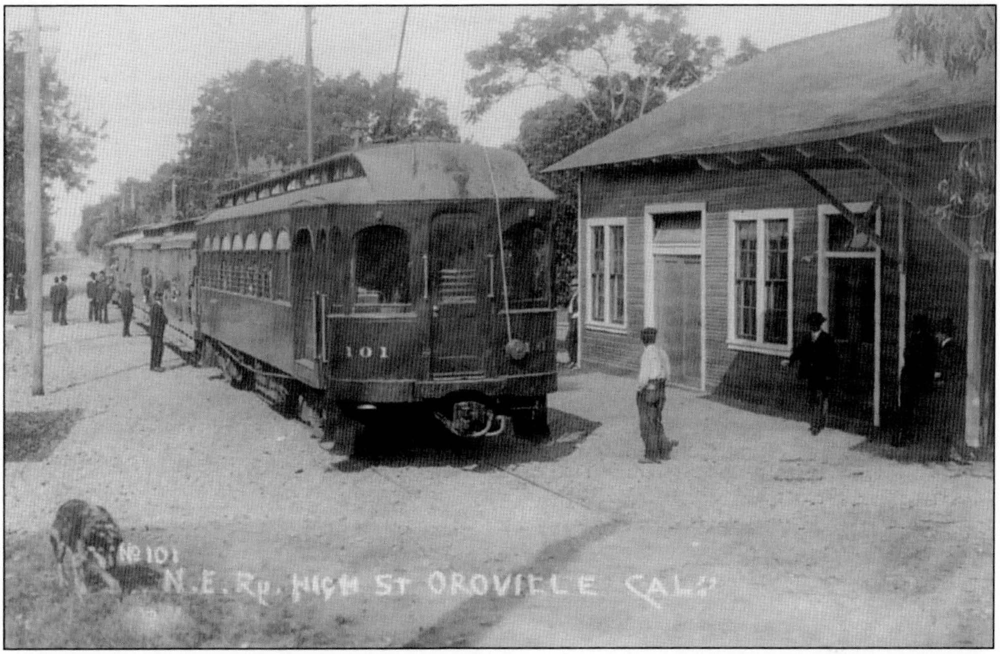

Northern Electric train is shown arriving at the Oroville depot located on the southwest corner of Myers and Robinson Streets.

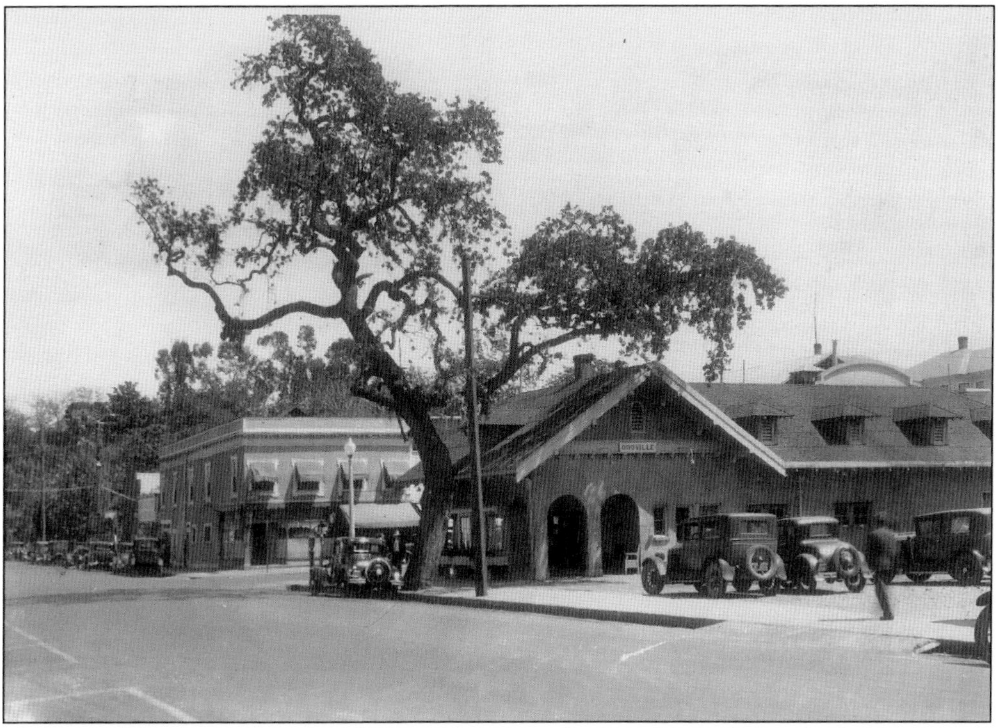

The original depot was considerably expanded as seen by this photo taken in the 1920s. Ancient oak still grew by the corner. Shown in the background is the building where Marcozzi Jewelers is located today.

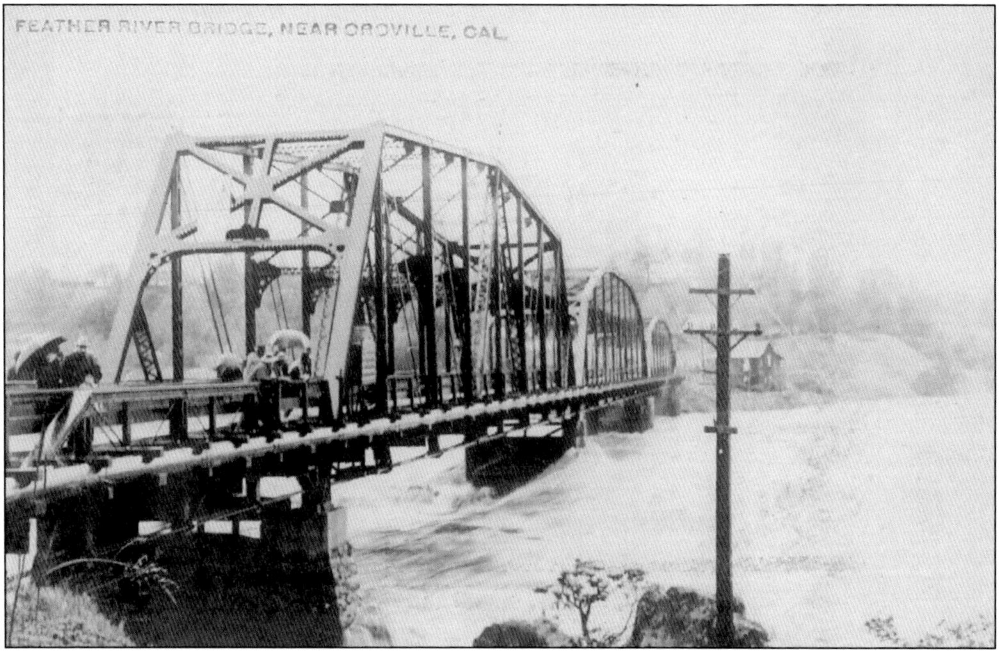

The flood of 1907 was one of the most devastating in the history of Oroville, washing out roads and flooding downtown streets. Shown above is the Upper Thermalito Bridge just prior to being washed away.

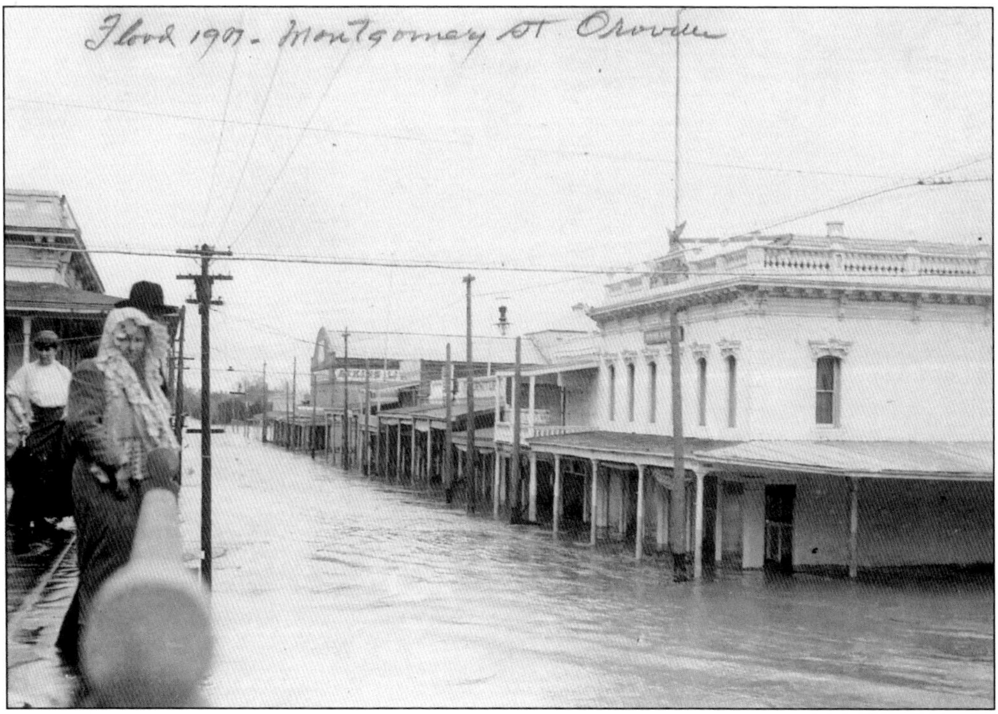

Looking down from the balcony of the Union Hotel, guests observed the water rushing down Montgomery Street past the Perkins Store and Atkins Theatre.

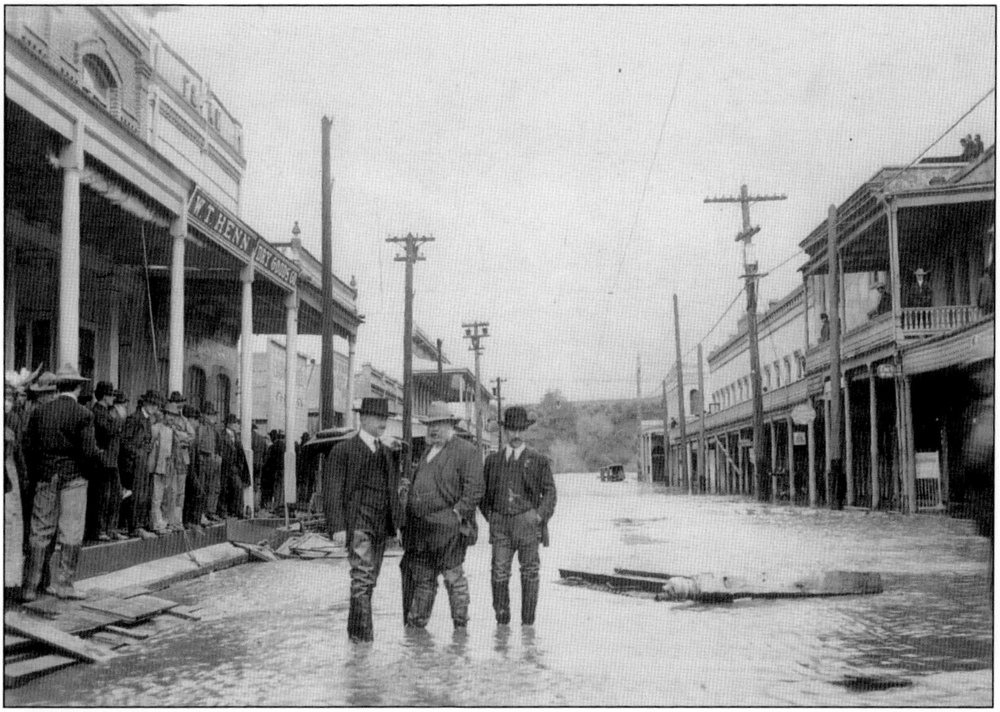

Standing at the corner of Myers and Bird streets, bank cashier L.L. Green and Major A.F. Jones survey damage caused by the flood waters.

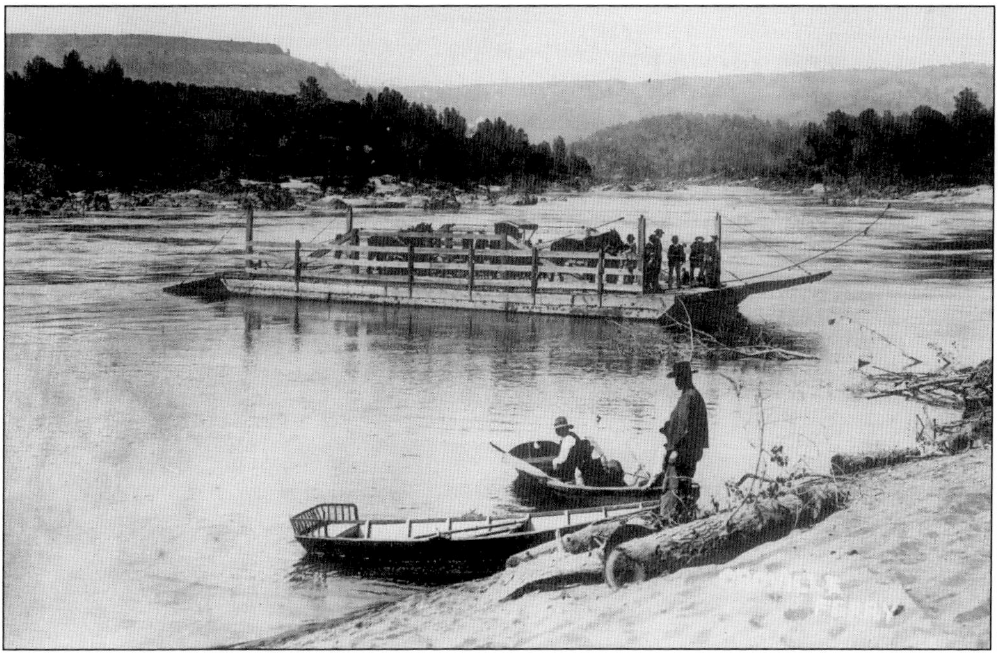

Until a new bridge could be built across the river, people had to use a ferry reminiscent of the early days in Oroville's history.

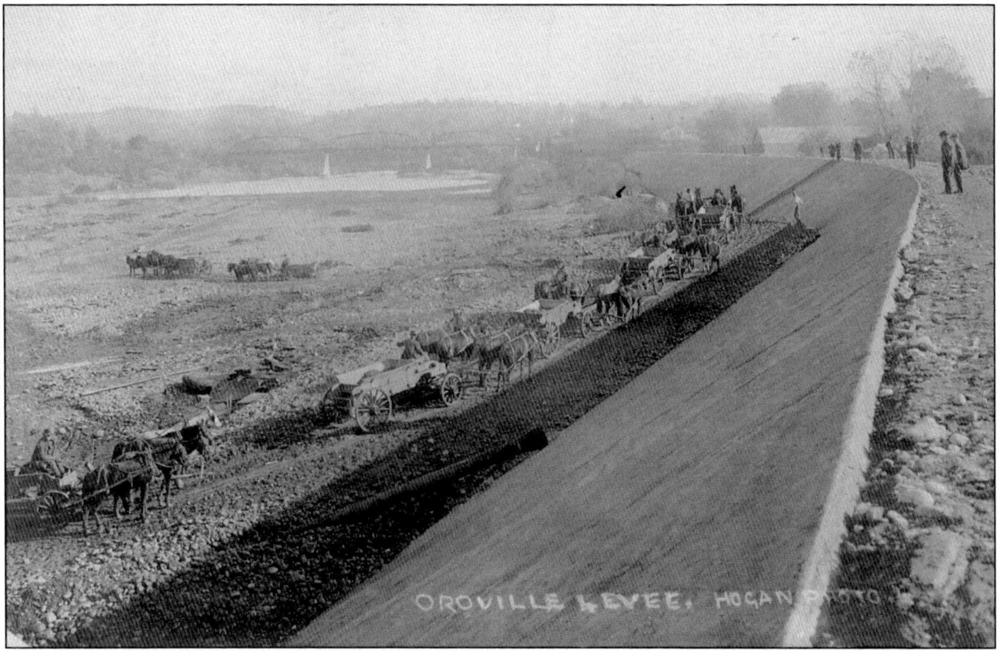

In an effort to avoid future floods, townspeople built a massive concrete-faced levee, which was raised even higher during the 1930s when a gold dredger narrowed and deepened the channel in order to permit water to surge past more rapidly.

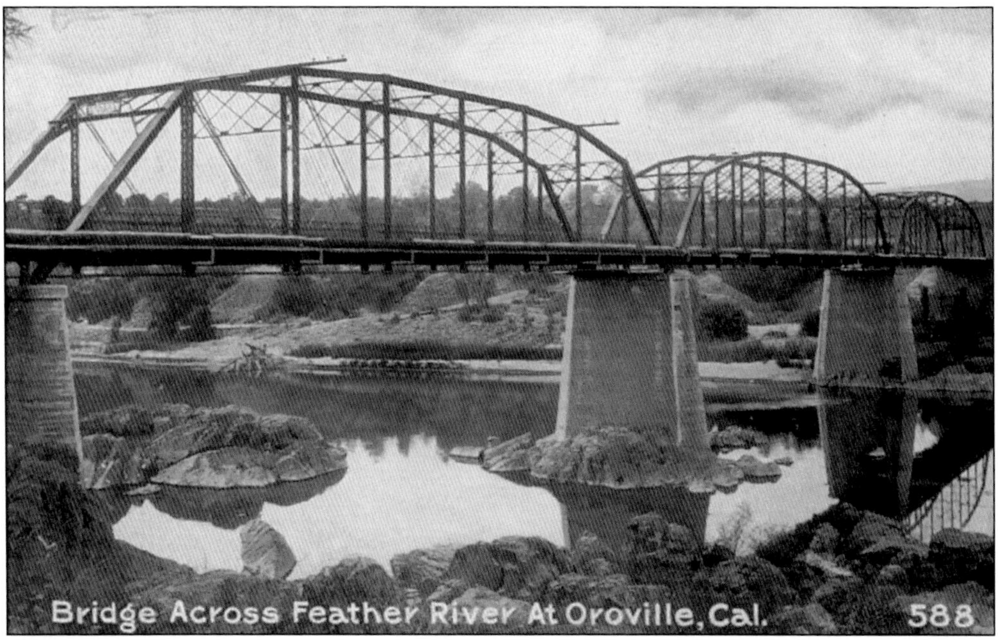

When the new bridge was dedicated in 1910, a grand electric water carnival was staged on the river and repeated annually for three years. Later, a second steel bridge was constructed across the river further downstream to connect the city with points west.

Seven

Agriculture and Lumber

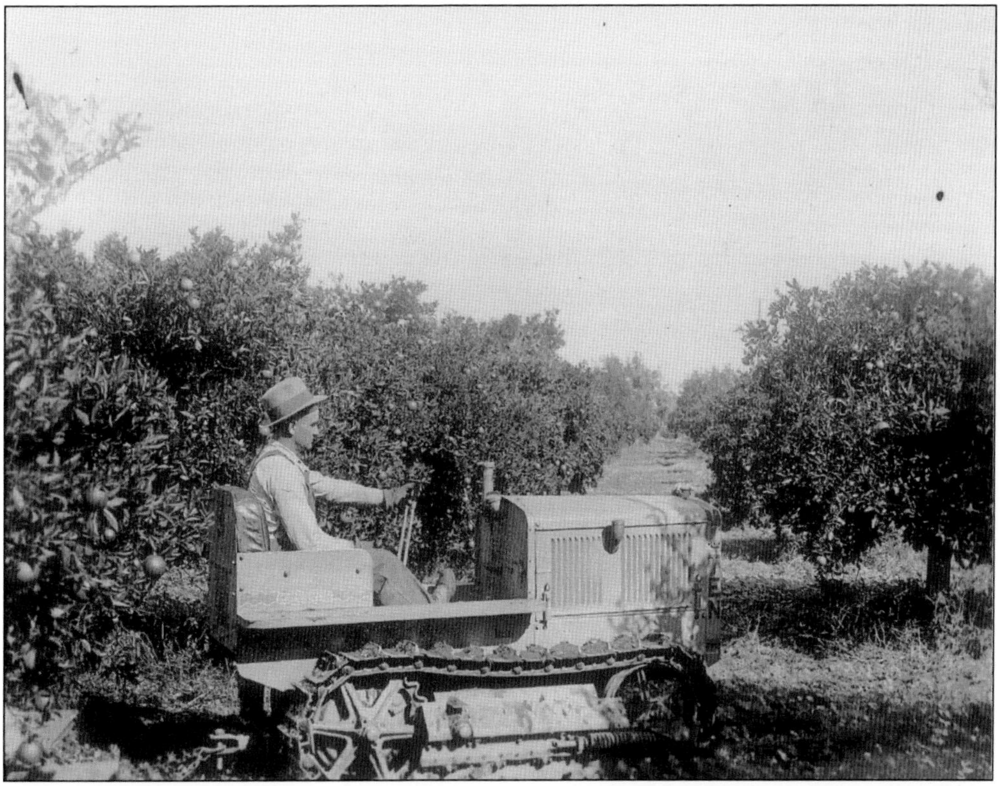

An Oroville farmer tries out a new tractor, plowing the ground around his prize young orange trees. Because of a mild thermal belt, local oranges ripen six weeks earlier than others in California.

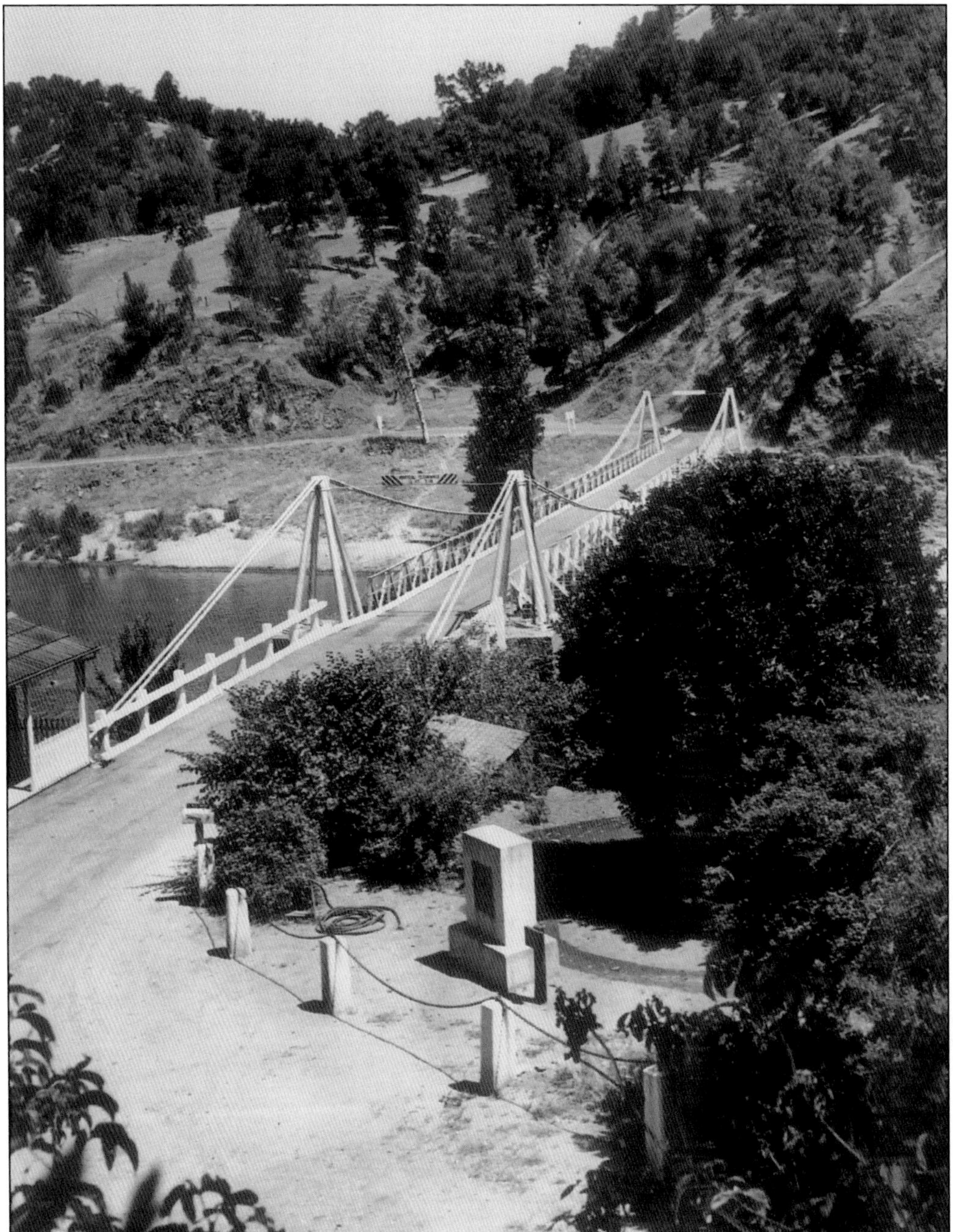

The citrus industry of Oroville was started with seeds from the first orange tree planted in northern California at the behest of 49er Joseph E.N. Lewis in 1856. Named the Mother Orange Tree, the seedling from Mazatlan was placed next to the Bidwell Bar Bridge, where it flourished for over 100 years before being moved with the suspension bridge and toll house to avoid being submerged beneath 600 feet of water behind the Oroville Dam.

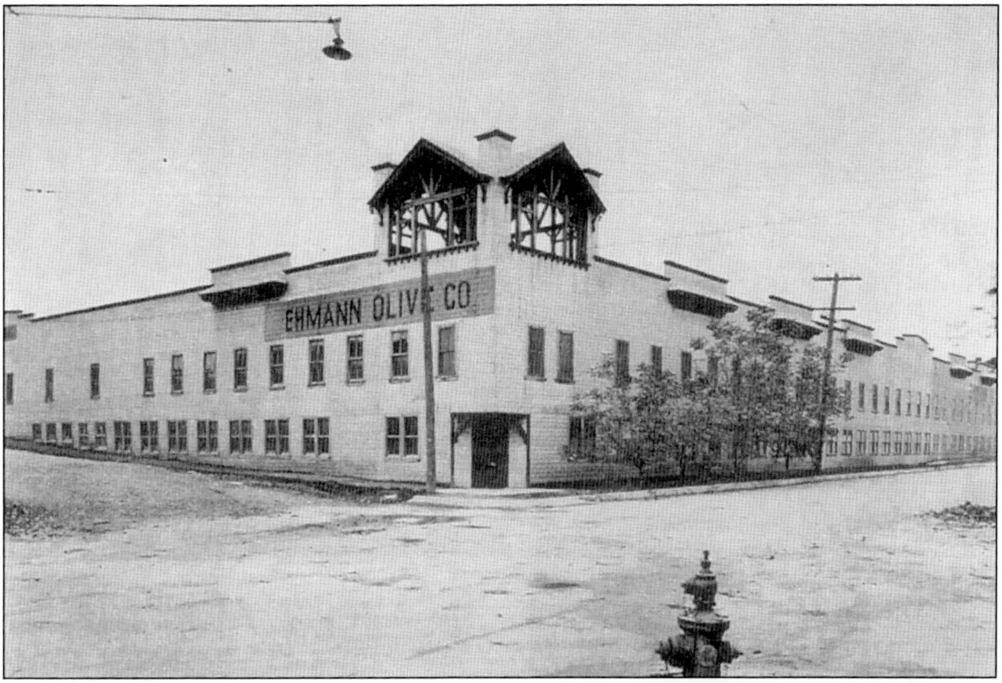

The olive industry made great strides after Freda Ehmann developed her black ripe olive, harvested from local orchards. Soon she moved her operations from a small shed in Thermalito to this huge processing plant located on the corner of Ehmann and Lincoln Streets.

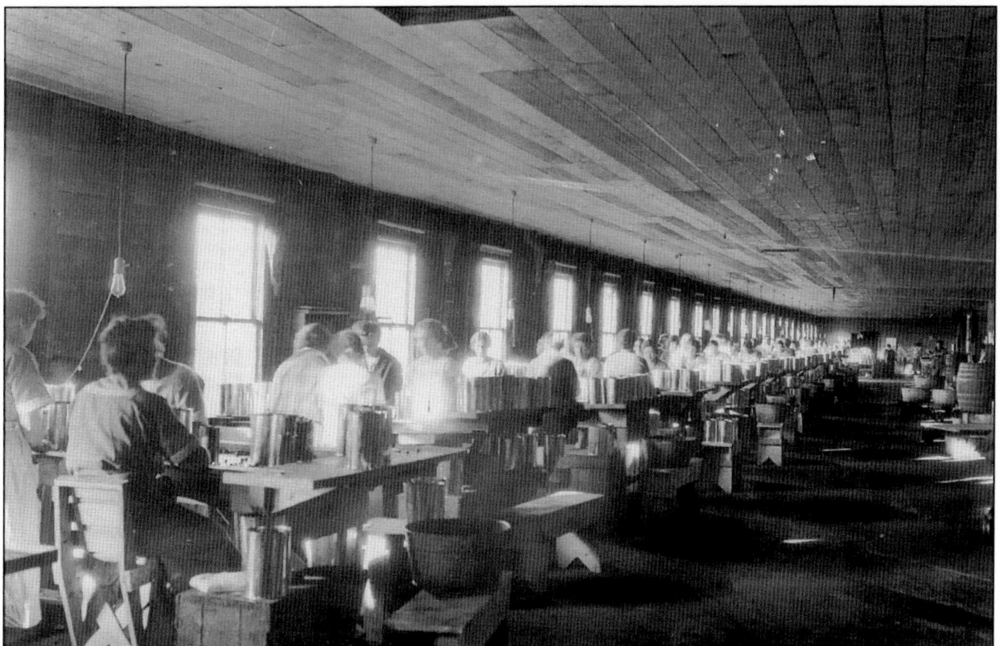

Mrs. Ehmann hired scores of ladies to pack her olives in cans that were then sealed, cooked, and distributed nationwide. Because of her efforts, she was later named the "patron saint" of the U.S. canning industry and even had a poem written about her by Elbert Hubbard.

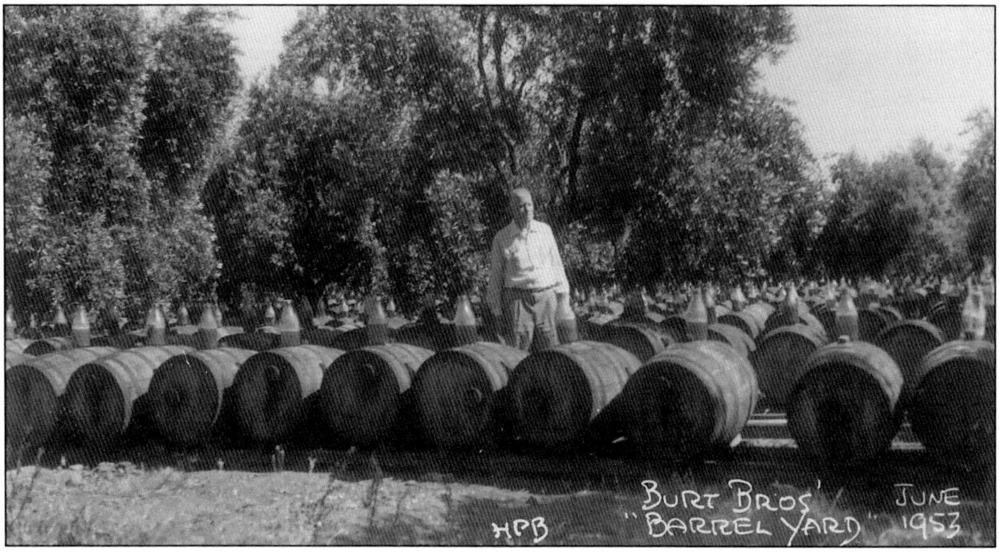

The success of Mrs. Ehmann inspired others to enter the olive business, including Pierson and Grinnell Burt who developed extensive holdings in Palermo and distributed under their own label.

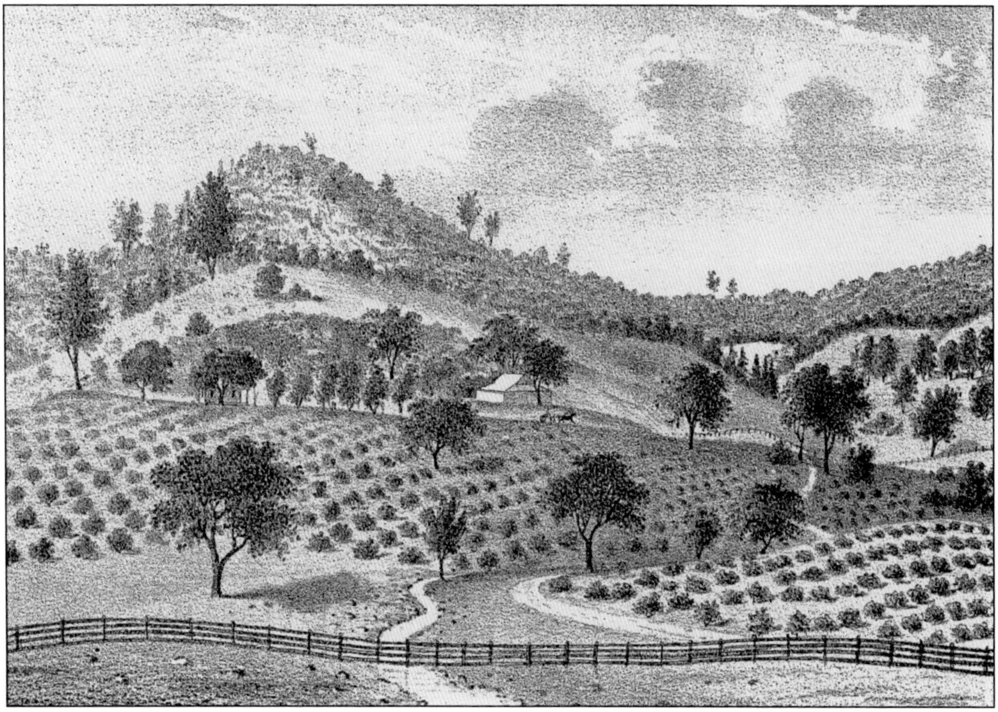
Rev. Jesse Wood was one of many who developed ranches in the foothills of Oroville, planting rows of orange and olive trees, plus other commercial fruit. (Wells & Chambers *History of Butte County*, 1882.)

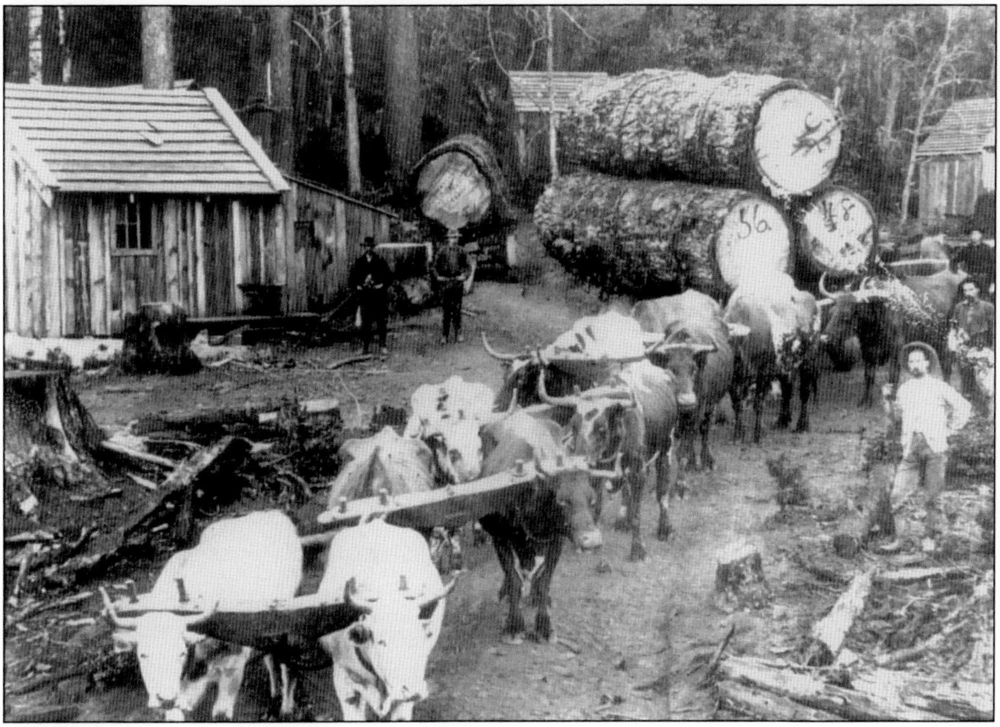

It took strong oxen to haul the giant trunks of virgin timber to local mills for processing into lumber. This view is at Lumpkin east of Oroville around 1880.

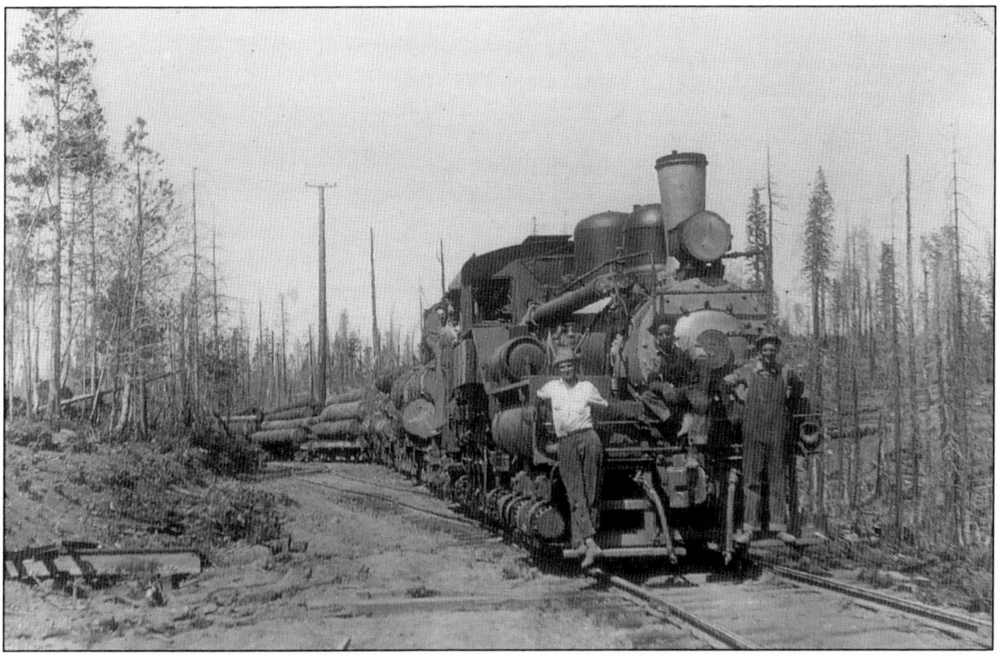

The advent of small steam engines allowed lumber companies to expand their operations on a grand scale. Besides two huge mills in Oroville, another was built by A.H. Land with its own town of Feather Falls.

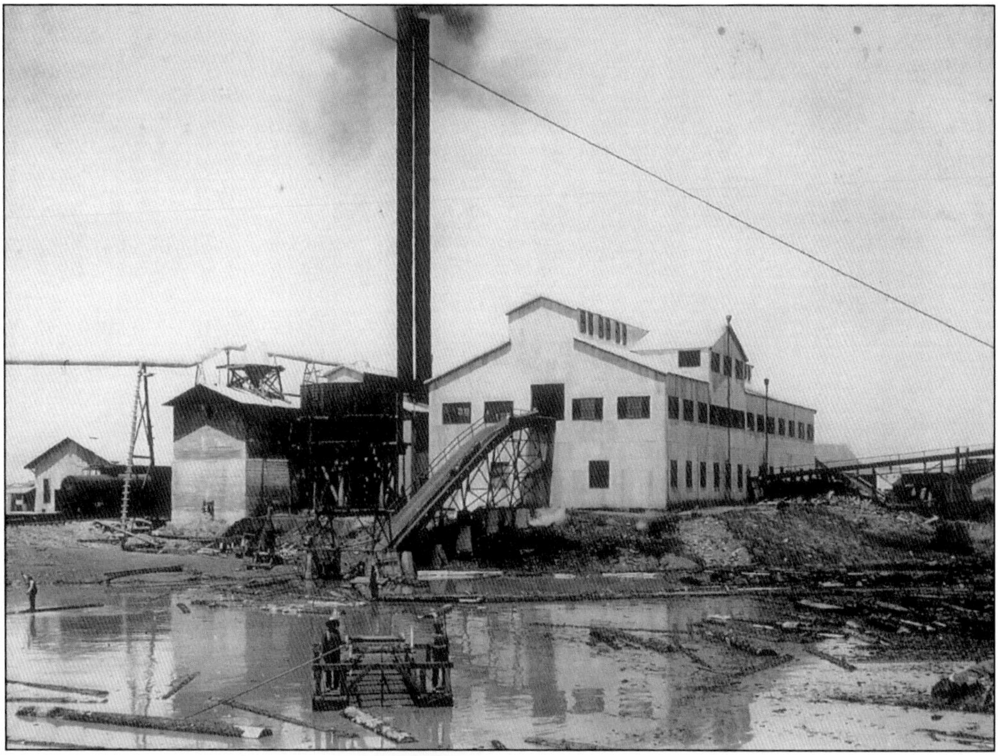

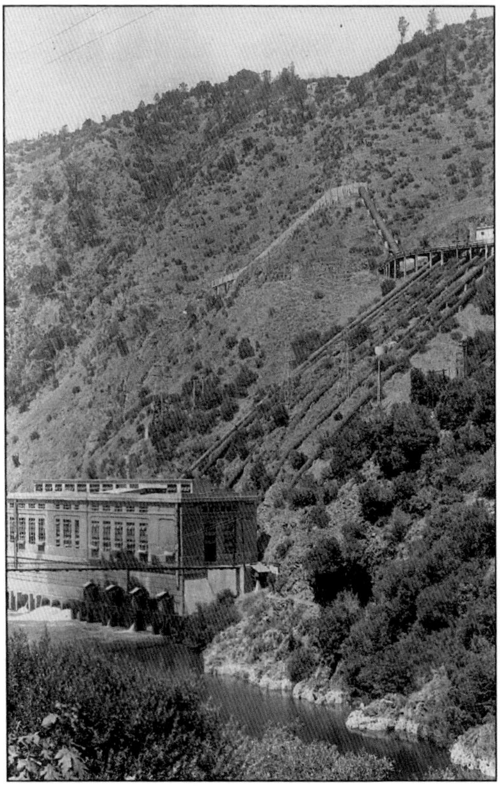

In 1916, the great Truckee Lumber Company was located just south of town on land now occupied by the cannery and other businesses facing Oro Dam Boulevard. It was later taken over by the Swayne Lumber Company. Further south was the equally impressive Hutchinson Mill.

In addition to supplying irrigation water for farms and other industries throughout southern Butte County, the Feather River was later called upon to power giant electrical plants. This first plant was constructed by Great Western Power at Las Plumas, utilizing the tunnel excavated by Major McLaughlin to divert the river in the 1880s.

Eight

Luminaries and Modern Times

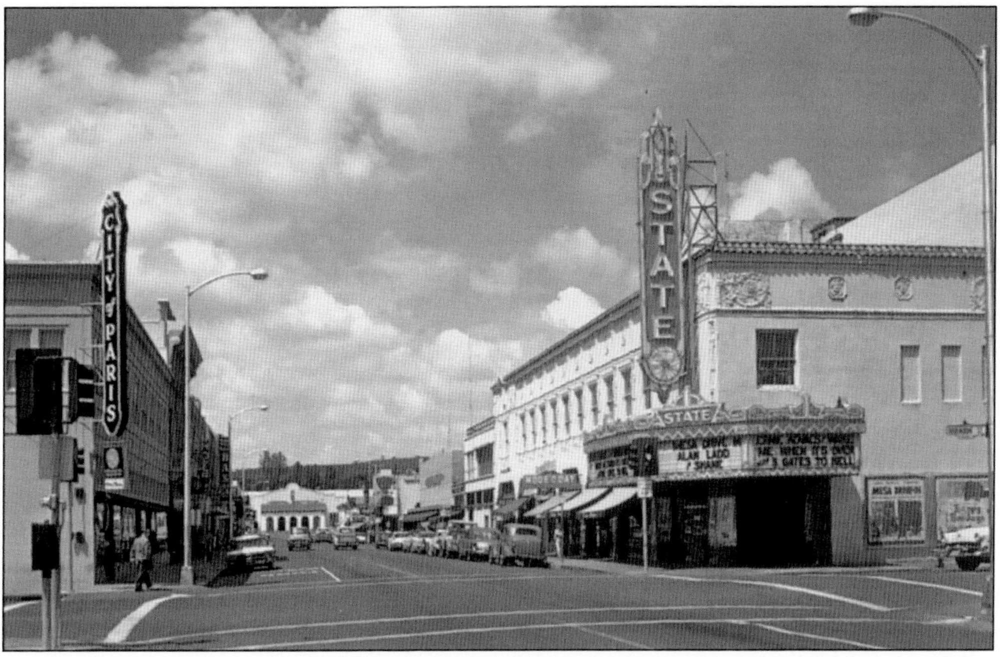

This is a view looking down Myers Street in 1953 after the Exposition Building had been remodeled and turned into a municipal auditorium. The marquee on the State Theatre advertised Alan Ladd was starring in *Shane* at the Mesa Drive-in.

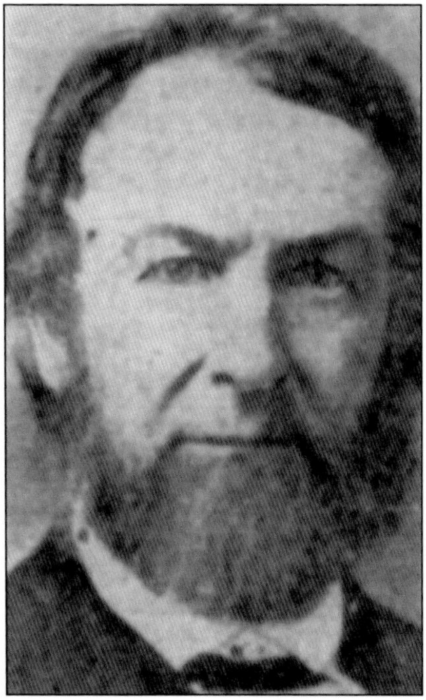

Among Oroville's most important luminaries was James M. Burt, who opened one of the first stores in the new city of Oroville, which he and Judge Lott named. His law office still stands on Bird Street.

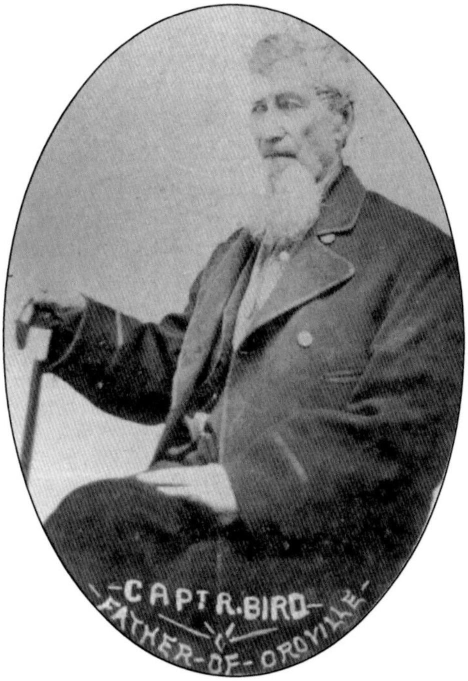

Forty-niner Captain Ralph Bird has been called the Father of Oroville because he laid out the new city of Oroville in 1855, naming the streets after himself and other contemporary associates.

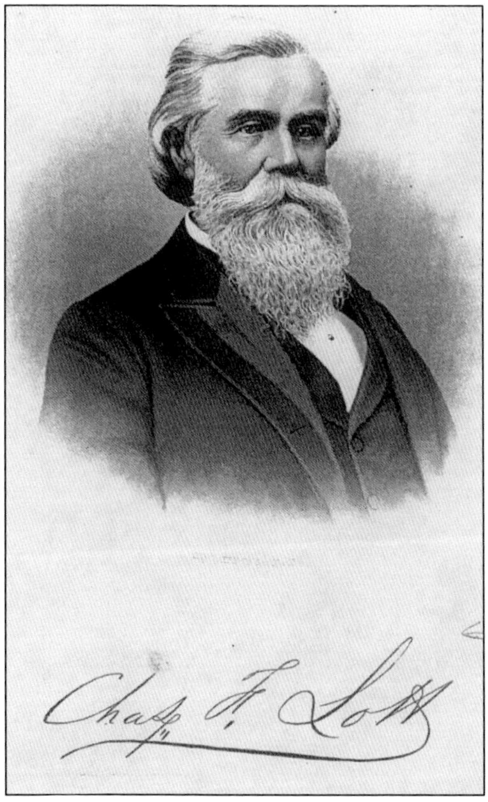

Charles F. Lott came to the Oroville area in 1849 and made his fortune in mining, law, and real estate. The building he erected on Bird Street in 1856 is still used for local mercantile pursuits.

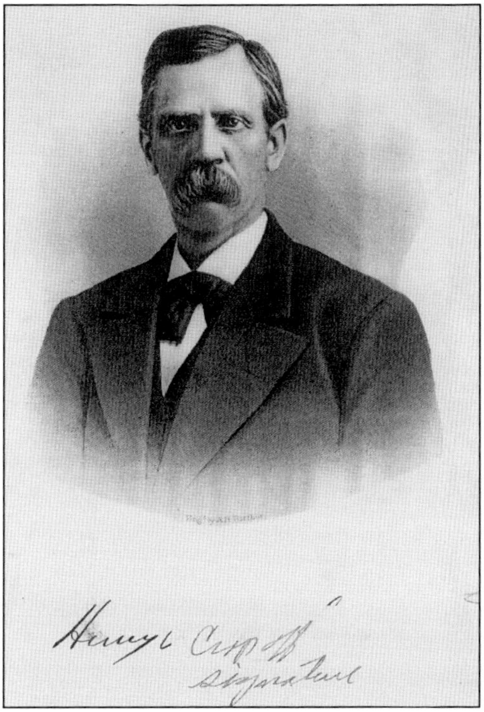

Pioneer artist Henry Mighels painted the drop curtains for Oroville's first theaters and later served as editor for newspapers in Oroville, Marysville, and Carson City, Nevada.

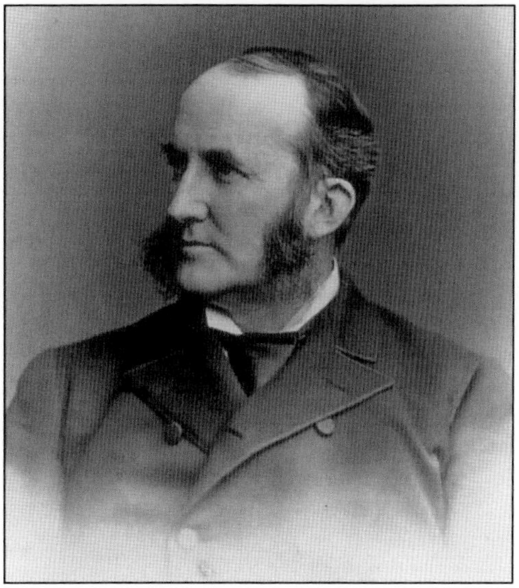

Charles Lincoln founded the first newspaper in Oroville in 1855, the *North Californian*, and was elected to the state assembly. He later returned to Vermont with his mentor, capitalist Trenor Park. Lincoln Street is named for him.

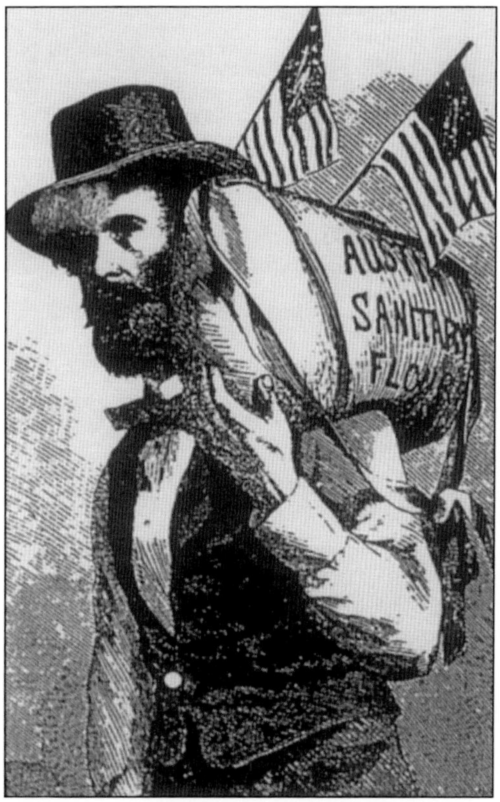

Reuel Colt Gridley owned a stage line in Oroville before moving to Nevada and achieving national fame, auctioning off his famous Sanitary Sack of Flour to aid wounded soldiers during the Civil War.

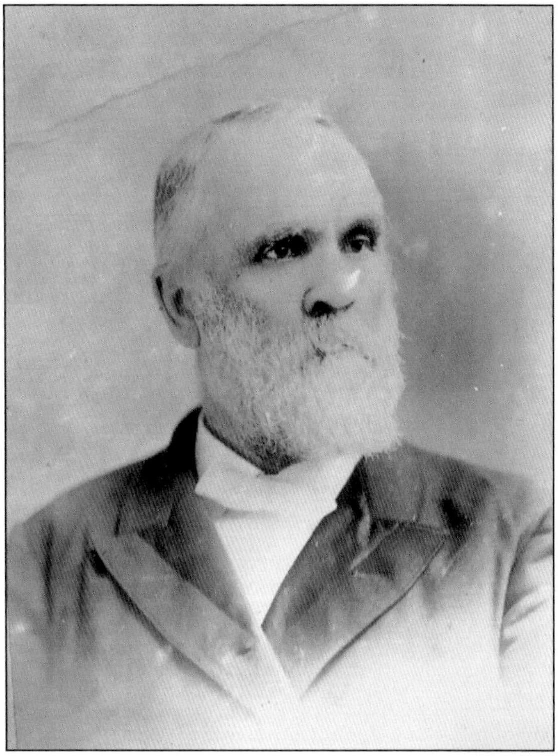

Rev. Bela N. Seymour preached beneath an old oak tree before rounding up enough support to build the first church in Oroville. Today, there are over 20 churches in the city.

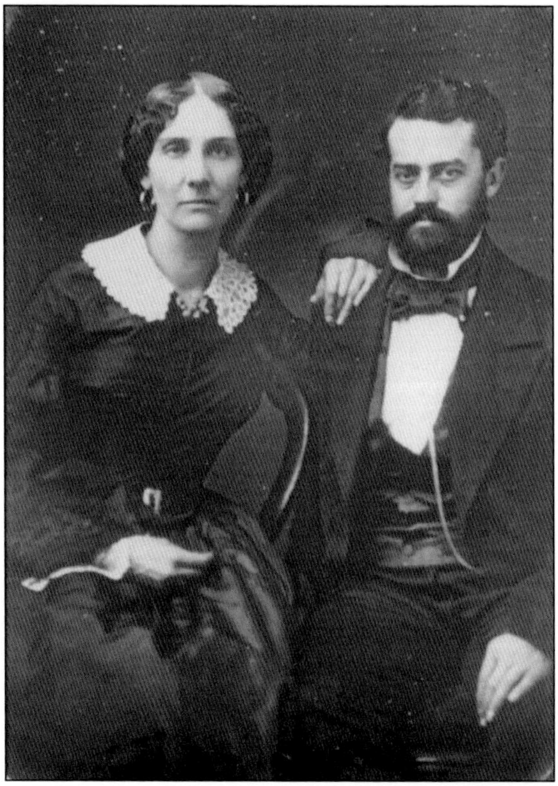

Forty-niner Warren T. Sexton was elected first Butte County Clerk, shared a law practice with Judge Lott, and later served as judge of the District Court. He is shown here with his wife Zobida.

James G. Fair of Comstock fame started his mining career in Oroville along the banks of the Feather River near the edge of town.

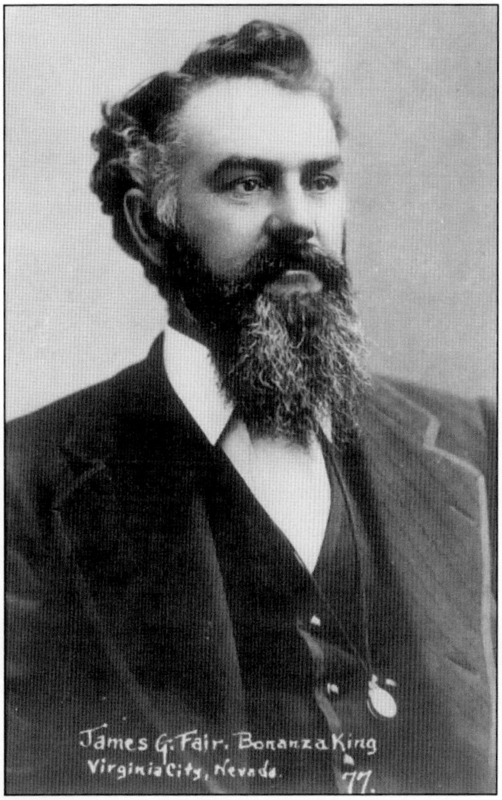

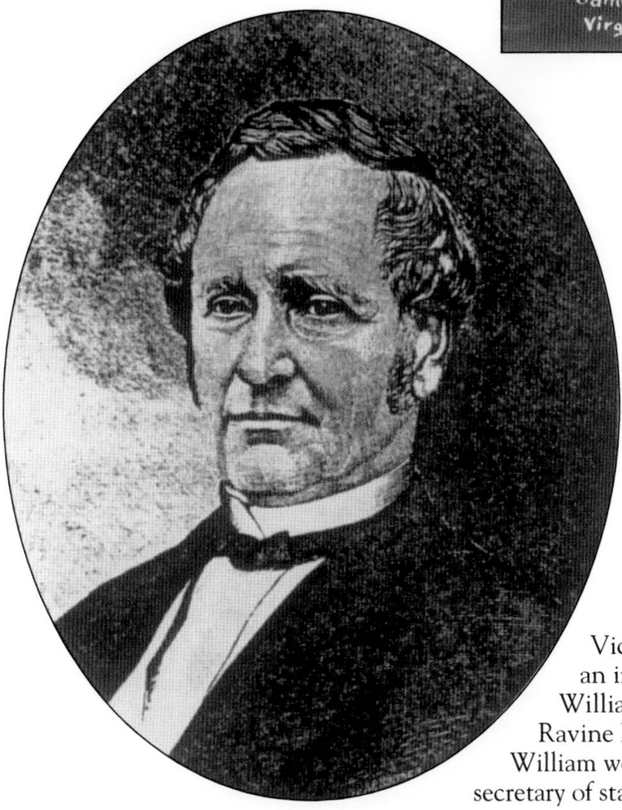

Vice President Thomas Hendricks was an investor with local family member William P. Hendricks in the Morris Ravine Mining Company near Oroville. William went on to be elected California's secretary of state.

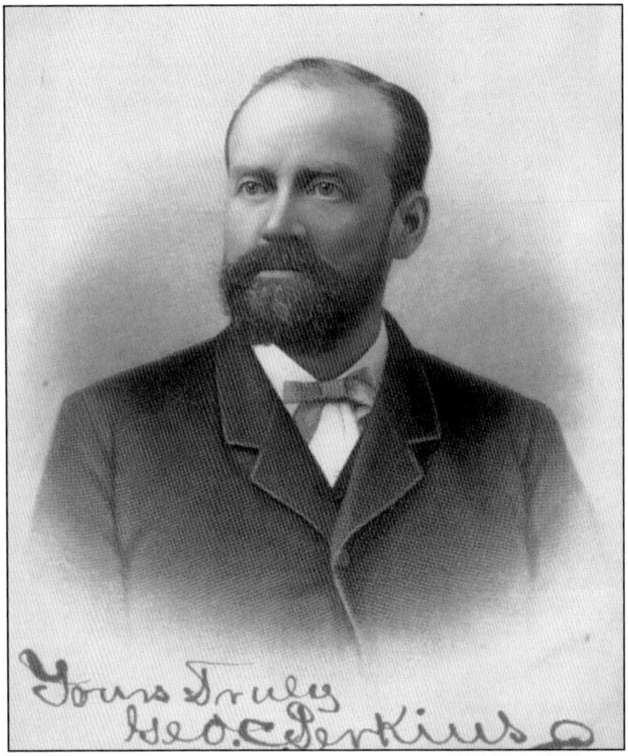

George C. Perkins is Oroville's most outstanding pioneer, going on to be elected governor in 1879 and serving as U.S. senator for two decades. His descendants still own large holdings on North Table Mountain.

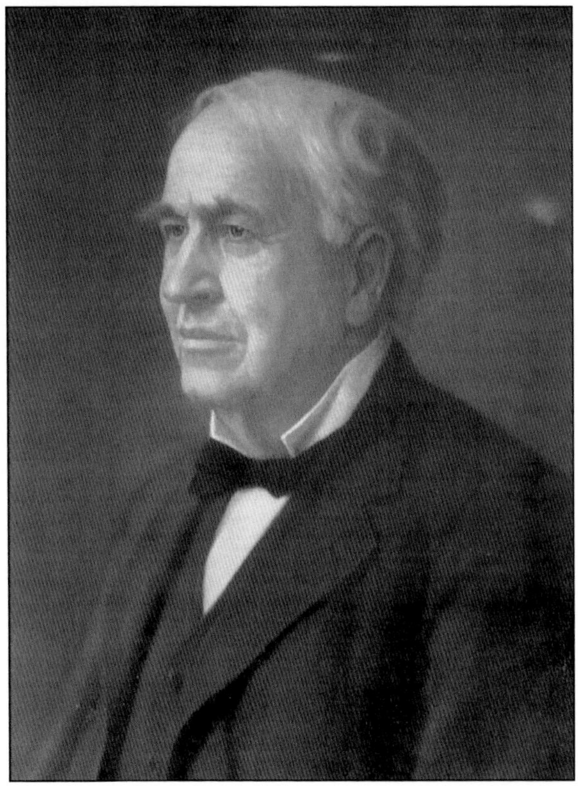

In 1879, Thomas Edison established the Edison Ore Milling Company in Oroville to promote his gold-separating machine and seek platinum for his new light bulbs. He also became involved in local agricultural enterprises and visited the town at least once.

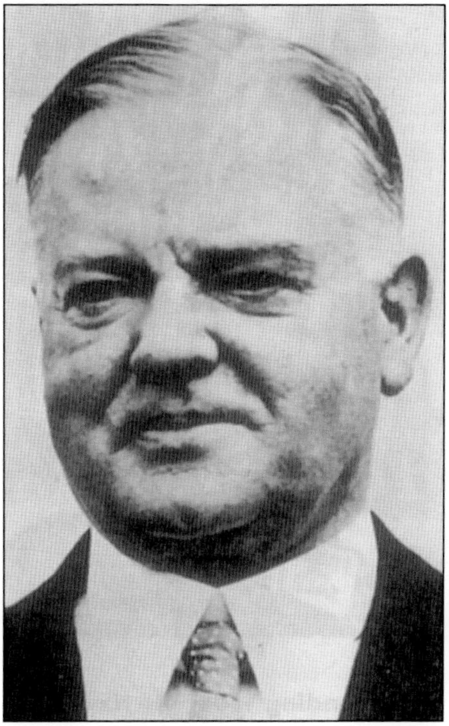

Future president Herbert Hoover was a mining engineer for the Oroville Gold Dredging Company and spent considerable time in town superintending operations.

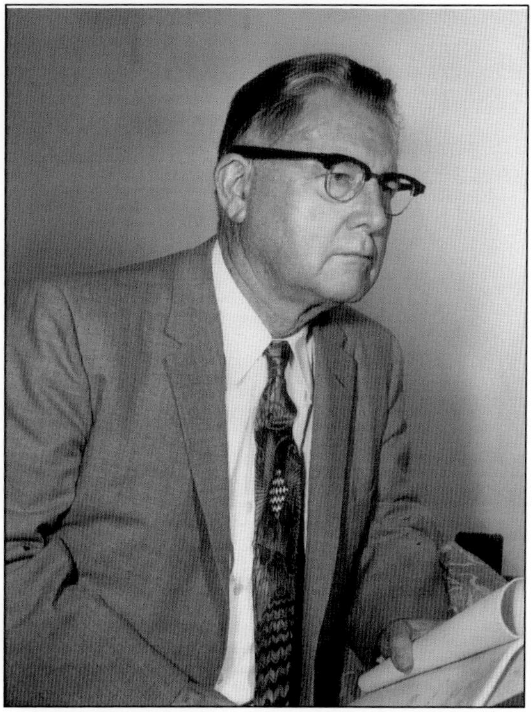

Famed mystery writer Erle Stanley Gardner was raised in Oroville. His father was a gold dredging engineer for Wendell Hammon. The family home still stands on Montgomery Street.

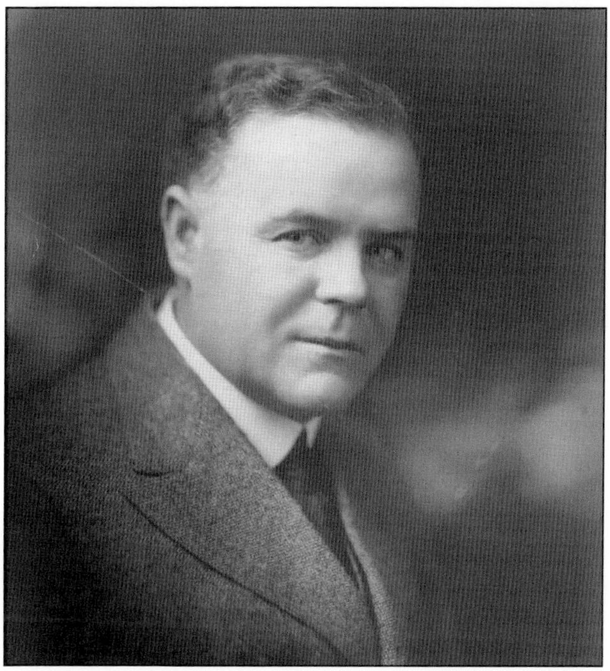

George C. Mansfield was a local newspaper editor who wrote a monumental history of Oroville and Butte County in 1918. It is a major source book and was reprinted in 1996.

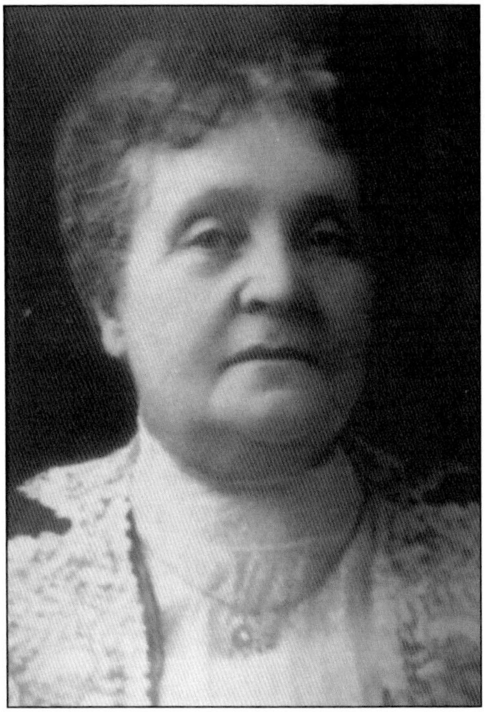

Freda Ehmann developed the black ripe olive industry of California, using her good fortune to help build the Congregational Church and endow the local YMCA. The processing firm she started continues to operate in Oroville today.

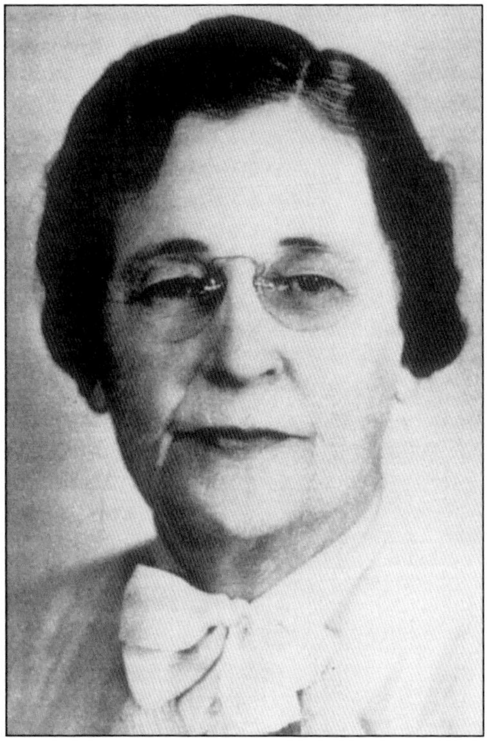

In 1919, local educator Elizabeth Hughes was one of four women elected to the state legislature for the first time. She was the first woman in Butte County to hold state office. Husband James was high school principal.

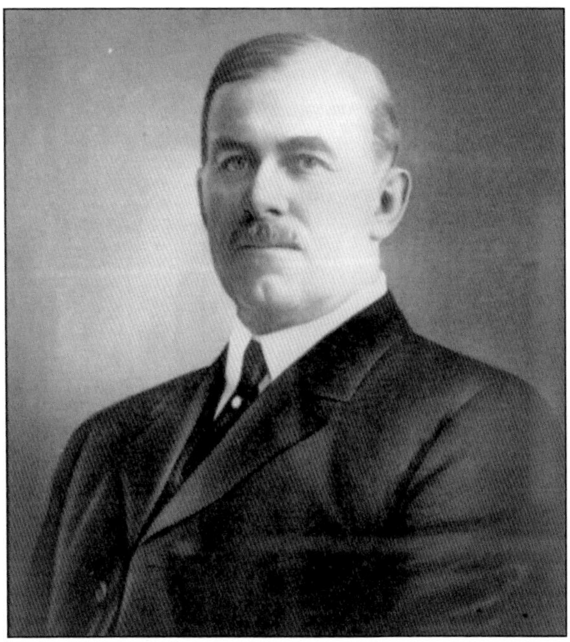

Agriculturalist turned "gold dredger king," Wendell Hammon went on to mining exploits around the world and was installed in the Alaskan Hall of Fame in 2001.

When Ishi was "captured" in Oroville in 1911, he created national attention that continues to this day. Books are still being written about him and his image appears on a giant mural at the jail site where he was held.

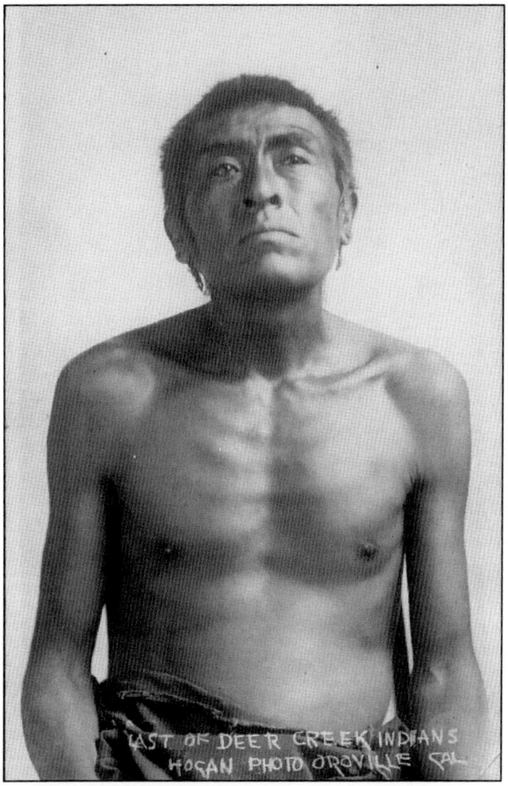

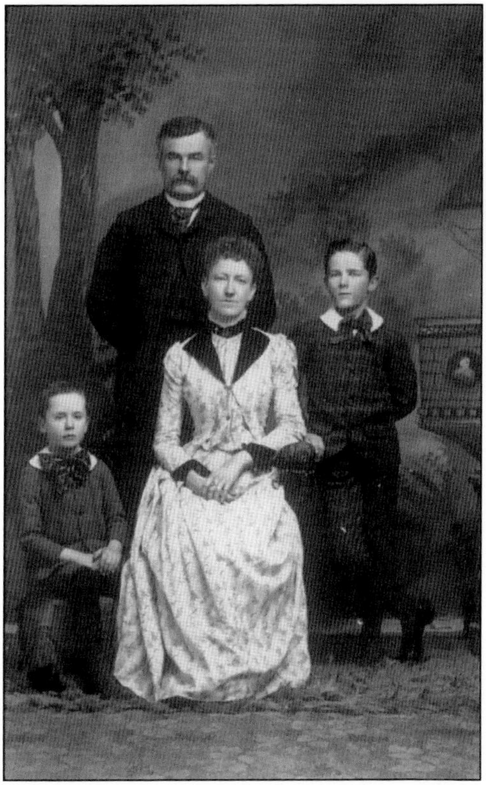

John H. Hogan was responsible for many of the pictures that recorded the history of Oroville during his 40-year career as the town's leading photographer. He is shown here in a self-portrait with his family.

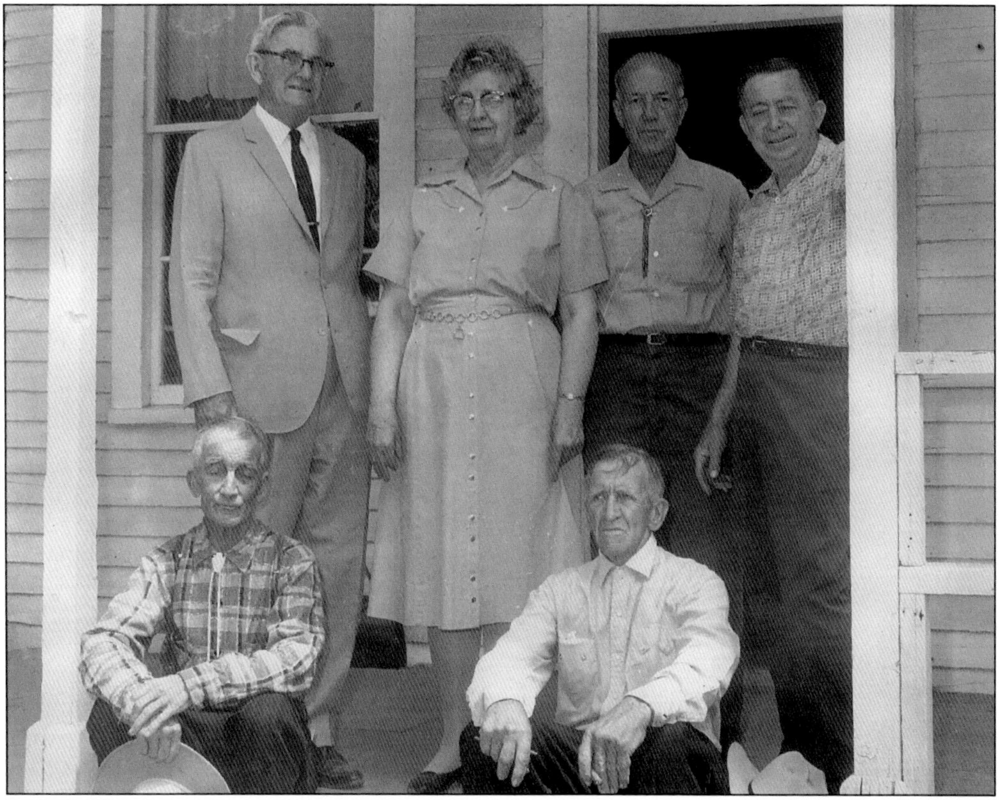

In 1966, former students of the little school at Oregon City met during dedication of a state monument nearby. Standing at left is venerated educator J.C. Nisbet. Next to him is Mattie Lund, first woman to gain public office in Butte County when elected treasurer in 1914. Others standing are Stanley Hedge and Ellmore Forbes. Tony Nunes and Charlie Johnson are seated.

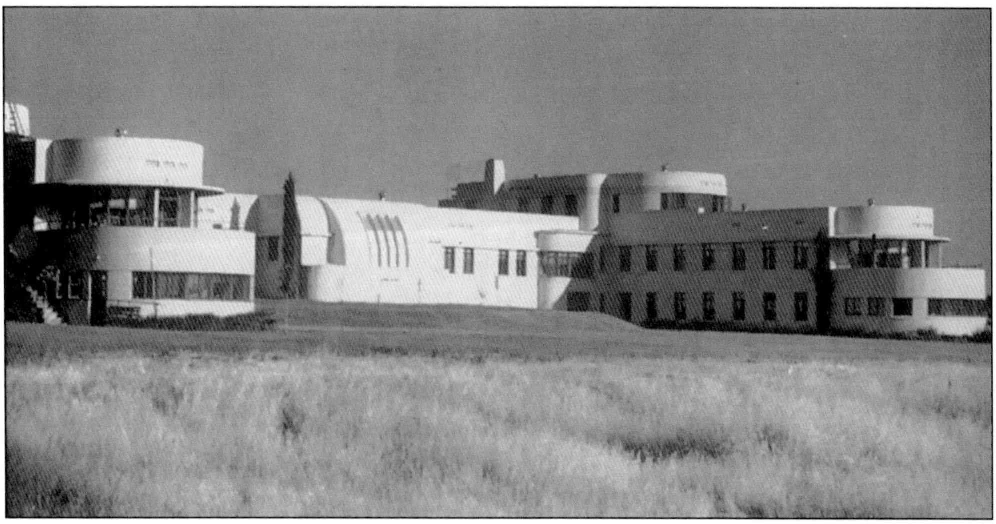

During the 1930s, a streamlined architectural design was selected for the new county hospital erected on a hillside overlooking the valley where the old infirmary stood. It is used for other county purposes today.

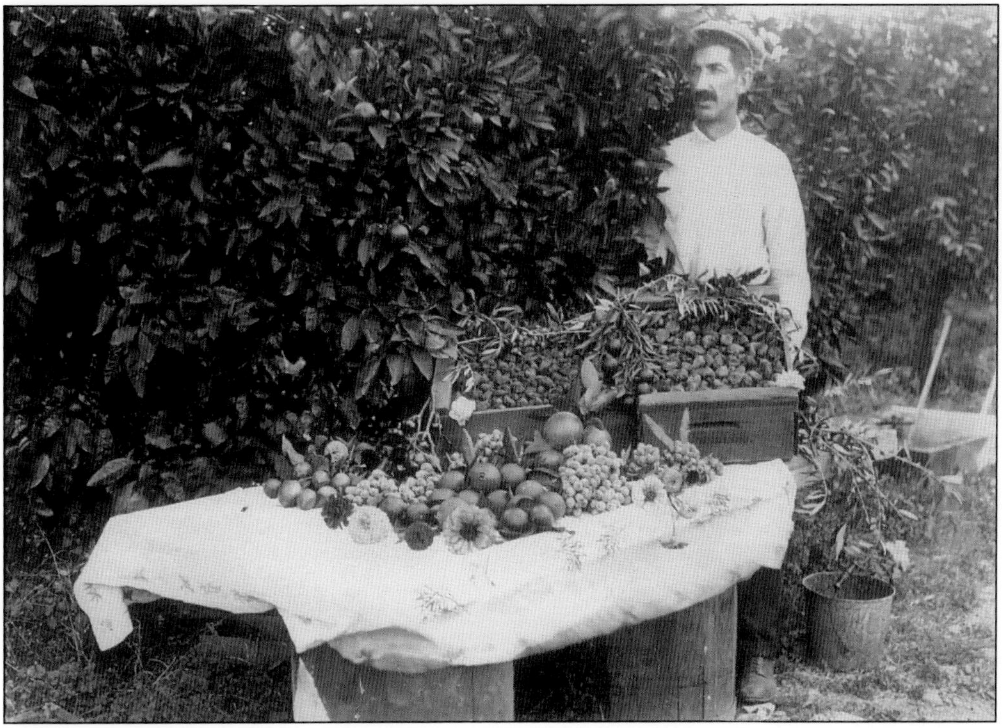

Americo Ghianda and his children were successful grape growers in Thermalito and marketed their own wine label for many years.

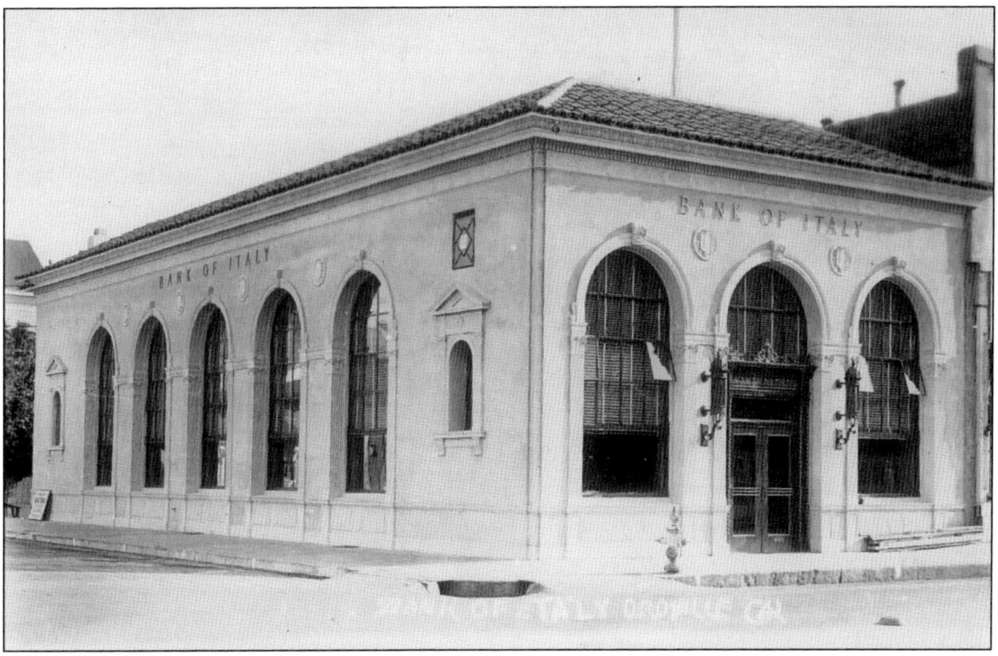

After the Bank of Italy (now Bank of America) bought out the Rideout-Smith chain in 1922, a brand new building was erected on the corner of Myers and Montgomery Streets. It is currently occupied by the Fraternal Order of Eagles.

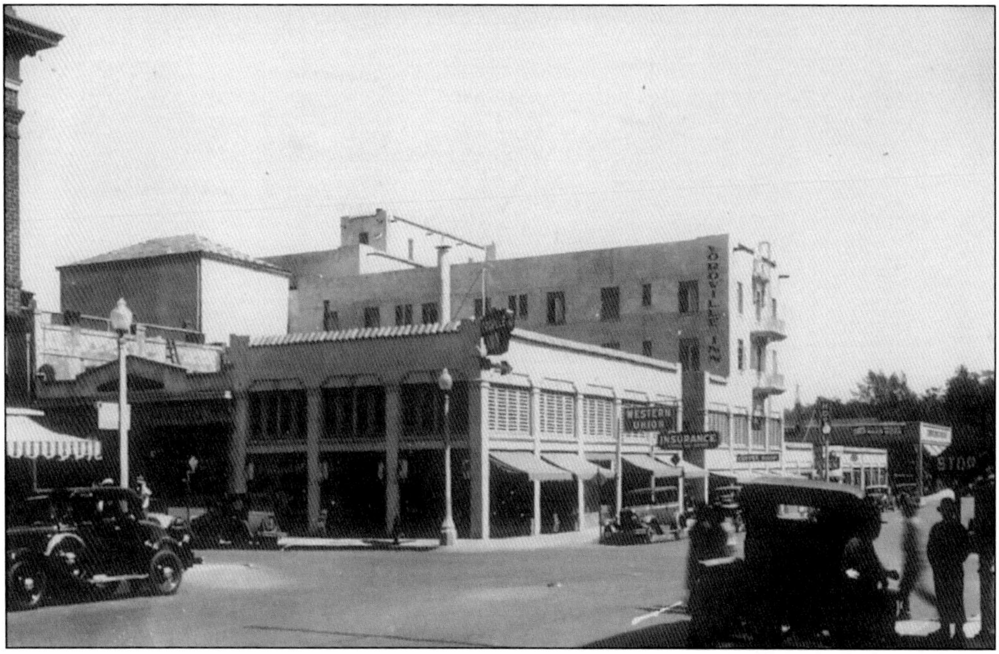

At the height of the gold dredging era, it was decided that Oroville needed a spacious new hotel to accommodate its many visitors. The Oroville Inn was erected in 1931, occupying an entire city block between Myers and Downer Streets. General Mark Clark, Randolph Churchill, and other notables have stayed there.

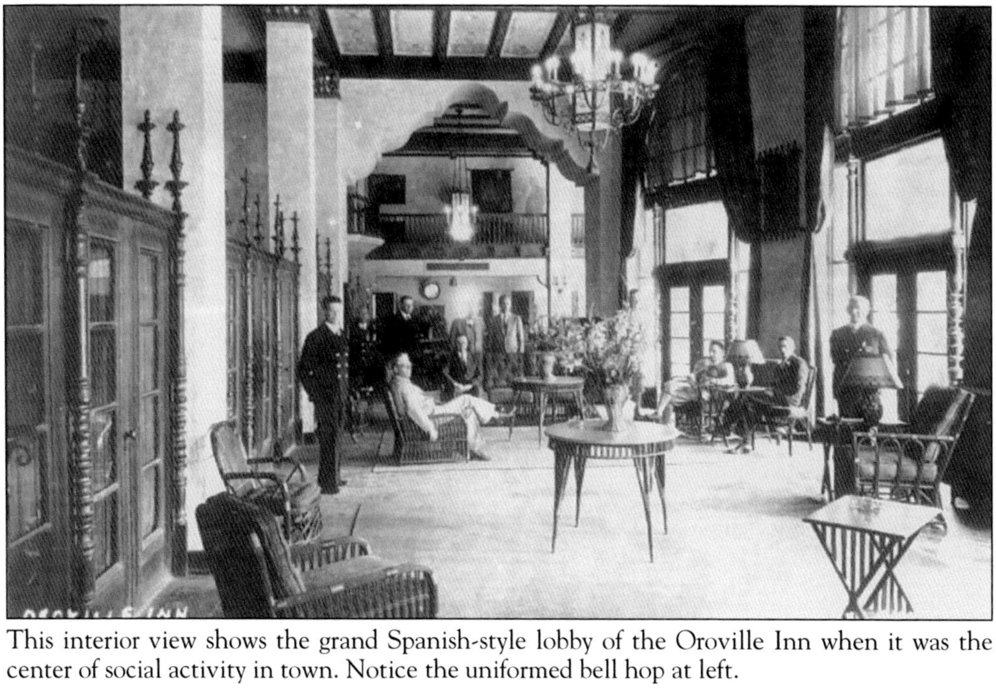

This interior view shows the grand Spanish-style lobby of the Oroville Inn when it was the center of social activity in town. Notice the uniformed bell hop at left.

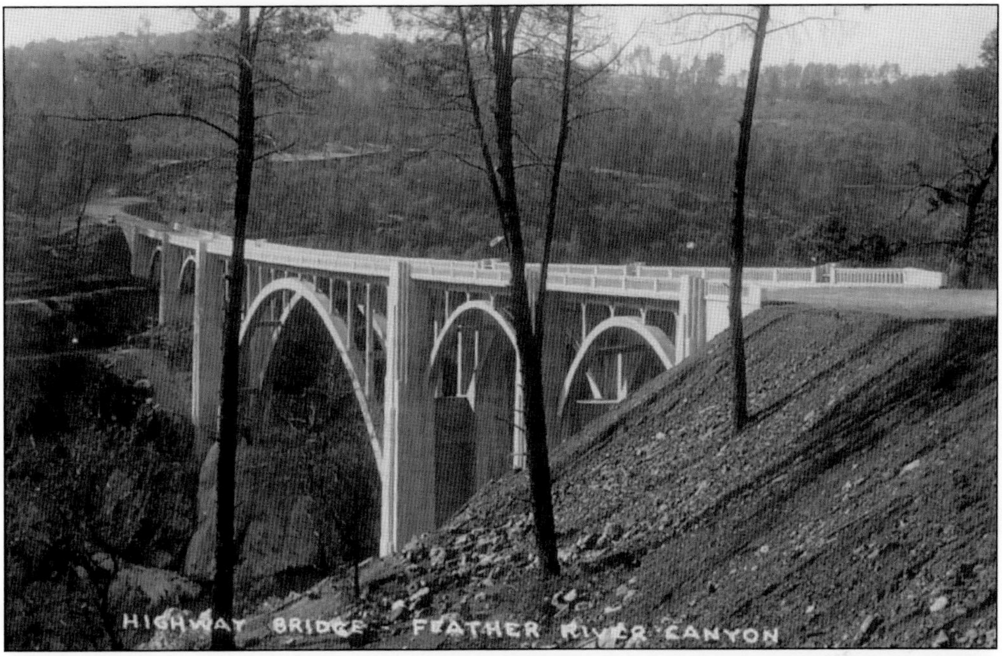

Construction of a new state highway through the Feather River Canyon was started in the 1930s, linking Oroville with Reno. Shown above is the concrete arch bridge which crossed the Feather River above Oroville. In the 1960s it would be blown up in order to build the Oroville Dam.

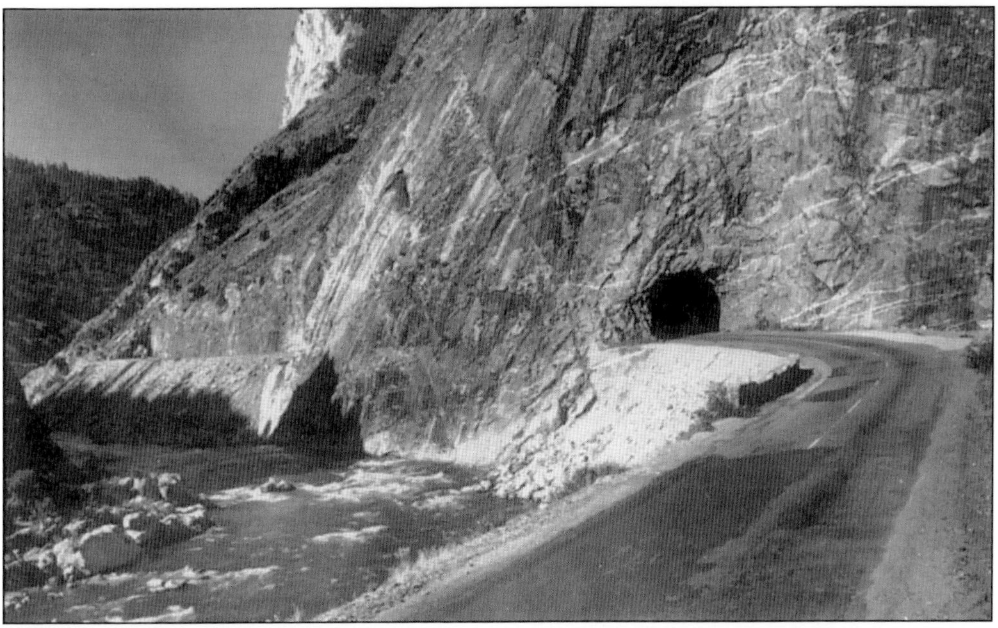

Unable to build around the massive granite mountains that jutted down to the canyon floor, highway engineers blasted tunnels through the Grizzly Dome area east of Oroville. These tunnels are still used today.

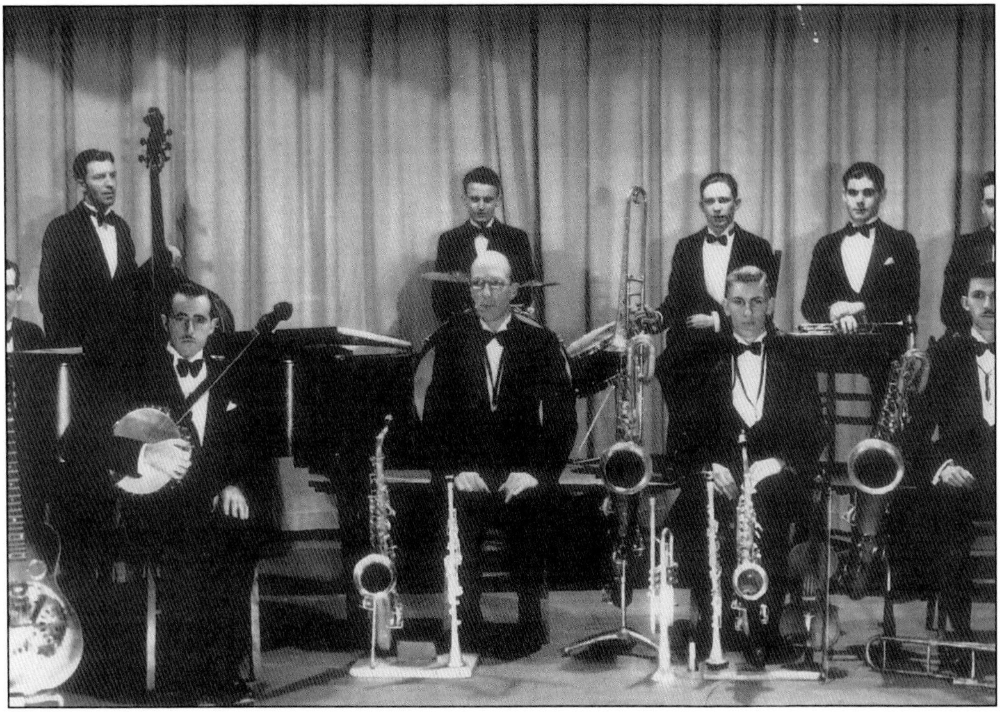

Local dance bands were popular during the 1920s, '30s, and '40s. Shown above is Harold "Dutch" Holub's band, which frequented Robinson's Corners a few miles south of Oroville. Seated at center is Harold. With banjo in hand is local haberdasher Eddie Costello. Two other popular bands were the Royal Tigers and Lester Casagrande's All Stars.

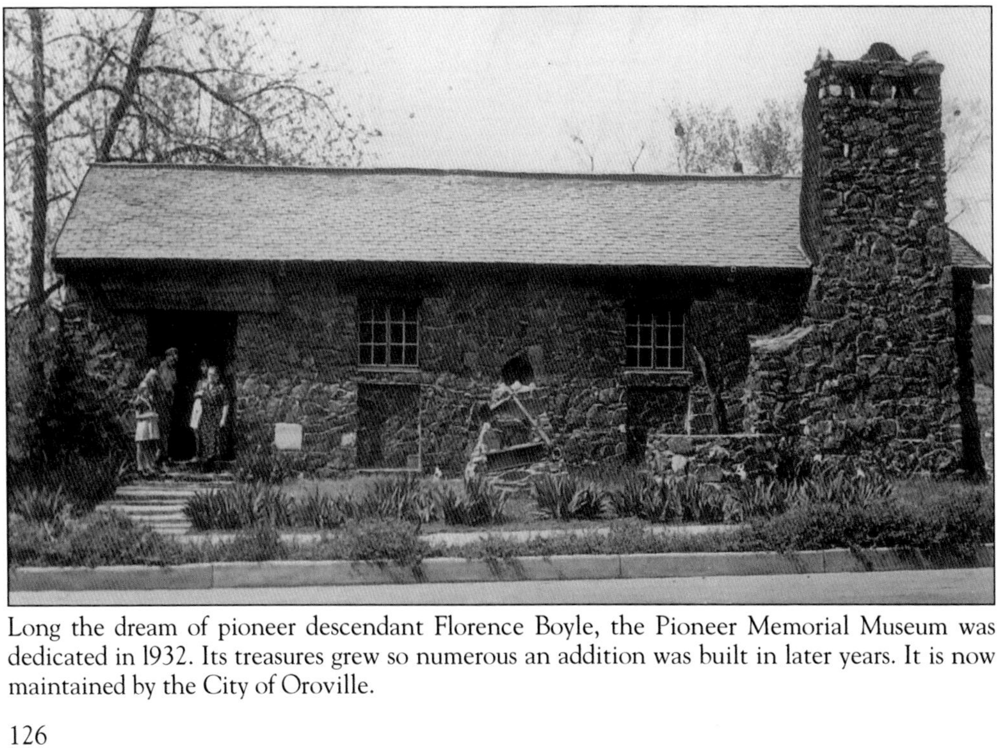

Long the dream of pioneer descendant Florence Boyle, the Pioneer Memorial Museum was dedicated in 1932. Its treasures grew so numerous an addition was built in later years. It is now maintained by the City of Oroville.

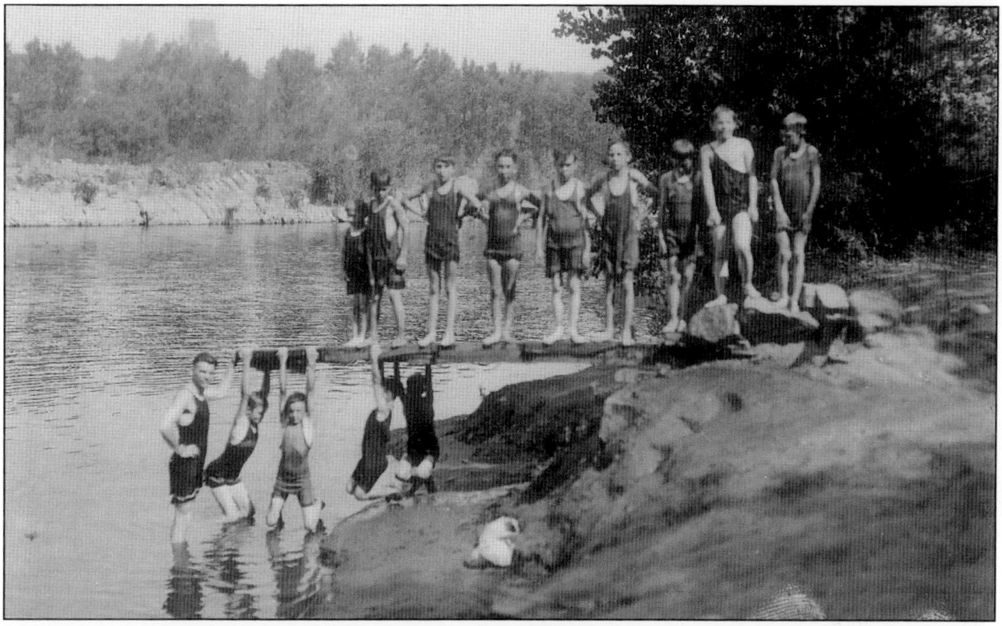

The Feather River has always been popular for swimming as seen by this photo taken in the 1920s. The city has maintained a public park along the river at Bed Rock for many years.

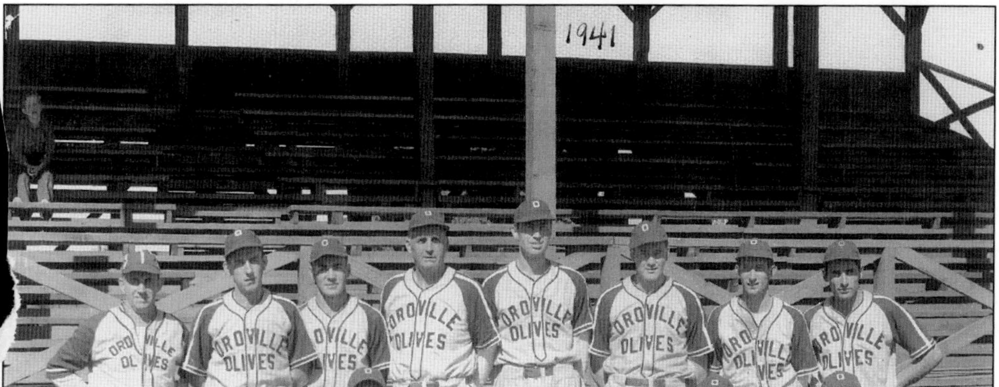

This photo shows the Oroville Olives baseball team in 1941. Kneeling, left to right, are: Gerald Openshaw, Fred Fehr, G. Blanchard, bat boy Tom Glaviano, Bart Smythe, and Oliver Ledford. Standing, left to right, are: Harry Gilbert, Russ Deforest, Joe Felipe, Bill James of Boston Braves National League Fame, Jack Andrews, Cliff Anderson, Bob Strang, and Val Quintana. (Courtesy Don Bloss.)

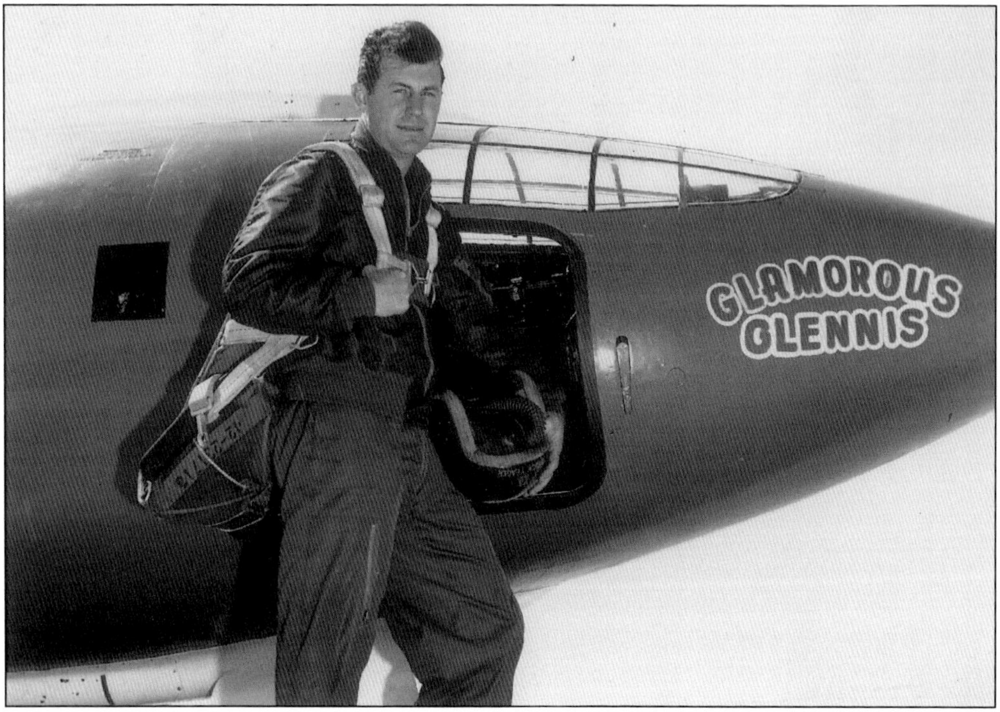

During part of World War II, flying ace Chuck Yeager was stationed at the Oroville airport. After marrying a local girl, he went on to break the sound barrier. A street at the airport is named in his honor.

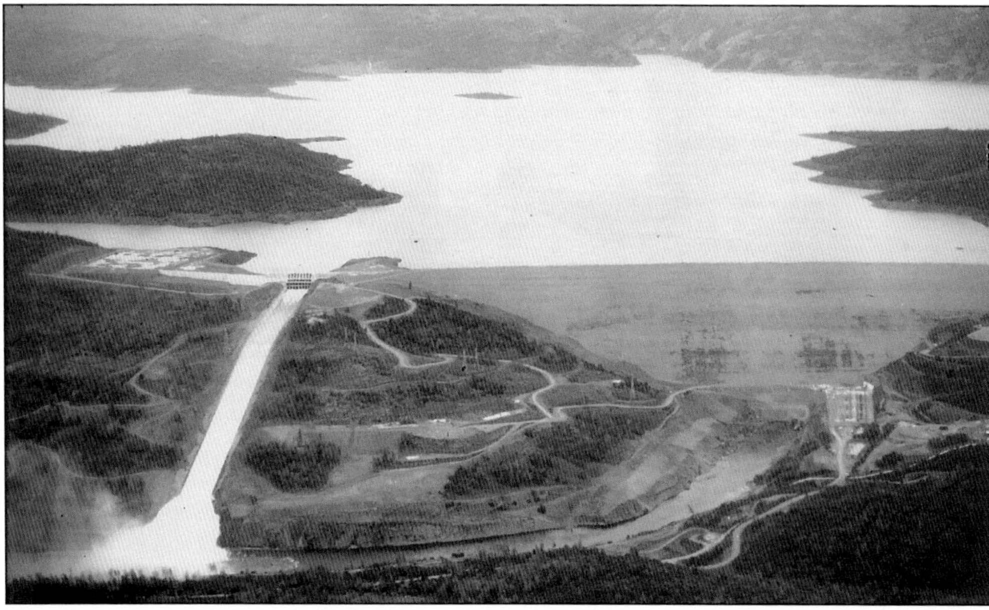

Everything centered around the building of the Oroville Dam during the 1950s and 1960s. Completion of the nation's highest and widest dam in 1968 ushered in a whole new era that has affected not only the lives of people in Oroville but thousands throughout the state. The project culminated an exciting 100 years since Oroville was crowned the jewel of the Gold Rush Era.